FRED PO

The Man and

Oh how the clichés come to mind when writing about a character like Fred Pontin.

'Hi - De - Hi', 'book early', 'value for money', 'thumbs up!' - they are all there! John Major when entertaining Sir Fred Pontin with other dignitaries at 10 Downing Street described him as a 'National Asset'. Lord George Brown thought he was an ideal candidate for the House of Lords when he was in power but the hint was not taken.

British holiday camps are part of the country's folklore and although Fred Pontin's business has changed hands on a number of occasions since he relinquished control in the late seventies and the concern was once again put up for sale and sold at the beginning of the twenty first century, deep down it is still the same operation catering for more or less the same type of customer. 'There's no place like Pontin's' can still be heard at Blackpool, Southport and Prestatyn and the future seems secure.

Days when Pontin's were delivering handsome dividends to shareholders are now long past but the show goes on and so did Sir Fred, until very nearly his 94th year. He had outlived all of his contemporaries and remarried very late in life to a long-lasting friend who had devoted many years to his wellbeing.

Sir Fred could look back on an eventful and fulfilling life which has had significant influence on other people.

This is the story of Sir Fred Pontin and his business. He had a meaningful impact on the holiday plans of many hundreds of thousands of people in the twentieth century. Not many people can make or even justify such a claim.

Peter Willsher had known Sir Fred Pontin for many years but his indirect relationship extends back to the early fifties when Peter counted himself amongst the close friends of Valerie Dean, the daughter of Leslie Dean who sold to Fred Pontin his very first holiday camp at Brean Sands, Somerset.

Lunching with Sir Fred at the Institute of Directors dining room at Pall Mall in the late 1980s Peter was enjoying many of Sir Fred's stories of his days in the holiday camp industry and remarked 'Fred, you should write a book and if you don't I'll do it for you'.

Author's acknowledgements:

Thanks are due to members of Sir Fred Pontin's family as well as to the management and staff of Pontin's both past and present. David Gywn, Jim Kennedy, Joyce Hey, Eddie Stamper, Joe Rubido, Trevor Hemmings, Stephen Haupt, Mike Austin, George Webb, Valerie Barnett, Ann Miller, Peter Hopper, Eileen Langridge, the late George Ross Goobey, Paul Rackham, Mr and Mrs Jack Sharples, Colin Homer and many others also assisted me in the research for this work.

FRED PONTIN
The Man and His Business

Peter Willsher

ST DAVID'S PRESS

www.st-davids-press.co.uk

Published in Wales by St. David's Press, an imprint of

Ashley Drake Publishing Ltd.
PO Box 733
Cardiff
CF14 2YX

First Impression – 2003

ISBN: 1 902719 220

British Library Cataloguing-in-Publication Data.
A catalogue for this book is available from the British Library.

Typeset by WestKey Ltd., Falmouth, Cornwall.

To my wife Beverley and my children,
James and Charlotte

CONTENTS

Chapter One

LIFE'S PAGEANT

The little boy opened his eyes and, just as quickly closed them. It must be a dream. This wasn't his usual bedroom; or was it?

Again John Sharples, aged five and half years, opened his eyes. Yes, he could hear the soft sound of his brother, breathing gently in the bed opposite but this really wasn't their usual sleeping place. There was no specially chosen wallpaper with the familiar elephants and giraffes; there were precious few toys on the floor; certainly not as many as there were last night, when he was put to bed by his mum.

Then it dawned on him! It was Pontin's! In that case it must be Southport, his favourite holiday camp; yet he had dropped off to sleep back home in the family's terraced house in Preston.

A shout of pure joy leapt from his young lips "Mum, we're at Pontin's. Come on mum, let's get out there!"

Anne Sharples had been waiting for the reaction of her children but she was just as excited as young John. Pontin's was a great place to unwind after a hectic week.

It didn't take long to have breakfast; the sun was shining and there was so much to do. Eating corn flakes was not a major priority.

The Sharples boys had been brought up, if not actually weaned on Pontin's. Their parents had, at first, been regulars at Butlin's but by the time that their children were of an age to appreciate what a genuine holiday camp had to offer Butlin's camps had become havens for rowdy teenagers who enjoyed group holidays with lots of, booze, noise and deafening music. This was not what Jack and Anne wanted for their active youngsters as far as the family holidays were concerned.

The Sharples soon discovered that it was Pontin's who catered for families who wished for nothing more than an all inclusive holiday where parents could be assured of comfortable accommodation, nourishing, wholesome food, something to do during the day as well as in the evenings and, as far as the children were concerned, all the day round entertainment and supervised activities.

Above all, they would be mixing with other families, many of whom had become firm friends, being regular visitors who tended to put down a deposit on next year's holidays before they had finished the current year's.

Jack Sharples had been having a particularly gruesome week in his self-employed occupation as a builder. Nothing had gone right; there were late deliveries of materials, the sub-contractors had left site without notice and the weather had been fine and sunny.

In normal circumstances the latter would have been good news when a new job had just been started. By Friday evening, however, he had had more than he could take and Anne's efforts in the kitchen had not been enough to encourage him to relax and forget the week's misfortunes.

He had reached for the telephone, explaining to Anne that he had a great idea.

"Hello, can I speak to Joyce please?" He spoke softly. He did not want to awaken the children.

"Who shall I say is calling?" rejoined the telephonist.

"Tell her it's Jack Sharples and he wants a chalet for the weekend" replied Jack, winking to Anne as he supped a glass of her home-made rosé wine.

Anne wasn't surprised. It wouldn't be the first time that Jack had decided on a Pontin's break at such short notice. Joyce Hey had been general manager at Pontin's Southport for some time and she knew Jack and Anne Sharples to be very keen campers. Indeed, they could always be relied upon to bring a little life to any, shall we say "limp occasion". Anne felt confident that Joyce would be able to find some accommodation for them and the children.

Jack and Anne had caught the holiday camp bug years ago and had been only too willing to participate enthusiastically in everything Pontin's had to offer.

"Hello, Jack, how are you?" Joyce's familiar voice was as welcoming, as always. "Don't tell me; you've had a bad week. Well, we could certainly do with the both of you. It's been so quiet. I think it's the weather. Everyone has had so much fresh air what with being on the beach and running around all day; they seem to be too tired to get the party going."

"Say no more" said Jack. "I take it you can put us up. We're on our way."

Packing didn't take long and within half an hour young John

Sharples and his brother were being bundled into the back of Jack's van and driven off to Pontin's.

Put to bed in Preston and waking up in Pontin's. That's what they called living in the 1970s.

The above is not fiction; it actually happened. It may not be exactly typical of a regular booking at a holiday camp but it's symbolic of what Pontin's meant to genuine holiday campers. It was pure escapism; not just for a short weekend but for holiday breaks of one, two and three weeks and upwards.

Pontin's was and still is an institution and before he was sixteen, young John Sharples was wearing the blazer of a Pontin's Bluecoat, as a prelude to making a still ongoing career in the entertainments industry.

It has to be said, however, that entertaining comes as second nature to the Sharples family in that Anne's father was an actor, the late Bernard Youens, who played the role of Stan Ogden in Granada TV's *Coronation Street* for many years. And as for Anne and Jack, they have been the life and soul of so many happy evenings at Pontin's. They could entertain just by being there. Their lively and fun-loving personalities as well as their unbridled enthusiasm for having a good time did the rest.

On the subject of popular television series, BBC's light entertainment programme *Hi-De-Hi* attracted regular audiences of up to sixteen million viewers, not all of whom had been regulars at Pontin's, Butlin's or any other holiday camp for that matter. But those who watched on Sunday evenings during the long winter months were well aware that holiday camps were places of fun and entertainment. Sir Fred Pontin, founder of Pontin's, was fond of admitting that he was certainly one of these millions of fans.

Watching the programme brought back many memories of the early days in the industry and Sir Fred was particularly intrigued by the fact that the entire concept of the series was based around the staff and not the holidaymakers, who, like absentee owner Joe Maplin, were never very much in evidence. However, there is one thing that could have been said about Sir Fred during the period of thirty three years or so he personally controlled his beloved holiday camps, his commanding presence was dominant; some would say, even when he wasn't there.

Previous programmes on life in post-war holiday camps were pathetic caricatures of the real thing. Tales of concentration camp atmospheres, being awakened by loudspeakers at the crack of dawn and the need to escape by digging under the perimeter fence were nothing more than corny music-hall jokes. It was refreshing, therefore, to see how David Croft and fellow Water Rat Jimmy Perry OBE captured the flavour of what went on behind the scenes – even though most of what was portrayed in *Hi-De-Hi* was grossly exaggerated.

This simply added to the entertainment value and tremendous popularity of the series, all episodes of which have been subjected to countless repeat showings on terrestrial as well as satellite television and, in the main, gave the fully justified impression that guests and the staff were all having a very good time.

Pontin's holiday camps have progressed immeasurably in terms of comfort and facilities over the years and investment in new buildings and refurbishment is still taking place. Sir Fred gained great satisfaction from the fact that today's Pontin's was under the control and organisation of some of the most experienced operators in the business but he had recognised that there was a need for change, of which more later.

This book is about not only Sir Fred's life and times but also regarding that particular segment of the leisure industry in which he played such an active part. In these circumstances, it would do no harm to pause for a moment in order to reflect on not only what he achieved but also just how fortunate he had always felt as a result of his rather curious entry into the business of making people happy.

Hi-De-Hi has been mentioned specifically because this programme served to remind Sir Fred of the origins of his business and how it came to change not only his own life but also the lives of thousands of people . . . members of his own family, the enormous numbers of staff who have worked and are still employed at Pontin's and, above all, "his" guests like the Sharples family, without the likes of whom there would have been no business and no happy times for Sir Fred, who was surely the doyen of the postwar holiday camp entrepreneurs in the strict meaning of these words.

If an ordinary chap from working-class origins can accompany Her Majesty The Queen's consort to an evening meeting at a London greyhound track . . . if this same man can lead in his own racehorses after they had won the Grand National and Schweppes Gold Trophy in the same season . . . then for this rather unlikely fellow to cap it all by acting as chairman at a memorable celebratory dinner attended by no less than five British Prime Ministers, there must be a story worth the telling.

Fred Pontin was no ordinary fellow and this is his story as well as that of the company he created.

* * * * * * * * *

A derelict and war-scarred holiday camp could perhaps be described as an improbable foundation for the good fortune which lies behind such a tale, but that is where it all started. If there is to be any moral which could possibly be attached to this account of Sir Fred Pontin's extraordinary life it must be related to the maxim that no one should ever fail to make use of their experiences. Good, bad or just indifferent, these are certain to come in useful at some further stage in what that delightful character, the late Arthur Marshall described in his own autobiography as "life's rich pageant".

The creation of wealth can lead a person down many different paths, any one or even a combination of which could result in the destruction of that individual for what may be a variety of reasons. Wealth is capable of creating power and power can lead to corruption in one form or another.

Wealth creates access to all manner of material substances; wealth can be squandered, it can be abused and it can lead to self-destruction by the abuse of the material substances. For instance, how many times do we read of successful pop stars and possessors of inherited wealth succumbing to hard drugs which have become available only because of the wealth of the individuals concerned?

How often do we learn that a wealthy person, so intoxicated with the sense of his own importance and infallibility, has taken just one chance too many and has seen his empire come crashing down around him?

These questions are posed to illustrate that the mere possession of wealth cannot automatically lead to the unique sequence of events described near the beginning of this narrative.

The foregoing was part of Sir Fred's personal philosophy and he was the first to admit that he had not led a blameless life, during which he had often been noted for his extra-ordinary staying power. What he achieved was the result of being aware of his limitations, learning and benefiting from his varied experiences, not to mention the odd adventure, and also by recognising that there were many others who had not been so fortunate in the course of their own progress through life.

It has been said that some successful people make their own luck. Sir Fred had always felt that he had been lucky enough to have been blessed with the necessary confidence when adopting such an approach. Consistency and strength of purpose have also been common factors and he had often made it clear that he had unceasingly possessed a sense of determination to achieve the required result without suffering too much from feelings of despair if things went wrong.

There was, however, a time when he felt that the right opportunity was being denied to him and he must have come very close to pursuing his frustrated ambitions in a different direction.

It was early in the Spring of 1946 and he was driving a large open tourer, which had been shipped over to England from America during the war. His companion was a young secretary who knew the area.

He stopped for petrol at a filling station, just south of the seaside resort of Weston-Super-Mare, feeling more than a little despondent. Fred Pontin and his companion were engaged upon what was proving to be an abortive search for readily available, de-requisitioned anti-aircraft or searchlight sites on or nearby the coast of Somerset. Fred Pontin had hit upon the idea of converting these types of property into holiday camps, a concept which had been developed on a national basis by people such as Billy Butlin and Captain Harry Warner in the 1930's.

Hostilities had ceased and, having been released from his wartime duties, of which more later, he was anxious to fulfil his ambition to make his fortune. He was then 40 years old; Fred Pontin was no young Turk, looking for easy money. Before the war he had been working on the London Stock Exchange where he came across many wealthy individuals. Hitler's activities had been an interruption in his quest to join the ranks of these affluent classes, so he was intent upon making up for lost time.

Former members of the armed forces had their gratuities to spend and were desperate for cheap family holidays, and Fred felt that if he moved quickly he could be among the leading contenders in that year's holiday season. This would be the first after six long years of hardship and sacrifice by the people of Great Britain.

Fred was not too ambitious in those early days. A small camp to cater for say fifty to sixty guests would provide a good start and get the cash flowing. There was no doubt that he knew what he wanted but the frustration was that he seemed to be getting nowhere in pursuit of what he considered to be only a modest objective.

He asked the garage attendant if he knew of any likely sites, but the chap shook his head. It seemed that all local positions had been cleared by a large party of French workers, who had dismantled the redundant buildings and transported the materials back home. These could be reassembled in Caen to provide temporary housing for local people who had lost their homes during the fighting.

If, on the other hand, Fred could possibly be interested in a pre-war, purpose-built holiday camp with about eight acres of land which had just been de-requisitioned by the Government . . . the garage man recommended that Fred should go and look up a Mr Leslie Dean, the owner. He lived just a few miles away in a village called Berrow, near Burnham-on-Sea, across the narrow roads which led to Brean Sands and what proved to be a very attractive stretch of coastline; just the right surroundings for postwar holiday makers.

Although he was not to know it at the time, the garage attendant had just launched Fred Pontin on a career which was to result in his becoming a household name, known throughout the whole of the United Kingdom and even in the sunspots of Europe.

This single incident led to Fred Pontin becoming a millionaire and earning a knighthood for what people have justly described as his enthusiastic charitable activities which are continued by his successors throughout Pontin's holiday centres even to this day.

Chapter Two

EAST END DAYS

To have engaged Fred Pontin in discussion at any time, especially over a glass of whisky or a crystal goblet of good claret, and he would tell you that he had always been proud of his Cockney origins, having been born in Shoreditch in the East End of London on 24th October 1906 although the family moved out to Walthamstow a few years later. In those days Walthamstow was considered to be a country area with much better surroundings for bringing up a growing family.

Fred was the eldest of six children and he was baptised with the same names as his father, Frederick William. Being the eldest, he would not hesitate to confess that throughout the whole of his adult life he had always tended to have a dominating influence on the rest of his kith and kin.

Fred's father was a cabinet maker of some distinction, following an equally distinguished line from his own father and the male members of two generations before him. Fred's mother was absolutely devoted to her husband and children, most of whom became associated with him and his future business activities.

In common with his younger brothers, Harry and Len, Fred was educated at the local council school in Blackhorse Road, Walthamstow before moving on to become a fee-paying day pupil at St. George Monoux Grammar School, Walthamstow. He had another brother, Stanley, who died at the age of ten, the day after Len was born in 1918. Fred's sisters Florrie and Elsie also took advantage of the good educational opportunities made available by their parents.

Len Pontin has assumed the role of family historian. Because Fred had been subject to a vast amount of publicity over the years, mostly of his own making, he had received many letters from people who claimed some form of family relationship, mostly for what were obviously pecuniary reasons.

Very few were able to provide any evidence of the alleged connection, though on one occasion what proved to be a genuine letter arrived from a distant cousin in Australia. This prompted Len Pontin to follow up some of the leads which were provided from this source.

As a result Fred and his immediate relations now have a detailed family tree dating back to John Pontin, who was born in 1793. It is thought that the Pontin family came over from Normandy in the seventeenth century, but Len has much more work to do before they will have a fuller picture of their ancestors.

It is known, however, that Fred and Len's father's skill as a cabinet maker derives from an ancestor dating back to the early nineteenth century. A George Pontin, born 1812 in Bethnal Green, was described as a cabinet maker in the parish records.

One of Fred's earlier memories was of his mother rushing down to the railway station at Blackhorse Road, Walthamstow every night of the week to meet her husband when he returned from his place of work in Shoreditch. While Fred's brothers and sisters were growing up the eldest son was expected to take on a position of some responsibility as far as looking after the family was concerned. Fred had a regular evening routine, which allowed his parents to enjoy the odd drink at the Royal Standard public house on their way home to put the younger children to bed before sitting down to enjoy their evening meal.

The Pontin family has always been very close and in those days they all made a frequent habit of calling in to see Grandma Belcher. She was the children's maternal grandmother, who had been widowed at a very young age. Her second husband, Tom Belcher, was a door-to-door collector for a coal merchant, but in the evenings he played the cornet with the orchestra at the very popular Collins Music Hall. Among the stars there was the cheeky comedian Max Miller, who was to become a close friend of Fred's during the course of his future career in the holiday camp industry.

Most weekends Tom Belcher would also be playing with two other musicians at the Royal Standard. He spent his last years as Fred's personal guest at the South Devon Holiday Camp at Paignton, where Tom enjoyed watching the various outdoor sporting activities as well as the billiards matches played there in those days.

Fred's parents were very much involved with the Walthamstow Avenue Football Club, an amateur football team which earned a national reputation as a result of their successes in the FA Cup.

His father and mother were enthusiastic supporters and took part in a wide variety of the club's activities. Their interest in the team was also shared by the entire family and it soon led to Fred becoming the club's treasurer and also their Press reporter. His match reports were regular features in the *Walthamstow Guardian*, the local newspaper.

In those days all of the players were officially described as amateurs and this status would have been compromised if they accepted payment for playing for the club. On the other hand, everyone who supported Walthamstow Avenue wanted success, so the club had to recruit footballers who were ready to exploit their superior talents for pecuniary purposes.

"Expenses" a euphemism for regular wages, were paid to members of the team and Fred became involved in all sorts of cash-raising activities to finance this extra-curricular, but very necessary activity. He organised the running of a tea and coffee bar, as well as selling programmes, to generate the necessary funds paid to the players in various surreptitious ways. Who was to know where these early catering and publicity activities would lead in later years?

The other local amateur football club was Walthamstow Grange and there was great rivalry between the two sides. Fred recalled a preliminary round in the FA Cup when the teams were drawn against each other and the Avenue, playing at home, were a player short. Fred managed to recruit Jim Lewis, who eventually captained England as an amateur player. Lewis had an outstanding match on the left wing, scoring seven or eight goals in a 13-0 win for Avenue. He later joined Chelsea as a professional and his son also played for the south west London club.

From a very early age Fred was never satisfied with second best. He very much wanted to be involved with the most successful amateur team in England, so he had no hesitation in working tirelessly, and enthusiastically for the club.

The family's enthusiasm for the Avenue club was undoubtedly generated by the fact that virtually every match seemed to have the atmosphere of a cup tie. Every opposing team wanted to beat the Avenue and this brought out the best in the players.

There seemed to be a never-ending series of celebrations as the Pontin family witnessed the club earn promotion from the Spartan League into the Athenian League and eventually to the Isthmian League. Fred's recollection was that the team was top of the league every year. This was a source of great delight to him, because nothing can be more rewarding than success in a competitive environment, regardless of whether it be of a business or sporting nature.

He also recalled when Walthamstow Avenue reached the Third Round of the FA Cup. They were drawn away to Manchester United after beating Stockport County and Reading in the First and Second

Rounds. The game was drawn with a goal each, a result which disappointed the fans who had travelled up from London. Groves, the centre forward, missed an open goal ten minutes from full time.

The replay could not be staged on Avenue's pitch and at the same time satisfy all of the two sides' many supporters, so it was arranged for the match to take place on Arsenal's ground at Highbury. Crowd capacity at Avenue was 12,000, but they seldom had less than 5,000 spectators, reflecting very well on the entertaining football played by this successful amateur club.

The match took place at Highbury on the following Wednesday afternoon before a crowd of 55,000 wildly enthusiastic spectators, most of whom were from the East End of London. Avenue lost by three goals to two in an exciting match which Fred Pontin had never forgotten.

Bearing in mind that Manchester United ended the season as champions of the First Division of the Football League, Avenue's performance could be considered as very impressive and it gave all of the Pontin family a lift.

It is sad that such a fine amateur football club is no longer in existence. Avenue's ground is now a residential housing estate and, as a result of a merger between several clubs in the area, Walthamstow Avenue's footballing activities were continued through the medium of Redbridge Forest, a team which once played in the Premier Division of the Vauxhall League and competed in the annual FA Challenge Trophy. In the 1990s a further merger took place and the team is now known as Dagenham and Redbridge, still competing successfully and finishing near the top of what is now known as the Ryman League in the 1998/1999 season.

Walthamstow Grange subsequently closed down as an active football team when their ground became a greyhound racing venue.

Fred's interest in sport, which survived to the last, was undoubtedly kindled at St George Monoux Grammar School, where he not only took part in boxing matches – suffering a broken nose – but he also won the Victor Ludorum Cup by winning every sporting event available to him as a junior.

Fred's brother Len reminds everyone who cares to listen that his elder brother also went on to win open events where he had to compete against the more senior pupils.

Because Sir Fred is considered as an extremely distinguished former pupil, the Victor Ludorum Cup was subsequently returned to the school, together with the photograph which recorded his success. This was framed in a very professional way by his father and both cup and framed photograph are now exhibited in the school's museum set up in 1977 after their 450th anniversary celebrations. Accompanied by brother Len, Sir Fred had the honour to attend the event as chief guest.

The school provided a very good education. Former pupils include a High Court judge, numerous chartered accountants, stockbrokers and high-ranking bank officials.

Looking back, Sir Fred felt that he did not reap the full benefit from his studies at St George Monoux Grammar School. He attributed this to the time lost when he had a form of nervous breakdown following the death of his young brother Stanley, to whom he was very close.

Stanley's death at the tender age of ten was a great shock to the entire family, especially Fred, and he was sent away to Clacton-on-Sea to recuperate. As a result he missed the greater part of his first term at grammar school. Although he was always near the top of the class and in constant competition with two other pupils – Ashton, who subsequently qualified as chartered accountant and Hughes, who became a tea planter – he felt that he never really caught up with them, as far as academic studies are concerned, anyway.

Fred was always somewhat behind in some of the more important subjects, such as English and French, but he maintained that he will always be thankful that he was lucky enough to have an aptitude for figures, if not for all of the finer points of mathematics.

Looking retrospectively, Fred felt that he did reasonably well, given the circumstances, but he had always tended to set his standards very high. Yes, even in his earlier studies, second best was never really good enough. His memories of St George Monoux included the name of the headmaster, Wally Topliss, who was stone deaf, but, as all mischievous new pupils soon learned to their cost, he was an expert at lip-reading!

Fred completed his schooling when he was not much more than fifteen years of age, but, despite his above-average performance in the classroom he left without any educational qualifications. The pressing need was to earn money for the family, not to stay on in an effort to matriculate.

Fred was conscious of the fact that his parents had made many sacrifices over the years in order to give each of their children a good start in life, even though the cost of providing higher education proved to be beyond their limited resources.

It should be borne in mind that Fred was just eight years old when the Great War started and his parents also had to provide for three other children. By the time he left school the family had grown to seven and his father was not able to work on a self-employed basis during the long period of hostilities.

Fred's father was a gifted and very skilled craftsman, but his war work was with Waring & Gillow, the furniture manufacturers, who were directed into the business of making wooden aircraft frames for both fighters and bombers being flown in combat by the Royal Flying Corps. This job – as important as it was – did not pay as well as making, restoring and repairing fine furniture for some of the grandest houses in England. It was important, therefore, that Fred should make a contribution to the family's income at the earliest opportunity.

Incidentally, Sir Fred came across an interesting little item of family history during the course of being interviewed for this book. Bob Shilling, who runs his own travel agency business in London, worked for Fred for many years. When his own father died Bob inherited some woodworking tools which were originally in the ownership of his grandfather, who was also a cabinet-maker at Waring & Gillow at the time Sir Fred's own father worked there many years ago.

Among the beautifully-kept tools was a spirit-level made from wood and brass bearing the initials FWP, carved very neatly on the side of the instrument. Bob was not aware that Sir Fred's father had even been a cabinet-maker, let alone having worked for Waring & Gillow, but when he heard Fred talk about his father's skills on a BBC national radio programme he contacted him and very generously returned the essential element of the cabinet-maker's craft to the family where he felt it belonged. A very charming gesture and I trust it will be agreed, a remarkable coincidence.

If Bob's grandfather had borrowed the spirit-level from Sir Fred's father around 1910, the fact that it was returned after all those years goes to show that there must be hope for everyone still awaiting the return of garden shears, books or other items loaned to neighbours and friends!

Fred's father wanted him to take up a career in banking and offered to arrange an interview with the Midland Bank. His son was adamant that he did not have the slightest interest in following a career which relied upon what he considered to be dead men's shoes.

Fred made it clear that it was the London Stock Exchange which had the most attraction as far as he was concerned. This was the place where fortunes were made. Even the most disinterested observer might be forgiven if he ventured to suggest that young Fred Pontin's attitude at that time was probably influenced by the wild, almost hysterical, boom which took place in the investment markets during the post-war period of 1919-1920 when the most successful of the many daring speculators became millionaires on a literally overnight basis.

These exciting events must surely have been in Fred's mind when discussing what career he would follow. He remembered very clearly telling his father that he wanted "to join the millionaires' club". He must have explained to a disappointed father that it was impossible to make that sort of money working for a bank. Banks were places to keep your fortune, not to make it, at least as far as the ambitious Fred Pontin was concerned in those early days.

Even at such a tender age, and with no direct knowledge of the workings of the City of London, he seemed to be very much aware of what he wanted by way of a future career. He got his own way, just as he did so often in later life, despite his father's misgivings regarding the uncertainties connected with something which he did not really understand.

The youthful Fred Pontin had long been an avid reader of the financial columns of the national press and he was certain that the Stock Exchange was where all of the wealthy people had made their money; by trading in stocks and shares, commodities and all manner of exciting pieces of paper. The City, he decided there and then, was for him and he could not be persuaded otherwise.

Chapter Three

SOMETHING IN THE CITY

As was usual in those times, it was a family connection which provided the introduction to a Mr Smith, who was employed as an office manager at a firm of gilt-edged jobbers called Gordon Askew and Biddough.

There was no time to enjoy the summer holidays that year, for it was the Monday following Fred's last day at school that he reported to the firm's premises in the City of London.

He had been there for only one week – doing very little and spending most of his time sitting with the messengers – when he was called over by Mr Smith. He handed Fred a one pound note for his wages, then broke the news that he was sorry but he was instructed to give Fred, his newest clerk, just one week's notice. Fred found it difficult to understand what was happening and asked what he had done to deserve the sack after such a short period of time. He felt he had done nothing wrong. In fact, he had done virtually nothing at all, although this was no fault of the young lad.

The office manager told Fred not to worry; nothing was held against him, but the firm, which had a staff of 80, was going into liquidation. Fred's immediate reaction was to return the money with the remark that perhaps the firm was going to need it more than him . . . Mr Smith laughed, then explained that it was to be a voluntary liquidation, purely for tax reasons.

It appeared that firms were taxed upon average earnings over a period of three years. Askews had enjoyed two very good years and voluntary liquidation was a perfectly legal and common tax avoidance device in those days.

Mr Smith seemed to be treating the whole matter very lightly. He announced, to Fred's enormous relief, that he would have no trouble in finding a similar job with another firm. Mr Smith further astonished Fred by saying that he would also qualify for a bonus – the lowest on offer, but of a sum of no less than £100. This was a considerable amount of money in those days and in terms of 1999 values this bonus was worth some £2,100.

So, after only two weeks of employment in the world of high finance, Fred was to receive (even he could not possibly say that it had really been earned) the magnificent sum of £102. It may not have proved to be a fortune, but it did make a jolly good start.

Fred couldn't wait to get home in order to tell his parents this splendid news. As far as he was concerned in recalling those far off days, his love of money started from that wonderful summer's day in 1921 . . . and the feeling had never left him, as he was the first to admit.

When Fred took up his job with Askews he was dressed in his grandfather's long, double-breasted jacket, which his mother had altered to match the latest trend in men's fashion. He soon learned that it was important to look the part, having seen the smart clothes worn by the partners and senior employees, so Fred had no hesitation in deciding to invest some of his newly-acquired wealth in a brand new outfit.

Hector Powe in Bishopsgate was a tailor's shop of some distinction as far as the budding City gent was concerned, so he lost no time in paying them a visit. He spent over £40 on an off-the-peg black jacket, striped trousers, hat, suede gloves, spats and rolled umbrella. He was now ready to face the world and his new employers.

These turned out to be Messrs Gow and Parsons, a recently-formed firm of stockbrokers seeking five senior clerks and two juniors. One of the juniors was to be the still inexperienced Fred Pontin. The other was someone he can only recall as Walpole, a lad of fourteen years of age who had one week's seniority over Fred because the young Pontin was the last member of the staff to be recruited to the new business.

The senior partners were John Barnett Gow, who came to London from a firm in Glasgow called Gow Brothers and Gemmell, and a Mr Parsons, who was previously with a firm of merchant bankers Fred remembered as Lathan & Roselli. Both partners employed their sons in their latest commercial enterprise. Albert Parsons was in charge of "names" clients and Ian Gow had similar duties in a basement in Throgmorton Street, close to the floor of the Stock Exchange.

Fred was given what he has always described as an "Irishman's rise". His wages were fixed at fifteen shillings per week (75 pence in decimal currency). Walpole and Fred had a routine which involved the daily collection of official and unofficial lists of share prices from the printers, who Fred clearly remembered provided a very erratic service.

The Stock Exchange ceased trading at 3.30 in the afternoon and five o'clock was when the lists should have become available. More often than not, however, Fred had to hang around until 7 p.m. before he could rush back to the office and prepare to post the information to the provincial brokers, for whom his employers were conducting regular dealing business on their behalf on the floor of the Stock Exchange.

These out-of-town brokers relied upon the lists in order to keep their clients in touch with the London share markets.

All should have been well except that the other junior and young Pontin were often at loggerheads about whose turn it was to be doing this menial, but important, daily task. The inevitable happened. Neither of them did the post one day, and to compound their misdemeanours the office was left with the lights on and the doors wide open.

They were given the sack. Fred started to appreciate that fortunes were not all that easily made in the City. Even keeping a steady job was proving to be a difficult task.

Perhaps junior clerks were difficult to recruit, so whatever the reason, both Fred and Walpole were reinstated by Albert Parsons, though Fred was determined that he was not going back to do the junior job. He succeeded in earning promotion to the task of assisting the son of one of the partners, who was then a "red button" clerk on the floor of the Stock Exchange.

Fred's duties consisted of handling "names", registering details of buyers and sellers of shares. He had, at last, been given a job which gave him an insight into the deals conducted in the share markets.

Fred began to understand terminology such as "bulls", "bears", "stags", highs and lows and middle market prices. Dividends, dividend cover, yields, price earnings ratios, capital issues – all of these terms became very familiar with his keenness to digest every scrap of information on offer.

He must have performed his duties in a satisfactory manner, because he was rewarded with a ten shillings rise bringing his weekly wages up to 25 shillings. Further increments followed and Fred was soon earning twice this amount.

He continued to be very ambitious. It must have showed, because he soon graduated to jobbers' ledger, a cash book record of transactions between jobbers and brokers. This promotion did not come without some prior jiggery-pokery, mainly on the basis that Fred thought that the man whom he eventually succeeded was far from efficient and had been promoted over his head. Fred was certain that he could do the job better. He bitterly resented the fact that the office manager had favoured the other person and would not listen to his urgent protestations.

A showdown was soon brought about when Fred contrived to "find" some names which appeared to have been "mislaid" by the party he was convinced was an incompetent incumbent as far as the much-coveted job was concerned.

It should perhaps be explained that the direct effect of Fred's employers not being able to pass on the names of the buyers of shares to the selling brokers was that the other firm then had the right to "sell out" the holdings for cash to a market jobber. As a result, Gow and Parsons were forced to finance any losses on the deals from their own resources.

In due course Fred was to receive the much-sought-after promotion and a rise in his weekly wage to four pounds ten shillings. The office manager was eventually sacked when the partners came to appreciate that Fred had been treated very unfairly.

Before not too much time had passed there was what Fred would almost certainly describe as a form of poetic justice. When he was employed on the clients' ledger Fred made a very serious error in mixing up the statements of account which were sent out to a father and son, both of whom had been dealing – with the benefit of insider knowledge – in the shares of a sugar refining company.

Fred recalled that his slip-up caused what he described as "a hell of a row". Both clients wrote and complained to the senior partner and demanded that young Pontin should be sacked! He was given one month's notice.

He had been with the firm for over four years, so the consolation was that Fred had gained some very valuable experience. Luckily he had enough common sense to take a realistic view in that, given the particular circumstances, the dismissal was undoubtedly justified. Although he considered that he had been entitled to take matters into his own hands on the earlier occasion, when he felt that his work had lacked proper recognition from the office manager, Fred did not see how he could possibly resent dismissal for what can only be described as incompetence.

In later years, when Fred was running his own business and dealing with large numbers of staff, he considered it essential that he should always be in a position to be able to justify any disciplinary action which was proved to be necessary and he sought similar realism from any transgressors. Whether or not he actually succeeded in meeting these ambitious and exacting requirements is probably best left to the judgment of others but there have been many tales of instant dismissal, long before the advent of industrial tribunals.

Out of a job and with the share markets relatively quiet after the industrial and rubber booms which followed the First World War, Fred approached the Stock Exchange Benevolent Fund, which acted as a type of employment agency. They directed him to Bristow Brothers, a firm of stock jobbers who were the third largest in foreign stocks. He must have impressed them at his interview by his knowledge and the extent of his experience, as he was offered a salaried clerical position at an annual salary £500 – subject to a good reference from Fred's previous employer.

Bearing in mind the enforced nature of his departure, Fred was more than a little apprehensive when he called on the new office manager at Gow & Parsons. He need not have worried. Despite the circumstances of his dismissal he was given a reference which was good enough to secure his new position with Bristow Brothers.

Fred was again employed on the jobbers' ledger, where the volume of work did not reach any appreciable level until after the firm's partners returned from the floor of the Stock Exchange after 3.30 in the afternoon. It was then necessary to write up all of the transactions conducted during the day's business.

Fred remembered the leisurely lunches and games of dominoes at J. Lyons' premises in Throgmorton Street while other clerks and the new recruit at Bristows waited for the partners and dealers to return to their offices.

He also learned new aspects of the business in stocks and shares, in that his employers were involved with arbitrage, the traffic in securities in order to take advantage of different prices in other markets. Most of Bristows' foreign transactions were conducted on the markets in Belgium, where bearer shares, as opposed to registered stocks, were the predominant feature.

Fred broadened the depth of his experience and knowledge, but, once he had assimilated and understood the precise nature of the day to day transactions, he began to find the work rather boring and far from inspirational.

He was still in no position to create and accumulate capital of his own, though, at least, he was learning how sterling and foreign currencies were being converted into paper and how this paper represented wealth, power and influence.

After a year with Bristows Fred felt that he was in a rut. Something had to be done about it. Although he was earning a reasonable salary, with bonuses of about £100, he felt that it was time to move on.

At least on this occasion, his projected move was not being forced upon him, so around about Fred's twenty first birthday he returned to the Stock Exchange Benevolent Fund to see if they could find him a better job with improved prospects.

Perhaps they felt that Fred warranted some form of challenge, because they ignored the conventional broking and jobbing houses and introduced the ambitious young man to a company called Rock Investments Limited, which was operated by Martin Coles Harman.

Within no time at all Fred was introduced to the man from whom he was to learn more about "paper" transactions than from all of his previous employers put together. It was a move that led him into a phase of his City career that was to have a profound influence on Sir Fred's future success, although he could never have known it at the time.

Harman was famous, or perhaps notorious, for owning Lundy Island situated off the coast of Devon in the Bristol Channel. He had entertained ambitions to declare some form of independence and create a tax haven on the lines of Jersey and Guernsey in the Channel Islands, but the authorities would have none of it.

Although it was contrary to British Law Harman went as far as to introduce his own currency, the bronze coins of which were called puffins and half-puffins, after the sea birds on the island. They also bore his portrait making him one of the few private individuals ever to achieve this status.

The Government were not amused, but only a nominal fine was imposed upon him in 1930. Souvenir sets of the offending coins were struck in 1965 from Harman's original dies. He also produced and sold Lundy postage stamps. This time there was no protest from the authorities and subsequent owners of the island have followed this practice.

His efforts created only modest returns for this enterprising and innovative businessman with whom Fred soon formed a good working relationship. In due course it could perhaps be said that Fred became his protégé and was to form a great deal of respect for Harman's business acumen.

Because of this Fred had never had any difficulty in being even-handed regarding Harman's eventual fall from grace, and his subsequent prison sentence, which resulted from charges of fraudulent transactions in stocks and shares.

At the time of Fred's arrival in the City Harman was controlling and operating a series of companies with grand sounding names, such as London Irish Trust, Oceana Consolidated and the British Bank for Foreign Trade. They were all dealing with each other as a method of keeping up the prices of various stocks and shares in which Harman's investment companies were interested.

Fred came to be very much involved with the entire process, which he came to describe as "dog eating dog". This type of activity certainly appeared to be legal in those days, when controls were not nearly as stringent as they have been in the scandal-hit 1990s.

Fred had his preliminary job interview with the office manager, Dickie Doyle, who figured very prominently in Fred's post-war business activities. Dickie Doyle subsequently became acting chairman of Pontin's Limited when Fred became incapacitated as a result of a serious motoring accident.

Fred was offered an annual salary of £800, which Harman immediately increased to £1,000 as soon as he realised the full extent of his new employee's considerable knowledge and experience. By the mid-1930s Fred's annual earnings increased to some £2,000 (some £63,000 at 1999 values) but he was expected to work very hard and not question the long hours which were required by his new employer.

Sir Fred had often reflected that if he had joined the Midland Bank on leaving school he would have been very lucky to have earned anything approaching this level of salary. Moreover, he would have been institutionalised to such an extent that his success and enthusiasm would have been lost to an important sector of the British holiday and leisure industries.

Fred's duties were far from routine. At the age of 26 he was dealing on a basis which he found both exciting and stimulating. As his experience became broadened he also gained increased confidence and learned to think for himself. So much so that at a later date he was able to warn Harman of the markedly dubious manner in which certain of his associates were conducting their activities in a series of stock transactions.

In doing so Fred earned his employer's respect and also what he hoped would be his admiration for Fred's timely spotting of a blatant attempt at deception. To say that Sir Fred had never held any ill will against Martin Coles Harman, despite the eventual criminal record, is to understate the case.

During the course of Fred's employment with Harman's organisation he learned virtually every facet of the capital markets.

Although his employer's career was to be ruined, Fred was able to take advantage of the opportunity to learn about finance by first-hand experience. When, in due course, Fred was to conceive an idea for a business which required capital investment, as opposed to an over-reliance on borrowed money, it was his former City connections which were to provide the means for the creation of his outstandingly successful business empire.

Chapter Four

CHAMPAGNE DAYS

Fred Pontin married in 1929, having met his wife, Dorothy Mortimer, at one of the social events organised at Walthamstow Avenue Football Club.

They were blessed with a daughter, Patricia Heather Mavis, who was born in November 1937. Fred did not have a lot of say in the choice of two of these names but he felt that Heather might bring them all some luck.

Being accustomed to annual earnings of up to £2,000 but now having increased family responsibilities, there was a pressing need to generate more income. Fred had no capital to invest as a partner in another City firm and he could not face the prospect of working as just another inconsequential employee.

Having experienced entrepreneurial enterprise when working with Martin Coles Harman, Fred felt that the time had come to start his own business. The question which faced him was what could he do to earn a worthwhile return without the need to invest capital?

Football pools were in their infancy, having been started by Littlewoods and Vernons. Fred decided to try his hand by setting up Smiths Soccer Totes Limited. Premises were obtained in Bride Lane, Ludgate Circus, very close to a boxing gymnasium where Primo Carnera was training for a title fight.

Fred bought a mailing list containing 20,000 names and he recruited some part-time employees as well as members of his family to send fixed-odds coupons to addresses all over the United Kingdom. There was a covering letter which intimated that the prospective customers had been recommended by "reliable clients".

This exercise in direct marketing proved to be reasonably successful. Turnover soon increased to an acceptable level and Fred was starting to earn some money again. He introduced various combinations such as "four draws" and "seven home wins" so that altogether there were seven separate pools.

Although he was not fully aware of the implications at that time, Fred's clients were actually being offered a degree of what amounted to "illegal" credit, which proved to be an advantage over the larger companies, who could not afford to anticipate an impending decision on a gambling case in the High Court.

Unfortunately, Fred's customers tended to offer payment in settlement of their accounts only when they won and not when they lost. Business could not continue to operate on such an uncertain basis. His description of this experience has always been "Skinners – No Winners" – He fixed the odds according to the number of "skinners" and took the chance of getting paid.

Other pools were formed and Fred was joined in this burgeoning business by his sister Elsie. He diversified into bookmaking and life became less precarious until the outbreak of war put an end to horse racing.

Hitler did not strike though before Fred benefited from some twelve months of relative prosperity. He had many regular clients, including John Cobb, the racing motorist, with whom he shared a regular bottle of Veuve Clicquot champagne at El Vino in Leadenhall Street. When Elsie talked about the old days, and this time in particular, she was inclined to say "You didn't do too bad".

She was right; her brother considered life to be very very tolerable. Fred was his own boss and he had some cash in his pocket. This form of activity was not likely to lead to everlasting prosperity, but, in the event, King and country had other plans for Fred and there was to be a dramatic fall in his standard of living.

He had suffered from deafness in one ear for many years so, as far as the Services were concerned, this was a disability which excluded him from active duties in the war against Germany's aggression in Europe.

Fred went to the appropriate authorities to register his availability for other work in the war effort and he was directed to the Orkney Islands, where he was instructed to report to the catering manager. This overworked individual was responsible for feeding what ultimately proved to be an enormous work force, many of whose members were to be mustered from the Republic of Ireland.

Fred had only recently been recruited as a reserve policeman and had reported to Mincing Lane in the City to collect an armlet, truncheon and helmet. He should also have reported to the Guildhall in order to be sworn in, but, after an altogether too-festive an evening with some of his bookmaking friends at the Trocadero restaurant and a Soho night club, he overslept and missed this solemn occasion.

One of his colleagues had, however, completed all of the necessary formalities and one of his first duties on that same night was to guard Southwark Bridge. This was a far from pleasant task in November 1939, being cold and damp and thoroughly unattractive.

Fred decided that this was no way to spend the winter nights. The posting to the Orkneys presented an opportunity to escape from the duties of a glorified air raid warden, even though he had never heard of the islands, let alone knew where to find them. He had some previous experience as a special constable during the General Strike of 1926 and, although his memories of those days were far from disagreeable, they were not to change his mind about the move northwards.

Rail warrant in his pocket, Fred caught the 3.30 p.m. train from Euston on the first leg of his journey to the Orkney Islands. By then he had a vague notion of where these islands lay in geographical terms. On arrival at Thurso the next day, in the company of two other luckless souls, Fred found a local hotel where they were able to spend the night in comparative comfort, albeit somewhat apprehensive about what they would be called upon to do when they reported for duty early the next morning.

Their first task was to escort 40 Irish labourers on the ferry ship to the islands, the southernmost of which lay just a few miles off the North West coast of the Scottish mainland. It so happened that Fred was dressed in his "City uniform" of black jacket, striped trousers, spats and a trilby hat.

The ferry ship travelled to Stromness and Hoy escorted by a Royal Naval frigate. When they were told that the Pentland Firth was swarming with enemy submarines Fred began to wonder whether or not Southwark Bridge would have afforded a more attractive proposition after all.

They were eventually put ashore on a jetty overlooking Scapa Flow. It was in very poor condition, not having been repaired since it was damaged in World War One and, needless to say, the weather was entirely predictable. A blizzard made the landing even more hazardous so they were not impressed by this inauspicious welcome.

Neither were they reassured by the state of the roads and the open lorries which were to transport the party to the accommodation site. All of the workmen were carrying their belongings in brown paper parcels or carrier bags, and when the lorries sank up to their axles in thick brown mud their possessions had to be temporarily discarded in order to push the vehicles on to firmer ground.

Fred's rather superior outfit appeared to single him out as a cut above the others in terms of sartorial elegance and he managed to exclude himself from such a strenuous and thoroughly messy activity.

They arrived at the accommodation camp, which was being constructed for the Admiralty by Balfour Beatty. Fred's quarters consisted of a little room measuring six-feet by ten feet six inches. There were no items of furniture other than an iron bedstead, a flock mattress and a pillow. There were a few blankets but no sheets and no pillow case.

He lost no time in complaining to Mr Sharpe, the site agent, on the basis that he was certainly not accustomed to such primitive accommodation and he would not stand for it. It was no surprise to receive the classic reply of "Don't you know there's a bloody war on!". Fred knew then that his hitherto comfortable lifestyle was to change on quite a dramatic basis.

This was the time of the "phoney war", but as far as Fred was concerned privation was to commence from that day onward. It was to be a long time before his life was to return to some form of normality.

His immediate superior, the catering manager, was soon the victim of a nervous breakdown so Fred was called upon to take over his duties. The living conditions of the construction workers could only be described as horrific. Fred was charged with the responsibility of feeding them on a weekly budget of one pound seven shillings and six pence (£1.37p) for each person. For those interested in comparisons with more up to date values this would be the equivalent of £34 in 1999.

The numbers in the work force eventually built up to 15,000 and this became Fred's first experience of mass catering. As well as the Irish there were Norwegians from Stavanger.

All supplies were subject to the rationing regulations, so he made use of every conceivable device in an effort to provide a balanced diet, despite the limited nature of the menus. He remembers buying excellent beef cattle "on the hoof" at Kirkwall and there were also plentiful supplies of eggs in the islands. Not all of the raw material was up to these standards and Fred soon came to rely upon the ingenuity of the cooks to make the grub more palatable to his ever-ravenous throng of manual workers.

Perhaps now is a good time to reflect on whether or not this early experience of mass catering was to have a beneficial effect, or otherwise, on feeding guests at Fred Pontin's holiday camps which he opened just after the war ended and in conditions where the rationing of food was to remain with the British people for almost ten years.

The work force in the Orkney Islands was building oil containers and dummy ships as well as accommodation units. These construction activities attracted numerous reconnaissance flights by German air-craft, which were sometimes followed by enemy air attacks. It appeared that the allied efforts to convince the Germans that our naval forces were greater than they actually were proved to be successful.

When an air raid killed three of Fred's workers he grew to under-stand that there could be no guarantee of survival – even in such a remote outpost of the United Kingdom.

It was at this time that Fred was fortunate to meet a person who has played a very significant role in his personal life as well as what was to be his post-war business career in the holiday camp industry. Ann Calder Scott Miller, who was then 24 years of age, was employed by the Civil Service as the Food Executive Officer for the Orkney and Shetland Islands. It was necessary for Fred to have to deal with her in connection with rations for the construction workers.

She was also the National Registration Officer with the duties of keeping personal records on the entire population of the islands, both indigenous and migrant.

Ann Miller was educated in the Orkney Islands and Edinburgh University, where she graduated with a M.A. and B. Com. Before the war she had spent a year with the John Lewis Partnership in London at their Oxford Street store under a graduate training scheme. She had been seeking commercial experience in order to complement her degree qualifications.

The outbreak of hostilities took her back to her parents' home in the Orkneys, from where her mother had applied for the civil service job on her behalf, even though Ann was very keen to join the Women's Royal Air Force and play her part in the war. Her father, a lighthouse keeper, would not countenance such a spirit of adventure so her wartime duties were confined to registration formalities and being responsible for controlling civilian and military food supplies.

Life was never conducted on a wholly routine basis in the storm-battered islands, but Ann Miller, being a local girl and having many friends, was able to introduce Fred to numerous social activities that were a pleasant divergence from life in the accommo-dation camp. Summers were short, but on the few days when there was no wind and the sun shone, the couple obtained a brief release from their onerous and tedious duties. They enjoyed the scenery together, trying to forget that there was a war on.

The austerity of Fred's life in the Orkneys was to be relieved to a considerable extent by his close friendship with Ann Miller. It would be unfair to describe their relationship in such hackneyed terms as "just another wartime romance". It was also the start of a personal and business partnership which has endured during a period of well over fifty years up until the day he died. Ann Miller's name will figure prominently in this record of Sir Fred's extraordinary life and times.

Fred left the Orkney Islands just after the Germans surrendered in May 1945. He was still of military age so there was no question of him being able to return to normal civilian life. Because of his wartime experience he was directed to a National Service Hostel at Coventry where he was to receive a week's training before being sent to undertake managerial responsibilities at a similar establishment elsewhere in the United Kingdom.

Fred's tuition was cut short when news was received of a riot at the Government's original hostel for manual workers at Jubilee Drive, Kidderminster, an accommodation unit of chalets for 950 male forge workers and 50 female land girls from nearby sugar beet fields. The manager, a retired colonel, had been there for only three weeks before being forced to pack in the job after he had been physically assaulted. He could no longer stand the strain of trying to keep the inmates under some form of acceptable control.

Fred Pontin had already arranged to take Ann Miller to the theatre to see *Arsenic and Old Lace* so he managed to delay the taking up of his new appointment until the last day of the week. Ann had broken her journey at Coventry on her way to an appointment in London with Lord Woolton, the Food Minister, to discuss her future employment in the Civil Service.

Fred was not given any details of the riot and the manager's forced departure from Kidderminster, so he arrived at the hostel in a state of complete ignorance as far as its grim reputation was concerned. However, he soon became aware of the hostility that was extended to people with any degree of authority.

The staff, including the catering officer, entertainments manager, matron and nursing sisters, took Fred on a tour of the site. In the assembly hall his attention was drawn to a crudely written poster bearing the text "Welcome to the new manager" under the insignia of the skull and crossbones.

That night, after members of the camp's population returned from the local pubs – alcoholic liquor not being available on the site – there was another riot with fighting between many of the men, various missiles being thrown and fire hoses played on the staff and inmates alike. Fred quickly retreated to a bungalow which had been allocated as his personal living quarters.

Having carefully locked all of the doors, he set about preparing a plan for dealing with the situation. Fred took the view that he had not come through the war just to be intimidated by a crowd of ruffians.

There was clearly a case for him to make his presence felt before he suffered the same fate as his predecessor. Next morning Fred went to see the person in charge of the local office of the Ministry of Labour. He announced to this astonished official that he was going to get rid of the main rabble rousers so that some degree of discipline could be restored in the camp.

This state of affairs could not be permitted to continue. The drunken festivities were causing nothing but mayhem as far as the manager's position was concerned. It was to be a question of if they did not go, Fred certainly would. He did not wish to suffer the same fate as the previous manager.

Fred was told that it would be very unwise to carry out such a policy as the men were engaged upon work of national importance involving the manufacture of weapons and ammunition. Luckily, reason and common sense prevailed and he was successful in getting his own way in the matter.

He warned the local police that he was sacking about twenty troublemakers and that they had better be on hand to supervise the arrangements, which ran the risk of violence. There was indeed a police presence when Fred dismissed the now sober ringleaders. There were the inevitable protests but he made it clear that his decision was final. There were to be no second chances under his new regime.

Perhaps Fred's height of six feet three inches and a heavy frame had something to do with it, but he got away with this course of action and he enjoyed a large whisky when it was all over.

These measures were not welcomed by Cadburys' management, who were responsible for the site. They complained of the "oppressive conduct" of the new administrator. Fred's response was to insist that as he was the ninth manager in four and a half years there was clearly a need for a new approach to discipline. If they did not support his policy then they had better start looking for number ten.

He got his own way again and, although the remainder of his stay was far from uneventful, he did at least last the course. Fred improved the living conditions and the quality of the food, as well as the entertainment . . . and he took the precaution of having a personal bodyguard who was always accompanied by an Alsatian dog.

However, Fred still had his problems. Some of the workers stole his car and abandoned it with housebreaking tools in Kidderminster. Then he had trouble from American servicemen mixing with the land girls causing racial tensions between the black and white GIs who attended dances at the hostel.

Looking back he felt that his experiences in the Orkneys and at Kidderminster were to stand him in good stead for his future career in mass catering and entertainment at the post-war holiday camps. The establishment of these camps was to change not only his own life, but that of Ann Miller and the lives of all members of his family.

Chapter Five

WELCOME CAMPERS!

Fred was constantly seeking a release from Kidderminster, and when this was granted he joined forces with the site's catering manager, a man called Youlton. The rebuilding of the city of Bristol offered opportunities for exploiting their wartime experience, so, after seeing the local authority, they tendered for the operation of a former 1,000 bed camp at Bedminster.

The council had imported large numbers of workers for the reconstruction programme. Unlike Kidderminster, their partnership could operate this camp on a commercial basis, with the council paying a fee for their services. The council entered into a fifty-fifty profit sharing arrangement with Fred providing the initial cash capital of £100 and Youlton the catering equipment that got them into business.

This was never likely to be a highly profitable venture, but it was a reintroduction to the spirit of free enterprise and capitalism. The Stock Exchange had not returned to anything like the prewar level of trading, so Fred's immediate future did not lie in that direction or with the fixed odds pools and other bookmaking activity. Throughout the whole of post-war Britain money was scarce and businesses then being released from their wartime activities were only just starting to think about peacetime trading and the manufacture of consumer goods.

Fred's ideas for the provision of "value for money" family holidays were taking shape. He needed a suitable site to make a start before too many other people came to the same conclusion . . . and his search led him to the front door of Leslie Dean's house at a village called, Berrow near Burnham-on-Sea, Somerset.

It would not be too difficult to imagine what was passing through his mind when he parked his car outside of Les Dean's house. There were fine views across the Somerset Levels to Brent Knoll and the Mendip Hills, home of the famous Cheddar Caves and Burrington

Combe, which provided inspiration for the well known 19th century hymn *Rock of Ages*.

A fine sandy beach stretching over seven miles from Burnham-on-Sea to Brean Down was only a very short distance away and the Brean Sands site, which had been recommended by the petrol pump attendant, was just down the road. Fred Pontin decided there and then that this was an attractive area for holidays and no mistake.

What's more, the coast of North Somerset was easily accessible from the highly populated areas in the West Midlands and Bristol. There were main line Great Western Railway stations at Weston-super-Mare and the nearby market town of Highbridge. Trains also ran direct from Paddington in central London.

Much of Britain's coastline had been out of bounds during the war years and Fred's considered view was that this would provide an added incentive to those seeking a break from an austere peacetime. Because of the intervention of the war, paid holidays were still a novelty after the passing of the Holidays with Pay Act in 1938, which gave all employees an entitlement to a week's paid leave, together with the usual public holidays.

Fred came to the conclusion that gratuities being paid to ex-servicemen would also fuel a demand for places in holiday camps that was sure to exceed supply. He could not wait to put his theories to the ultimate test – the ownership of a seaside holiday centre.

He had been somewhat dismayed when seeing "his" site for the first time. Many of the wooden huts had been badly damaged when the US army had taken part in a little fun with their tanks before they quit the place just before the Normandy landings. They had been training for the invasion by carrying out exercises on the nearby beach, which resembled those in Northern France.

Fred took the view that some form of compensation would be payable by the Government and perhaps this could be part of the deal; that is if there was going to be a deal.

The unknown factor troubling him was: could this Mr. Dean be persuaded to sell the holiday camp site from which he had been trading before the war? Perhaps he was keen to get back into business. It did not look, though, as if a start had been made on repairs.

Every man is supposed to have his price, even though Fred was not immediately familiar with Walpole's famous quotation, but, with a fully utilised overdraft limit of £500 at the Corn Street branch of Barclays Bank in Bristol, he was hardly in a position to be too generous. What should he be offering? He had no idea of land values but the site was exactly what he had been hoping to find during his searches along the Somerset coastline.

All manner of thoughts were racing through Fred's mind when twelve year old Valerie Dean answered his knock on the front door and she called out to her mother that a gentleman was asking to see her daddy. There was something of an anticlimax as far as Fred's anxious expectancy was concerned. Leslie Dean was not at home. He was at the other of his holiday camp sites at Osmington Bay, near Weymouth in Dorset, where he was making preparations for a reopening.

Fred was a little apprehensive at this news. Would he be re-opening the site he was interested in? Mrs Audrey Dean reassured him by saying that she felt that her husband could well be interested in selling the Brean Sands property. It was arranged that Fred would return at the weekend, by which time Leslie would be back from Dorset.

He would then be in a position to organise a conducted tour of the site so that Fred could gain a better impression of the condition of the buildings. Mrs Dean explained that her husband would also be able to provide details of the claim which had been submitted to the appropriate ministerial department in connection with the dilapidations.

Within the next few days a price of £23,000 (some £510,000 by 1999 values) was agreed, but this was to be for control of all the shares in the company which owned the site, not for the purchase of the actual property. On this basis the new owner would have the benefit of any monies received from the government by way of compensation for the damaged buildings. This was the sort of deal that Fred liked to put together and he felt that his mentor from prewar days in the City, Martin Coles Harman, would have been proud of him

Fred's former employer was very much on his mind when he started his new business, because he now had to find the money for the deal.

He had arranged to pay this significant sum of money for what amounted to no more than eight acres of land with about 100 wrecked and derelict buildings, including the dining hall, kitchen and ancillary offices. Yet Fred was absolutely convinced that he was about to enter a growth industry with enormous opportunities for expansion.

His experience in the City had led him to believe that investment capital was always available for really worthwhile propositions and Fred was determined that his newly purchased company would not only be successful but the shares would be quoted on the London Stock Exchange, thus realising one of his long-held ambitions.

He decided to set up a syndicate of personal investors to subscribe for 50% of the capital in the company and lost no time in making contact with some of his prewar City connections, including Harman and Reginald Binns, both of whom agreed to give their support to Fred's new venture. Another investor was Bill Smith, who was in the meat trade, and he was joined by a plastic button manufacturer called Alex Bernstein. Fred also persuaded Rex Randall, one of his bookmaker friends, to make an investment. Together this group of indi-vidual investors put up the sum of £12,500 for 50% of Fred's new holiday camp company.

This cash-raising exercise took place before Business Plans became a vogue term, yet Fred managed to persuade everyone that this was a proposition that was well worth a modest investment.

Looking back, they could well have thought that Fred was suffering from some form of Orcadian madness, but, no doubt recalling the ability he had demonstrated in his prewar days, they had the necessary confidence to back his foresight. The lure of a prospective quoted investment was an important consideration after a period of financial dormancy as far as the capital markets were concerned.

This small band of investors was relying upon Fred to produce an attractive return on their investment. They were not to be disappointed.

Fred quickly sold out his interest in the Bedminster business to his partner and this raised a somewhat gratifying amount of £2,000. His bank manager, Mr. Collins at Barclays Bank in Bristol, was not only impressed by Fred's infectious optimism but he was also prepared to admit to taking a liking to his customer's blue eyes. He agreed that the bank would lend the sum of £10,500. For internal technical reasons associated with individual discretionary powers in lending money without reference to Head Office, this was initially made available by contributions from other branches in Somerset, including Highbridge and Burnham-on-Sea. Perhaps even Mr Collins was taking a risk by seeking to disguise his largesse in such a manner. Fred Pontin was not to let him down.

The financial support from Barclays Bank enabled Fred to acquire control of the remaining 50% of the shares in Brean Sands Holiday Camp Limited. He then changed the name to Pontin's Holiday Camps Limited . . . Fred had plans for future expansion.

After a year or so the bank's lending was consolidated in one account at the Corn Street branch. Mr Collins did not know it at the time, but he had acquired a first-class customer for his employers and he did well in his future career with Barclays. He eventually became a

local director and joined the board as a non-executive director of
Pontin's on his retirement from the bank.

The company now had an authorised and issued capital of
£5,000 represented by 5,000 shares, each with a par value of £1. As
Leslie Dean's asking price was almost £5 for each share, the new
owners had already awarded the shares a premium rating even
though the underlying asset, the debutante to the post-war holiday
camp industry, was still a shambles, let alone open for business.

Fred was appointed Chairman and Managing Director at the
first board meeting and each shareholder was invited to become a
director of the company, although Harman and one of the others
were to be represented by nominees. The Harman nominee, Dickie
Doyle, was to stay on the board for many vital years

Leslie Dean also joined the board so that everyone could have the
benefit of his experience. He was, after all, the only person among
them who had the faintest idea of how a holiday camp should be
operated. Fred was, however, a quick learner and soon proved that
he had an inherent instinct for what the public wanted.

Urgent repairs were needed at Brean Sands and a work force was
recruited from the accommodation camp in Bedminster. Because of
their five-day working week, the men were available on Saturday
mornings, so Fred hired three coaches to take them to Brean. Renovations took place over three consecutive weekends in June.

The construction workers received cash and as many sandwiches
as they could eat. There was also a ready supply of the local ale,
which seemed to help get the task completed in good time for the
start of the season in mid-July.

Fred had been busy, meanwhile, in acquiring furniture, bed linen,
pots and pans and cutlery from the war-surplus sales being held by
the Ministry of Works. These items were not exactly of the highest
quality but he was working on the basis that people would be
prepared to make allowances after the privations of the war years.

Attracting the first customers proved to be no trouble at all. Just
one advertisement was placed in the *Sunday Express* and thousands
of enquiries poured into the hastily furnished office at Brean Sands.

Members of staff were recruited locally, but the lack of experience
was becoming only too obvious. After two weeks of rather dis-
organised operations Fred decided that he needed some help from
his family. His brother Len had gone back to his old job with Tote
Investors after he was demobilised from the army, but, at the age of
27, he was soon looking for a position which offered better prospects.

When Fred's "rescue" telephone call came he did not hesitate in
making haste down to Weston-super-Mare railway station, where

his elder brother picked him up in the car at eight o'clock in the evening and they drove to Brean Sands. Len still remembers finding the camp absolutely bursting with people and activity but nothing but chaos as far as the administrative side of the business was concerned. This was why he was needed and he had no time to enjoy the local scenery.

Fred and Len worked together on the mass of paperwork which had accumulated, but at midnight they took off to the dining room, which doubled as a dance hall. This was so they could assist in the preparation of the sausage sandwiches and hot coffee which were offered to the guests at the end of each evening's entertainment.

This little routine became a firm favourite with the holiday-makers and resulted in a welcome boost to the cash takings. It also illustrated Fred's willingness to turn his hand to any task which brought him into regular and direct contact with his guests. This would be an important feature of his future policy.

Thousands of Sir Fred's most loyal customers have always appreciated this accessibility and of his readiness to have a drink and a chat whenever they came across him during the course of his regular visits to each of his future sites. If he had any secret when establishing this type of relationship with his guests it must be what could be described only as an instinctive perception of what his clients were seeking on their annual holidays. Long gone are the days when personable characters such as Fred Pontin, Billy Butlin and Harry Warner could be seen having a pint with their campers during the course of the evening's social activities. Today's holiday centres, formerly controlled by these stalwarts of the industry, are owned and operated by vast conglomerates and the personal touch of anyone who could be affectionately described as "the guv'nor" is non-existent. Some site managers may still retain this common touch but it is not the same and it is no wonder that such colourful characters are not only missed but also remembered with such affection.

Despite his advanced years, Sir Fred Pontin had not completely lost touch with his former business. When Pontin's celebrated half a century of operational trading in 1996 Sir Fred visited several of the holiday centres and was greeted with much enthusiasm by the guests of the mid-1990's, some of whom have been visiting the camps since Sir Fred first started out in the business in 1946.

In *Good night Campers*, sub-titled "The History of the British Holiday Camp" by Colin Ward and Dennis Hardy and published by Mansell in 1986, it is stated that holiday camps were popular because they met aspirations which involved "the popular utopia, food and drink are plentiful, there is constant entertainment, and chores are done by others".

Holiday camps on a highly organised basis are very much a British innovation, first introduced on what he had always planned as a major scale in the 1930's by the late Sir Billy Butlin, who specialised in very large units running to hundreds of acres and thousands of beds.

However, it is not generally known that the first holiday camp in the British Isles was established in the Isle of Man by Joseph Cunningham, son of a Liverpool baker who became something of a philanthropist, devoted to the well being of the poor youths of Liverpool, of which in 1897 there were said to be many.

Mr Cunningham's innovative idea was to take these underprivileged children on a week's camping holiday each year, as a complete change from their normal surroundings. Unfortunately, he and his wife, who assisted her husband in his good works at various venues, did not receive the necessary level of support from an associated charity so Mr Cunningham took a lease on some land at Howstrake on the Isle of Man. At this site he created a camp which was used by a variety of organisations such as Sunday Schools, Harriers clubs and Temperance leagues who each sent parties of boys for Summer breaks.

The accommodation was bell tents and all meals were provided at an all-in weekly cost of the ten shillings (50p) for each person, although it has to be said that these ventures were run at a deficit and were heavily subsidised by the Cunninghams.

However, the ugly face of commercialism could not be kept at bay forever. In due time, the charges were raised to seventeen shillings and six pence per week and the camp attracted more affluent customers who were attracted by the novelty of outdoor holidays with tents already set up in an organised manner with meals provided, just as they were in hotels.

By 1904 a more permanent camp site was established at Little Switzerland in the Isle of Man, where Mr Cunningham erected all the buildings necessary for a large holiday camp.

Before long the Howstrake site was taken over by others who proceeded to run the camp on the same lines as the Cunninghams, albeit for more up-market open-air enthusiasts from the professional classes or members of Old Boys Associations of Public Schools.

Wooden chalets soon augmented the tents and by the time that World War II had commenced the site was capable of being utilised by units from the services, when the accommodation and facilities were not only occupied and utilised by regular and enlisted personnel but also by their families.

It is quite remarkable how these early beginnings on the Isle of Man led to the immediate prewar and post-war holiday camps founded by the big three operators, namely Billy Butlin, Fred Pontin and Harry Warner, whose companies became the market leaders.

Their common aim was to provide all-in entertainment at a low price in chalet-style accommodation which would be largely unaffected by inclement weather. A common policy which was by no means too far removed from what was taking place on the Isle of Man.

The catering was probably best described as canteen-style and entertainment as best reflecting the needs of the recognised market segment which, before the war attracted a largely lower-middle-class clientele, but in the post-war period the customers became significantly more working class.

Each of these companies had quite a distinct image for its guests who tended to be strongly brand-loyal and booked regularly with their favourite operator.

Looking back, it can be said that Fred Pontin must have got it just about right as far as his "small unit" camps were concerned. It has already been stated that people keep going back for more, year after year. There were, however, certain social geographic reasons for the success of businesses such as his and this subject will receive more attention a little later.

Catching on quickly to this camp business, Fred realised before too many weeks had passed that established sites were a far better basis for expansion than developing derelict properties.

Leslie Dean's other holiday camp at Osmington Bay was, therefore, soon to become the subject of some hurried negotiations. Osmington, which had a fine coastal position overlooking Portland and Weymouth Bay, was not too far away from Brean Sands, so providing efficient management and supervision were not likely to be insurmountable problems.

Although the Dorset camp had also been requisitioned during the war the chalets and other buildings were in far better condition than those at Brean Sands, so Leslie Dean and his partner George Harrison were determined to extract a much more favourable price than they had achieved for their other property. The camp had been newly decorated and was fully furnished. Their opening figure was £50,000, but, after a short period of bargaining, Fred managed to obtain an agreement for them to sell at the price of £46,000.

Osmington, with 220 beds, opened just a few weeks after Brean

Sands, which had 198, and both holiday camps operated to virtually maximum capacity.

As early as the second year of operations Fred became aware that the growth of the business required sound administrative control, so he lost no time in persuading Ann Miller to accept a position with the company. She was then 31 years of age and had continued her career with the Ministry of Food.

She had been posted to Winchester, where she found life to be very monotonous and uninteresting.

Their relationship was such that Fred had kept in very close contact. Ann became very enthusiastic about the prospect of joining the rapidly expanding group at a time when bookings were coming in at ever increasing levels.

She was commercially qualified, having graduated from Edinburgh University just before the war, and she shared Fred's enthusiasm for the acquisition of more holiday centres to satisfy the demand for family holidays.

Her first duties were to travel around the sites to supervise the complicated rationing procedures still in force. She set up home in Berrow, near the golf course and just a short distance from Brean Sands.

Sir Fred had never had any hesitation in recognising that without Ann Miller his business could never have achieved such an outstanding trading performance and spectacular growth. He had confirmed this publicly on several occasions.

It eventually became clear that Osmington would be an ideal headquarters for the entire business operation. Ann's organisational capabilities and her talents as a sound administrator were soon very much in evidence with Osmington Bay becoming her prime responsibility as an operational holiday centre as well as its role as the group's head office.

She was appointed to the local board and, although Osmington was being advertised as a camp "under the owner's personal supervision", it was Ann Miller who was responsible for its efficient operation until Colonel Walter Rowley took over in 1961.

During the 1946 holiday season the off-peak, all-inclusive tariff at both the Brean and Osmington holiday venues did not exceed £7 per week (£155 in 1999 values). Fred was determined to live up to his well-publicised slogan of providing "value for money". His pricing policy was based upon a belief that a holiday at one of his camps should not cost more than a week's wages for an average working man, a formula which still tended to hold good even in the late 1990s. Indeed, it could be said that with some of the bargain breaks available at the present time the level of pricing is well below the average weekly wage now on offer.

However, at the end of that first season, Fred increased the peak weekly tariff to £10. Captain Harry Warner, one of Fred's closest competitors and a prewar pioneer in holiday camps, told him that "he would ruin the business" by charging what Fred described as a worthwhile premium for the peak periods of school holidays. Fred was quick to reply that holidays would never again be so cheap.

This proved to be correct and others were soon to be adopting his policy, although Sir Fred always believed that he gave the best value for money.

Fred Pontin's "team" decided to celebrate their first Christmas in a big way after their hectic, but profitable inaugural summer season of 1946, when they had already earned a reputation for being a close-knit, family-operated company. They found themselves responding positively to suggestions that they should open Osmington Bay for what could be described as a "Christmas reunion" for some of the friends they had made during the summer months.

Fred's staff had been breeding ducks, chickens, geese and turkeys at Brean Sands so these were slaughtered and transported down to Osmington in an old military ambulance which they christened the "Blood Wagon". This vehicle was extremely prone to regular breakdowns so Fred took the precaution of bringing up the rear in his own car.

It should be remembered that these were times of rationing: even bread was rationed and in short supply and meat, in any shape or form, was available in only minute, strictly controlled, portions. Fred's prime aim was to create goodwill for the 1947 season, bearing in mind he already had plans for expansion, with the acquisition of a camp at Bracklesham Bay within his sights.

Between three and four hundred bookings were taken for Christmas at Osmington Bay, but three days before the guests were due to arrive large areas of the country were in the grip of harsh winter weather. Osmington was snowed in and everyone was at panic stations.

The approach road was narrow and winding to a site perched on the top of a cliff. Not the best of conditions when the ground is covered by six inches of snow. Miraculously, there was a thaw and it was a great relief when everyone reached the camp in time for Christmas Eve. Very few people had a car in those days so it was arranged to meet the various trains with coach transport.

The weather improved to such an extent that the guests and staff enjoyed conditions which could be likened to springtime. Fred and his staff were determined to give everyone a Christmas they would never forget. They had log fires, seven and eight course meals and food the like of which had not been seen since before the war.

Fred could not recall how they entertained everyone, but he did remember that there was a marvellously unique atmosphere which couldn't possibly be recaptured. The circumstances were perfect . . . everyone had a lot to celebrate and much to look forward to, though the risk of bad weather was very much on the thoughts of everyone present at such a memorable event.

No attempt was made to repeat the exercise on a large scale throughout the Pontin group until the 1970's, by which time all of the company's facilities were vastly improved and communications generally were far more reliable.

Fred's sister, Elsie did, however, experiment with a Christmas opening at Barton Hall in 1958, but this was considered to be a failure because she felt that the premises were inadequate. She resumed operations when the new wing had been built and her camp was provided with a new ballroom.

From then on Elsie had many years of successful Christmas festivities. There was always a waiting-list and she was known to boast: "You can't get into a Barton Hall Christmas unless some-one's died!"

Her standards were such that the male staff always wore dinner jackets, with the Pontin's girls in evening dress. Guests also rose to the occasion with the majority dressing for dinner in the traditional way.

By today's standards, the accommodation offered at Pontin's holiday centres during the 1946 season was very primitive. Very few, if any, of the wooden huts had cold water plumbing. Lavatories, baths and showers were available in purpose-built blocks, but even when some of the chalets were provided with wash basins for the 1947 season, hot water was obtainable only from a steam pipe usually located on the side wall of the kitchen. Guests were invited to take their water jugs to this facility if they wished to wash and shave in the comfort of their own accommodation.

Food continued to be rationed until 1954, but Fred's wartime experience was to serve him well when he consulted his chefs about the daily menus. Fred Pontin's camps provided three meals each day: breakfast, lunch and dinner, all served by waitresses in the main dining room.

Most of his customers were happy and he felt that he really was giving value for money in those far-off days of post-war shortages.

Chapter Six

TYCOON AT LAST

Harking back to the time in 1946 when the enterprising Fred Pontin set out to realise his ambition of launching a publicly quoted company on the London Stock Exchange, he lost no time in consulting Martin Coles Harman, who, after referring the matter to Barclays Bank, recommended a provincial stockbroker to handle the share issue.

The name put forward was the Bristol firm of Laws & Co. There had been a long connection and close association with the main branch of Barclays Bank in that city. Thurlow Laws, the senior partner, was introduced to Fred and they travelled down to Brean Sands together.

In later years, when Thurlow and Fred reminisced on the early days, he made reference to Fred's description of Brean Sands as a "proud collection of dog kennels". "Kennels" which nevertheless proved to be the foundation stone of a great empire.

Brean has always been Sir Fred's first love, but it was not until 1963 that the original huts were replaced by brick-built, self-contained chalets, each complete with kitchen, bathroom and television set.

The senior local director of Barclays in Bristol was the Hon. "Bill" Bathurst, who was soon to become infected with Fred's undiminished confidence and enthusiasm. Barclays agreed to act as bankers to the issue, and it is an indication of Sir Fred's penchant for loyalty that they remained his personal bankers to the end.

The company also needed auditors and reporting accountants. Leslie Dean and George Harrison introduced Fred to Percy Cansdale, whose firm, Cansdale & Co continued to act for the company until the time of the merger with Coral in 1979.

Laws & Co organised support for the issue in the City of London, Thurlow Laws having previously prepared a prospectus which made use of the earnings records of all quoted holiday camp companies.

On the basis of their profit-earnings ratios the prospects for Brean Sands and Osmington looked attractive. The issue was poised for success.

Fred's founder shareholders decided to raise the money to buy the Osmington camp by issuing at par value 45,000 new shares of £1 each, all of which were fully subscribed by the original members. These shares were subsequently placed with new investors by Laws & Co. and Fred Pontin derived a great deal of satisfaction at the confidence being shown in his new venture by the investment community.

On the other hand, he recalled that a partner in Clifford Turner, a well established firm of solicitors with an excellent reputation in the City of London, exclaiming, after listening to Fred's plans to take the company to Stock Exchange: "Well Pontin, we will do our best to keep you out of prison". The future Sir Fred was not put off by this cynical response to the – admittedly ambitious – proposals of Clifford Turner's prospective client.

Prior to the placing, the whole of the issued capital of 50,000 £1 fully-paid shares in Pontin's Holiday Camps Limited was divided into 500,000 shares, each with a par value of two shillings (10p). The shares were soon starting to be traded quite actively at a price of seven shillings and six pence (37.5p), compared with the placing prices, which ranged from three shillings and six pence (17.5p) to six shillings and six pence (32.5p), providing some of the new body of shareholders with some useful profits.

The company satisfied all the requirements necessary to obtain a quotation in the days immediately after the 1939-45 war, and the upward movements in the share price soon brought Pontin's some respectful attention in the City of London.

Fred was more than happy to reward Thurlow Laws with a seat on the board of the newly-quoted public company and he continued to be Sir Fred's firm friend and loyal supporter up until the time of Thurlow's death in the 1980s.

Thurlow's own autobiography made generous references to his connections with Sir Fred. He described the Pontin's issue as the most memorable of his long career, in that it gave him the most pleasure and satisfaction. Laws & Co, is still very much in existence as much-respected provincial stockbrokers, located in Queen Square, Bristol but the firm has now been renamed as Greig Middleton, following the retirement of Thurlow's son, Mr Charles Laws, who was the Senior Partner for many years.

Early in 1947 the shareholders were delighted to learn from their proud Chairman and Managing Director that the trading profit for the first operational season was some £17,000, thus producing an excellent return on their newly invested capital. It was at this time that a grateful board of directors demonstrated their appreciation by awarding Fred a service contract, which, if it was intended to work as an incentive, certainly produced the required results.

The contract provided for Fred Pontin, as their Chairman and Managing Director, to receive, in addition to a basic annual salary of £2,000, no less than five per cent of the company's net profit before tax at the end of every year in which he held this position until he reached the age of 70.

In 1976, the year in which he celebrated three score years and ten, and 30 years after taking over Brean Sands, the pretax profits of the group were £4,764,000, which would have resulted in Fred earning over a quarter of a million pounds – which would have made him the highest paid company director in the United Kingdom. In 1999 values this is the equivalent of Pontin's profits approaching £20 million with Fred's percentage earning him just under £1,000,000. It is worth bearing these figures in mind when making comparisons with the company's performance at the end of the 1990s, of which more will be written later.

In the event, and as was the case in previous years, Fred felt that the company could put the money to better use than him, especially as the Government would help themselves to a large slice of it in the form of their penal rates of personal taxation. He therefore, quite typically, waived his rights to the full entitlement and was content with his basic salary, which by then had been increased to some £50,000 per annum. What a remarkable contrast to the cases of personal avarice and greed shown by various "fat cats" and which have been so much in evidence in recent years.

The above facts on Sir Fred Pontin's former remuneration arrangements were probably not well known, despite being publicised with the annual results. Although he had no hesitation in not taking full advantage of the terms of the contract, it did give Fred cause for much satisfaction at a time when his directors had been prepared to be so generous to someone who had yet to prove himself in a new post-war career.

The presence of this service contract in his favour was a significant deterrent as far as unwelcome predators were concerned. In the 1960s and early Seventies any takeover bid for Pontin's would have had to take into account such a hefty prior charge on the company's annual profits, and compensation for termination of the contract would have undoubtedly cost the purchaser a great deal of money. It was not until Sir Fred had passed his seventieth birthday that this inhibiting factor was removed.

Although Fred Pontin had always enjoyed the personal rewards and nationwide recognition which his charitable and business activities had earned over the years, he was of the opinion that a close inspection of the underlying circumstances would reveal the tremendous benefits which had accrued for the benefit of the company's many shareholders.

At one time, these were numbered in many tens of thousands, but towards the end of its existence as an independent company the numbers were considerably reduced to a figure of less than 30,000.

Financial institutions, which have an enormous flow of cash that needs to be invested on a basis of creating a well-balanced portfolio, have taken much greater control of public companies, and not always on a basis which has been acceptable to the minority shareholders.

Sir Fred's personal shareholders were always a great source of joy. Large numbers took the trouble to attend the Pontin's annual general meetings, which were usually held on or around the date of his birthday, when he had much pleasure in giving an off-the-cuff and purely informal report on the company's activities, once the formal proceedings had come to an end. This always seemed to be appreciated and it created a form of family atmosphere at what would normally be a rather stuffy occasion.

During 1947, faced with applications for more holidays than the company could supply from their two camps, Fred set about the acquisition of four additional sites: Sand Bay, Weston-super-Mare; Buckleigh Place, Westward Ho! near Bideford, North Devon; the South Devon Holiday Camp just outside of Paignton at King's Ash Hill; and Bracklesham Bay, Sussex.

With his empire growing he was thoroughly enjoying himself and certainly making up for lost time in his efforts to make his personal fortune.

Sir Fred had never been a modest man in any sense of the word and he had always liked to think that he became a firm favourite with his guests. Even in those early days he lost no opportunity in publicising his new business. Leisure was fun not just for the holidaymakers but also for the management.

He was given a free rein by his shareholders and board of directors. It was his business as far as he was concerned and Fred was able to run it his own way without any hint of interference. To all intents and purposes he *was* the company and it soon showed, not only as far as his staff and guests were concerned but also at meetings of the National Federation of Permanent Holiday Camps, where other members soon became aware that there was now a new force on the scene. The industry soon came to realise that it would have to change for the better, whether the members of the Federation liked it or not.

It proved to be very hard work for a comparatively short season, but success can become an addiction. Fred was only too willing to succumb to the temptations associated with prosperity and he was the first to admit that he had remained an addict to the end.

Twelve months of travelling and skilful negotiating had added a total of 910 extra beds which, together with Osmington and Brean Sands, now gave Fred Pontin control of over 1,300 units of holiday accommodation at six separate locations.

Compare this with Billy Butlin's ownership of Pwllheli Holiday Camp, which as far back as 1948 could accommodate a total of no less than 5,500 holidaymakers in one location, and the differences in their business philosophy will be readily appreciated.

At that particular time Fred took the view that to have the task of filling literally thousands of beds on one site for every week of the holiday season, as well as to entertain and feed all of the guests with food rationing still very much in evidence, were managerial problems of such insurmountable proportions that he felt that he had no wish to be in that particular market.

Although Butlin's was to prove to be a successful company, the business never enjoyed the cachet of Pontin's more manageable centres. This was the key to Sir Fred's considerable personal success and the rapid growth in popularity of every one of his company's holiday centres. Pricing policy did, however, have its part to play.

In 1948 Billy Butlin was offering a total of 21,500 beds in five separate locations. These were large sites, some of over 300 acres, and more than half of the chalets had hot as well as cold water facilities. Organised entertainment was on a large scale, though his guests were being asked to pay at twice the rate charged at Pontin's camps.

Fred Pontin was at the other end of the market, yet Billy Butlin was worried enough to take the trouble to see what his newest competitor was up to. With one of his colleagues, Basil Brown, he just happened to be photographed taking a drink in the bar at Brean Sands.

Jack Sullivan was the camp photographer at the time and, some years later, he recognised Billy's face in a batch of proofs and brought the photograph to Fred's attention. His boss was quick to take advantage of this somewhat unauthorised intrusion by a close rival by publishing the picture in the Pontin's annual brochure – with a caption drawing attention to where Billy Butlin spent some of his leisure time, using the slogan "All the best people come to Pontin's".

It was very much a tongue-in-cheek type of reaction, but an excellent example of Fred's aggressive marketing techniques. Billy was none too pleased, but he did not take it too seriously once he got over his initial irritation at Fred's effrontery.

Billy Butlin once offered Fred control of Butlin's. He talked of taking less interest in his holiday empire because of the penal personal taxes he was having to pay. In the event his overtures, and Fred's qualified response, were not to be tested. Billy was not able to secure the agreement of his board, who seemed to be very much against any thought of Pontin's being in control of their sites.

With a good team and an ever-increasing demand for their brand of holidays, Fred was determined to add to the assets of Pontin's Camps Limited, but felt that he could not expect the board to back his judgment until such time as the new acquisitions were seen to be profitable.

The audited accounts of each prospective purchase provided little justification for optimism in terms of future success, though Fred was certain that he had the right formula and that a period under his management could transform a previously indifferent trading performance. He decided to shoulder the risks and embarked upon a policy of using his own as well as the bank's money to finance the expansion programme.

The method was quite simple. A camp was identified and it was Fred Pontin who decided if it met his requirements in terms of location, facilities, accommodation, staff and atmosphere. Above all, however, he was looking for potential. If a site met all of these requirements it would be purchased and operated outside of Pontin's camps until such time as it was considered ready to be added to the expanding group.

Leslie Dean and, on occasions, George Harrison became Fred's partners in these projects. When they sold the newly acquired businesses to Pontin's, usually at the end of the first year of trading, it was at cost price plus the equivalent of the first year's profits. These were paper transactions with each partner taking shares in Pontin's in exchange for the new sites. In this way Fred, along with the others, was able to build up his personal share holding in Pontin's and at the same time consolidate and increase his influence within the company.

This arrangement also suited Pontin's as to acquire camps before they were profitable would have diluted group earnings and caused the shares to falter in their upward spiral. Pontin's weren't paying over the odds for the new acquisitions and the purchase of the camps had no adverse impact on cash flow as a result of the share transactions.

The quality and quantity of food were always important factors. For the 1948 season Fred hit upon the idea of opening a small unit camp in Trabolgan, County Cork in the Irish Republic, where there were no rationing restrictions. He acquired, with some Irish partners, control of a 120 acre private estate where they were able to accommodate 200 guests in brick-built chalets. All units had hot and cold running water. There was additional room for 60 visitors in the main house, previously the home of Lord Fermoy.

This holiday centre proved to be very popular for only a year or so, because its popularity amongst the British took a turn for the worse when food rationing restrictions were eased and an overseas travel allowance became available to a population which had been starved of holidays outside of the United Kingdom.

The Irish never seemed to take to the holiday camp concept, but money was not too plentiful in Eire in those days anyway. It was to be many years before this Irish venture ceased to be a problem, though there was some personal consolation as far as Fred Pontin and founder shareholder and director Bill Smith were concerned.

Fred enjoyed regular visits to Eire, where he was fortunate enough to meet the world-famous racehorse trainer, Vincent O'Brien, and his brothers at one of the very popular hunt balls which were held in the main house at Trabolgan. They became firm friends, and as a result Bill Smith, always a staunch betting man, and Fred became the owners of several victorious National Hunt horses recommended by Vincent from his training stables in Mallow, Co. Cork.

This was to be the start of a very successful racing career for Fred Pontin, culminating in being the winning owner in the 1971 Grand National at Aintree, but more of that later.

Following the introduction of Trabolgan, making a total of seven holiday centres, Pontin's entered a period of consolidation that lasted through the early 1950s. Some of the surplus cash flow was utilised in upgrading the accommodation and other facilities.

Fred was constantly on the road, driving long distances in his newly acquired Bentley to make weekly visits to every holiday centre. This form of transport served him well for many years until 1963, when the company acquired an American Brantly helicopter for £10,000.

The new form of transport took away a lot of the strain and it made his visits much more spectacular. Large numbers of guests used to take photographs of the helicopter's approach and gather around the machine after it landed. Some people even asked for his autograph. If Fred was not a celebrity up until then, he certainly became one as a result of flying to his various camps.

Photographic concessionaires would also do some good business because guests liked to have a record of being seen chatting to the Chairman who had just flown in.

Fred kept this two-seater helicopter for about three years and it proved to be a great time-saver.

Pontin's were always being hampered in the 1950's by building restrictions, the Government being more concerned in diverting resources elsewhere in what they described as the national interest. Fred took to making a point of criticising this policy in his annual statements to shareholders, just to let them know that it was not his fault that improvements were being effected only on a long drawn out piecemeal basis.

As late as 1950, only Buckleigh Place and Trabolgan were advertised as having hot water available in the chalets. Other sites were brought into line as soon as it was possible to undertake the necessary improvement work.

There were some shortcomings, bearing in mind that Pontin's were dealing with prewar structures, untrained staff and a general lack of expertise in mass-catering for people who wished to have nothing more than a jolly good time. There were elements of dissatisfaction and this was reflected in Fred's post bag. He had kept a few letters dating back to 1948, during his third season, and they make interesting reading.

Water figures prominently. Pontin's advertised running water in the chalets – but some of Fred's correspondents took exception to this being effected through the wooden roofs of their accommodation!

The Pontin camps would often be near a caravan site and the increased number of summer visitors to the area was putting pressure on the water supplies. The water authorities had no money for investment so their answer was to reduce consumption by cutting off supplies or reducing the pressure during the course of each day. This had an unpopular effect as well as an unsavoury influence on the lavatories as well as the showers and baths.

Food was always a problem. It was impossible to please everyone all of the time but Fred always did his best to give his guests plenty to eat, even if the quality did leave something to be desired. Those were the days of rationing, with some of the effects of war still being experienced.

Tinned Spam was not a popular item and it is strange that this processed food appeared to be making a comeback in the late 1990s. One person complained that a fish course should "always be followed by a substantial pudding", no doubt some form of hangover from his school days. Another felt campers were not getting enough cups of tea for the value of the ration coupons Pontin's were collecting from their books.

Another grumbler decided that cutting her soap coupon, but not laundering her sheets on more than one occasion during the course of her visit, was a grossly inadequate service.

People also objected to paying for extras such as transport from the local railway station, an early morning cup of tea and afternoon tea with sandwiches and cakes – a service which was made available only in response to popular demand – so Pontin's decided to bring some of these features in on an "all-inclusive" basis.

Fred tried to respond in a positive manner to all justifiable complaints and even went as far as to offer the compensation of half-price holidays in off-peak periods for the following season, but the letters still came, especially from what Fred would describe as "professional bleaters" who could never be satisfied, let alone silenced. Being a member of the National Federation of Holiday Camps, Fred soon discovered that some names were known throughout the industry, so Pontin's devised an unofficial black-list.

By and large Pontin's experienced great loyalty and understanding from the vast majority of their guests. When restrictions were removed the company set about improving all services and facilities. With this in mind, Fred explained to his shareholders that he was not in favour of increasing the dividend on an automatic basis every year because he would rather build up the company's cash reserves.

Whatever the nature of some of the complaints from their guests, Pontin's could not have been too unsuccessful in their efforts. The level of bookings continued to grow on a thoroughly satisfactory basis and Fred was anxious to meet the increasing demand for what they had to offer.

By the 1960s the weekly dinner menus at Pontin's establishments tended to be based upon two roast beef, two roast chicken, one roast pork, one roast lamb and, on the last night of the week's stay, invariably roast turkey, with all the usual trimmings.

This type of traditional fare stood the test of time, and after the problems associated with rationing were behind them Pontin's got very few complaints.

Chapter Seven

BOOM YEARS

With the benefit of hindsight, it is clear that Fred Pontin, in seeking to expand his commercial empire, was not merely responding to demand but also benefiting from a social revolution in the post-war years.

Clement Attlee's Labour administration of 1945 had enormous problems to contend with, but it must be conceded that the policies of his government certainly assisted the working classes over and above other members in our capitalist society in the years that followed the Second World War.

When the Conservatives were returned in the early 1950s there was a continued improvement in living standards for working people. A phenomenon which led to Harold Macmillan's famous speech at Bedford in 1957, when he informed the British population that ". . . most people have never had it so good!"

This state of affairs was certainly to Fred Pontin's benefit, because by far the majority of his guests were made up of British workers which was not the case in the 1930s when it was commonly held that meaningful numbers from the lower-middle-class population were appreciating the delights of what holiday camps had to offer.

There was a significant redistribution of incomes in post-war Great Britain, and the people who benefited were Fred Pontin's regular customers. He was not slow in recognising where some of this fresh spending-power was being directed. By 1958 wage earners were 27% better-off than they were in 1949 and even office workers were enjoying ten per cent more disposable income.

These were golden years as far as Britain's post-war living standards were concerned. Economists have written that these improvements were both absolute and relative, the advance of ordinary workers being truly remarkable.

It was not long before Fred was able to add to the number of holiday camps under his control. Three rights issues by the company in 1954 and 1955 raised additional cash capital of £125,000 from Fred's enthusiastic shareholders, who, in common with tens of thousands of Pontin's customers, felt that they were getting value for their money.

A beauty queen contest with prizes totalling 100 guineas (£1,620 by 1999 values) was announced for both 1954 and 1955, and the reunion dance at London's Seymour Hall was billed as featuring Geraldo and his Orchestra.

The boom years of the 1950s attracted one particular investor on behalf of a major pension fund that is probably still benefiting today from this earlier shrewd decision.

In February 1959 Fred was persuaded to part with a number of Pontin's shares from his personal portfolio by transferring these to the Imperial Tobacco Pension Fund. Their Investment Manager, George Ross Goobey, was introduced to Fred by Thurlow Laws, the Bristol stockbroker and a director of Pontin's from the early days.

Pontin's had received the seal of approval from the Pension Fund Trustees on the recommendation of George Ross Goobey and his immediate superior, Mr P.V. Roberts, who was a director on the main board of Imperial Tobacco. These gentlemen had travelled down to South Devon with Thurlow laws to see how Pontin's operated and Fred recalls that they all enjoyed a riotous evening together.

Fred's three distinguished visitors, two of whom had hardly heard of holidays camps, let alone visited any, went back to Bristol convinced that Fred Pontin and his team were dedicated to their work as well as to the future prosperity of the holiday camp industry.

As a result of this meeting the pension fund acted as sub-under-writers to a succession of rights issues over several years by Pontin's Limited. The proceeds of these share issues were utilised to finance some of the more significant future acquisitions together with camp improvements.

Unfortunately, and to the intense disappointment, not to say chagrin of George Ross Goobey, as a result of these rights issues being so successful the pension fund was never left with any shares in Pontin's. If it wanted to invest in the company it would have had to be done on the open market, where any large purchase would have driven up the value of the shares.

One evening at Murrays Club in London's West End, where Fred had become an habitué, George took advantage of his companion's good humour. Before they had consumed their last drinks he had secured Fred's personal undertaking to sell the pension fund no less

100,000 of the Chairman's personal holding of Pontin's shares at what was then the middle market price of three shillings and nine pence (18.75p) – an investment of £18,750.

During succeeding years there were various rights issues, capitalisation issues and scrip dividends, which, at the time of the later Coral takeover of Pontin's in 1978, left the fund with a total holding of one and a half million shares at an average price of two shillings and seven pence (approximately. 12p) – a total of £193,650.

In exchange for this holding in Pontin's the fund received £368,000 in cash and 614,000 shares in Coral. In January 1981 Bass took over Coral and the Imperial Tobacco Pension Fund received 283,000 shares in Bass in return for the Coral holding.

By February 1991 Bass shares were quoted at £9.35 in a depressed market, but leaving the fund's original investment in Pontin's with a capital value of £2,646,050. This represented a profit of £2,452,400.

If any Imperial Tobacco pensioners find themselves reading this book, Fred would no doubt have suggested that they should be truly thankful and pay tribute to the investment expertise of fund managers like George Ross Goobey. He was a leading pioneer in persuading institutional investors to put a proportion of their portfolios into equity (ordinary share) investments, as opposed to government securities.

It should, however, be borne in mind how difficult the task was for George, having regard to the activities of people like Martin Coles Harman in the 1930s who gave "risk taking" by way of equity investment a bad name.

Incidentally, George's son, Alistair Ross Goobey, has also earned a fine reputation as a fund manager as well as an analyst in the City, and is often heard acting as a stock market pundit on BBC Radio 4's *Today* programme. He held a position as the head of Hermes, the pension fund giant and in recent years he held a similar position with Postel, the Post Office Pension Fund. He could also be found taking part as a most entertaining panelist on the BBC Radio 4 programme, *The Board Game*.

It appears that at least some part of the Imperial Tobacco's Pension Fund's original investment in Pontin's, as now represented by shares in Scottish & Newcastle Breweries, the present owners of the Pontin's business, is still intact. Without even a hint of sour grapes, Sir Fred Pontin may possibly have reflected on what additions there may have been to his personal wealth if he had decided not to sell the shares to his dear old friend, George Ross Goobey all those years ago.

Sir Fred and George kept in touch with each other until George's death in March 1999 at the age of 87. He had celebrated his golden wedding anniversary in 1998 and lived with his wife Gladys in Clevedon, a coastal resort on the Bristol Channel, not too far away from the site of Sir Fred's first holiday camp, at Brean Sands.

In its obituary notice *The Times* described George Ross Goobey as a stock market legend, often referred to fondly in City circles as "the father of the equity", or "the man who invented the yield curve" thus justifying his reputation for trailblazing the notion that shares are a better long-term investment than fixed-interest government stocks.

When building up his most famous publicly quoted company Sir Fred Pontin would always insist that it was very useful to have friends who enjoyed influence in high places, especially in the investment community. Having been associated with a succession of companies with listings on the Stock Exchange over a period of some 50 years he became accustomed to being able to rely on some loyal supporters. For a considerable number of years after the sale of Pontin's there appears to be no doubt that his reputation as a businessman was as sound as it ever was.

If he had one regret it is in connection with the outcome of the earlier efforts of Thurlow Laws to establish the Pontin's name in the City. The holiday camp industry had not really achieved any measure of respectability in the investment world in those early days. Thurlow wrote in his autobiography that he was not helped by the fact that, in his view quite wrongly, the Harman "image" behind the Pontin's company was unpopular in the City.

Although the Harman interest in Pontin's was through his nominee, Dickie Doyle, the investment community is close-knit and Martin Coles Harman's spell in prison was not to be easily forgotten. He enjoyed Fred Pontin's complete confidence, but Harman had nothing whatsoever to do with the running of Pontin's. That appeared to make little difference to attitudes generally, and Thurlow Laws had to fight what he termed an uphill battle in promoting, but never defending Fred Pontin's interests.

Eventually Thurlow hit upon the idea of seeking the sponsorship of a top London stockbroker and, after a sustained period of lobbying, he persuaded Simon & Coates to take a close look at Fred Pontin and his expanding company. A luncheon was arranged and, according to Thurlow, Fred Pontin made a very good job of selling himself.

However, Fred maintained that, as a matter of principle, he made a point of never offering any apologies for the actions of his former employer because he did not consider that such apologies were by any means appropriate. Loyalty, had always remained a very strong attribute of Fred Pontin. His memory could be prodigious as far as the more important people and events in his life were concerned and although he could be a stern critic of people who he felt had let him down he was seldom, if ever, guilty of criticising anyone who had earned his friendship and support, whatever the circumstances.

Fred Pontin's presentation of the Pontin business philosophy during the course of the meeting with the prestigious London stockbrokers must have been well received because, as a direct result of his efforts Simon & Coates duly became London brokers to Pontin's. The company then enjoyed the backing of a first-class firm when making a succession of capital issues in the years that followed.

Pontin's did not let anyone down and neither the brokers nor the shareholders had any cause for complaint. The company went from strength to strength. Both before and after the 1978 Coral takeover of Pontin's Sir Fred's own relationship with the company became the subject of much comment in the financial press... usually on the lines that he was the dominant personality, had been able to out pace his rivals and competitors, and that the management had consistently revolved around Sir Fred's personal commitment as Chairman and Managing director.

Financial pundits in the press were unanimous in contending that the company was well-managed and that to all intents and purposes Fred had always nurtured Pontin's like a child. Those who knew Fred Pontin would not have expected him to challenge these contentions, and he was justly proud that they are now a matter of record.

As well as the money men, others were drawn to Pontin's in the 1950s. Growth in the business was soon to attract, also, other members of Fred's family. His brother Harry, then aged 39, joined as manager at the newly acquired camp at Bracklesham Bay. He stayed there for a few years before assuming the role of a general factotum-cum-public relations officer for the burgeoning commercial enterprise.

Fred's sister Elsie had been employed as an Assistant Food Executive Officer with the Ministry of Food in Bristol and her husband Bob Brown, had seen active service with the Irish Guards. Fred persuaded Bob to give up his "pen pushing" (in his prewar printing works) to take up the more challenging position as secretary at Brean Sands in time for the 1947 season.

Elsie did not join Bob when he went down to Somerset, but she did take mother and her niece down to see what a holiday camp looked like. Fred confessed to being amused when she admitted being horrified by the rudimentary accommodation and refused to sleep in one of the chalets. She was found a room in the bungalow occupied by the manager, Arthur James, who was Leslie Dean's brother-in-law.

Elsie recalls that the chalets measured about eight feet by six feet "just like bathing huts", but she conceded that as these small, frugally furnished structures were being treated merely as places to sleep, it made good sense to keep the guests occupied throughout the day and spending money in the bars in the evenings.

Fred's father had died during the war years. He had been employed as a Ministry of Works inspector and was based in Bristol to where the rest of the family moved from a temporary home in Brighton. Frederick William Pontin, senior fell, quite accidentally, from a train just outside a local railway station and was never to fully recover from his injuries.

The eventual cause of death was cancer of the lungs – he had been a heavy smoker – but Fred, his mother and brothers and sister all felt that the accident was an important contributory factor to an early loss of the senior member of the family.

The Pontin family still enjoys the use of many items of fine furniture made by the former head of the household and often recall the times when in the course of his employment he stayed at stately homes and historic houses restoring important items of antique furniture.

It was not long before Elsie was persuaded to make use of her experience in food and catering and she and Bob moved down to the South Devon site to take over the respective positions of Catering Manager and Camp Manager.

They were to stay there for ten years before Elsie persuaded Fred to acquire, for the sum of £60,000, Barton Hall, Torquay. This acquisition was to prove to be of outstanding significance to the group. Elsie was not attracted by anything that was second-best, so she was determined to make Barton Hall a holiday centre with a difference.

She persuaded her elder brother to introduce a number of luxurious "Imperial" suites, which were fitted with carpets and named after the leading hotel in Torquay.

Barton Hall soon acquired a unique reputation for being the jewel in the crown of the Pontin's empire, even though in the early days it never had the benefit of the national publicity machine. It generated business by the guests returning year-after-year. More than 50% made their bookings for the next season before their day of departure. Press articles referred to it as "the executives' holiday camp", where Jaguars and Bentleys were parked alongside Minis and Cortinas,

Elsie and Bob established and maintained very high standards, putting exceptionally good food at the top of their list of priorities, followed very closely by comfortable accommodation. Excellent sport and recreational facilities included the country's first artificial ski slope.

The late Lord Ted Willis, the writer, was a frequent visitor who appreciated the sparkling white linen, superb four and five course meals, wine waiter service and piano music during dinner. He continued with his regular holidays at Barton Hall, after his elevation to the Peerage and he even arranged for an episode of *Dixon of Dock Green*, his popular BBC TV series, to be filmed there.

Pontin's had the entire crew at Barton Hall, including the stars, who it may be remembered were Jack Warner, Arthur Rigby and Peter Byrne. PC Dixon and his family were portrayed as staying at a holiday camp and the producer gave Fred Pontin an Alfred Hitchcock type cameo role.

Fred was seen with his mother leaving the camp pub as PC Dixon and Sgt. Flint were making an entrance. All he could remember of this event was that they kept shooting it over and over again. As a result of this experience he felt quite sure that he would never have made a film or TV star although Fred did become famous for his "Book Early" TV advertisements for Pontin's in later years. These made him a household name.

As a result of the Dixon episode shot at Barton Hall Fred was able to count the late Jack Warner amongst his friends. He succeeded him as president of the Thanet Dramatic Society in 1982 and donated holidays at his Farringford Hotel on the Isle of Wight as prizes for their fund-raising activities.

Pontin's by now had sixteen holiday centres, in the Channel Islands, the South of England and Blackpool in the North.

Fred's family took on ever-increasing responsibilities within the Pontin organisation, and Elsie, Len, Harry and Peter Hopper, who married Fred's daughter, Patricia in December 1958 were rewarded with appointments to the board of the parent company. Ann Miller also became a director and, although Fred did recruit senior executives – including some from the Butlin organisation – who also joined the main board, he always had the comfort of "family" control.

This ensured support for any important and sometimes controversial decisions. These board appointments from the ranks of his family were, in general, replacing the majority of the original board of director/founder shareholders. It may well have been nepotism but it had a purpose which suited Fred Pontin very well indeed.

Bill Smith and Alex Bernstein retired from the scene in the 1950s but Rex Randall and Reggie Binns continued as directors until both died in 1962. Dickie Doyle retired in 1964, following many years of loyal support leaving Fred the sole remaining member of the original group of investors.

Thanks to Elsie and Bob, Barton Hall became an instant success so, in accordance with Fred's standard practice, he offered it to Pontin's Camps Limited and in due course the site became a major contributor to the group's results. The deal was done against the issue of 300,000 ordinary shares, which further increased his stake in the public company.

This was one of the last deals Fred was to arrange on this basis because, after he had passed on Little Canada, his site on the Isle of Wight, on a similar basis, the major shareholders, particularly the institutions, severely criticised this type of transaction. They did this on the grounds that Fred was trading outside of the company's influence and then making a profit on the subsequent disposal.

Fred felt that their attitude was unfair and unjustified, bearing in mind that he had been taking the commercial risk, but he had to admit that he had not had to bear any losses.

Managers recruited by Fred Pontin in the early days came from a variety of backgrounds and it is quite impossible to detect any common factor. What Fred wanted, when looking for a new manager, was someone who had not only good administrative potential but, more importantly, also a person who was prepared to work hard on a virtual round-the-clock basis.

Fred Pontin required total dedication to the job and anyone not ready to make this sacrifice to the cause did not last long in the growing organisation.

One of the more unlikely applicants for the secretary's job at Sand Bay, Weston-Super-Mare was Bronislav Jerzy Baczkowski, a former lieutenant in the Polish army who fought with the British Eighth army under General Montgomery in the Second World War.

After Fred Pontin had decided that Bronislav could well meet his exacting requirements he remarked "You'll have to do something about that name you know. How on earth do you think my campers are going to get their tongues around Mr Baczkowski?"

Bronislav felt more than a little bemused by this implied stricture. His previous postwar employment had been as a teacher of English at a school in Stamford, Lincolnshire. He had encountered no particular difficulty there but he was attracted to working for Pontin's, a company which appeared to have a dynamic owner and was set for continued expansion.

When he got home to his wife, Elsie and discussed the matter with her the immediate response was positive. "You must use my maiden name" and from that day Bronislav Jerzy Baczkowski became George Webb, George being the English equivalent of Jerzy.

Fred Pontin has changed many lives but this was the only known occasion upon which he could be held responsible for changing the entire name of a person.

George did very well at Pontin's over a period of some 18 years but his first task and at the age of 28 was to work alongside Len Pontin, manager at Sand Bay. Within seven years George took over as manager when Len Pontin was appointed manager at Paignton. Elsie Webb, as she once more became known, joined her husband at Sand Bay and became very popular with the campers as well as the other staff. In due time she also worked for the company as a food buyer.

It is significant that George Webb, in common with other long serving managers, described the early pioneering days at Pontin's as experiencing the feeling of being part of the family.

Fred Pontin had been joined in the business by his wife, brother, sister and various in-laws and Les Dean had also introduced several members of his own family to the organisation. For managers and staff to feel that they were also part of the family must surely be due to the spirit generated by Fred Pontin and not forgetting Ann Miller whose influence on the founder and company policy was quite formidable. Fifty years later management and staff with long experience at Pontin's talked with considerable awe about Ann Miller when reminiscing about the period of expansion at Pontin's.

Fred Pontin made two very significant site purchases in 1960 and 1961. He had always been keen to get into the Channel Islands, not just for low taxation but also because of the cheaper prices for alcoholic drinks which were more or less duty free . . . a great attraction to the vast majority of his traditional clients.

A holiday camp at Plemont Bay, Jersey was owned by a former showman, Stanley Parkin, who sought a purchase price of £500,000. Fred remembers haggling with him because it was clear that the premises were in a very dilapidated condition and would require the "Pontin's treatment" before they could get a worthwhile return on the required investment.

They eventually agreed a figure of £375,000 (almost £5 million in 1999 values) after Fred learned that the Jersey Tourist Board were keen to have Pontin's on the island. The camp was virtually rebuilt and before long the expanding empire had another highly attractive holiday centre which became very popular.

Fred's Channel Island guests also entered into the spirit of Jersey's traditional Battle of Flowers, which is often described as one of the most joyous and colourful holiday spectacles anywhere in Europe. The visitors to Pontin's during that particular week of the year always made a great contribution to the fun by manning the company's bloom-laden float in the procession through St Helier and along the Esplanade. Fred took the wheel of the vehicle on several occasions and not just for the publicity he would assure everyone.

The Jersey centre also figures in David Gwyn's curriculum vitae and it is worth pausing a while to recount some of his experiences there, if only to illustrate the need for Fred Pontin to employ a team of unofficial trouble shooters during the boom years of his business.

David Gwyn, a Pontin's manager for many years, certainly became a member of such team and although most of his calls to duty under this heading were made on the basis of very short notice he did welcome a change from whatever he was doing at Pakefield, always his first love, at the time.

His first tour of duty at Plemont Bay, Jersey came about as a result of one of Fred Pontin's visits to Pakefield in the summer of 1969. The manager at Pakefield at that time was Derek Smith and he conveyed the news to David that he was required by the guv'nor for a private chat.

Intrigued by being granted an audience with the great man he was quickly brought down to earth and told that there was a crisis in Jersey and that he was being transferred there as soon as possible.

Within a matter of only a couple of days David was being greeted by a welcoming party which included Fred's sister, Elsie and his brother Len. He was shown around a site in an enviable position with views of the coast of France and other Channel Islands.

Sandy Nash was the manager in those days and he was suffering ill health as a result of too much work, long hours and no reliable back-up. Certain members of the staff were found to be on various "nice little earners" as David describes them and looking back in later years he felt that some of his experiences there would have served creators and scriptwriters David Croft and Jimmy Perry well in writing the odd episode of *Hi-De-Hi*.

At every Pontin establishment the management do what they can to get on well with the local population but in places like Jersey and the Pontinental sites something special is called for and considerable effort is made to ensure that there is no cause for hostility or ill feeling amongst the immediate resident population.

At some of the larger centres well over 3,000 people can descend on the locality in a matter of hours. This calls for good planning and lots of understanding of local needs. In general, however, Pontin sites were made welcome, if only for the employment opportunities created by the boost to the local tourist trade.

Plemont Bay camp was owned and operated by a Jersey company, so when Billy Butlin retired to the island Fred was very pleased when he accepted his invitation to join the board of directors in a non-executive capacity. Other local directors were required under the company law of the States of Jersey and these included the previous owner, Stanley Parkin.

It must have been a unique company in the holiday industry with two of the previously competitive United Kingdom holiday camp magnates sitting down together in the same boardroom. It would have been interesting to learn how Sir Billy Butlin reacted to Fred's style of management. One is tempted to speculate that Billy still looked upon Fred Pontin as a novice in the business, bearing in mind that Butlin's had enjoyed a head start before the 1939–1945 war, but this is probably far from the truth. Fred Pontin's success would have earned the respect of a sensitive man such as Billy Butlin and all the evidence suggests that the two men got on very well indeed when socialising in each other's company, whoever was paying for the drinks!

As a footnote to the Jersey acquisition, the now late Stanley Parkin had demonstrated his loyalty to Pontin's over the years by his continued presence on the local board and he often flattered Fred by recounting the story of his purchase of his site. "What I like about Fred Pontin is that if he shakes your hand the deal is done," he was fond of saying.

Fred would be the first to appreciate what is meant by this remark. In his personal experience when the lawyers and accountants got in on the act both purchaser and vendor were invariably thrown into confusion and what had looked like a perfectly straightforward deal was seen to assume the proportions of a new constitution for world government!

The second important acquisition during this period of expansion was Blackpool, an operational unit with a coastal frontage half-a-mile in length. The entire share capital of Squires Gate Blackpool Holiday Camp Limited, was acquired in what Sir Fred rates as his best-ever deal.

It happened really by chance. Fred had flown from Blackpool to the Isle of Man to view one of the original holiday camp sites dating back to nearly the start of the century. The premises were dreadful and in his opinion beyond redemption so he flew back to Blackpool with the feeling that the day had been wasted. Someone mentioned the Squires Gate site in the Borough of Lytham St Annes and very close to the airport.

Fred had only a brief look at the property but this was enough for him to make early contact with owners, with whom he agreed the purchase of the company which owned the site by an exchange of Pontin's shares, which were issued at a slight premium. Although Fred had to arrange to pull down most of the chalets, replacing them with modern units, as well as carry out a large-scale rebuilding programme, the purchase price of some £375,000 proved to be an absolute bargain.

Fred had always described the site as the best "free house" in the country.

He was surprised, though, at the extent of the local opposition to his move into Blackpool. As late as March 1969 the *Sunday Express* was telling its readers that Fred Pontin was upsetting the local landladies by describing his new site as "Pontin's, Blackpool". The property was, in fact, just a few yards over the boundary in Lytham St Anne's and had previously been known as "Squires Gate Blackpool Holiday Camp".

This was enough for them to allege that the new name was an infringement of the Trade Descriptions Act. Fred was, of course, delighted by this response. It demonstrated, as was subsequently confirmed, that the centre was going to be much more successful under the new ownership and, as usual, the free publicity could only be welcomed.

One of the Pontin's executives responsible for establishing the Blackpool site as a strategically important centre in the early days was George Webb. His job was to get it "on the map". This was achieved by lobbying a local councillor who arranged for Pontin's Blackpool to be featured in the all-important Blackpool Guide.

George described the newly-acquired site as a "Foreign Legion Outpost", not because of its location but due to the sand storms experienced when the strong winds blew from any point of the compass featuring west.

This sand was a major problem which was partially overcome by erecting two storey chalets on the windward boundary. These buildings cause much of the sand to be deflected over the top of the roofs before being deposited in the nearby airport. However, the writer discovered during the course of a visit to the site just after Christmas 1998 that the difficulty with the sand had not been solved after a night of near hurricane force winds. The general manager, David Roberts had not only to deal with structural damage but also with a covering of several inches of sand on the centre's roads, path-ways, lawns and gardens.

The early 1960s saw another significant move northwards. Fred acquired a holiday camp at Middleton Tower, Morecambe from a

Japanese gentleman who had built it from scratch, some say from a load of old packing cases which were once used for transporting gliders. Fred said that he could readily believe such a story, given the condition of some of the chalets.

As this camp could accommodate 3,000 guests, it was necessary to recruit someone who had experience of such numbers. Butlin's was the obvious source and Fred managed to sign up Eric Bennett who came with a sound recommendation from Tim Moorcroft, who had himself left Butlin's to join Pontin's only a few months previously.

Large unit camps required a different philosophy, but, although Eric Bennett, had the necessary experience, he will admit to having had quite a struggle during the course of the first year or so with Pontin's. He soon came to appreciate that Fred's emphasis had always been on the quality of accommodation and catering, whereas the Butlin's accent was on entertainment.

Eric Bennett represented a new breed of manager for Pontin's at that particular time and he undoubtedly joined his new employers at a turning point in their progress towards big company status. He started work at Butlin's straight from leaving school at the tender age of fourteen and left only because he felt that their centres were getting too large to handle. When he left Butlin's Filey in 1960 there were 8,000 beds and such camps were operated by controllers, not managers, of whom Eric was one of Butlin's best. He soon appreciated that Pontin's were still a family company, but one which was going places.

Eric saw an opportunity for advancement and he took it, moving on to become General Manager at Blackpool, from where he retired in 1985.

Fred Pontin and Eric Bennett had their differences – Eric would always speak his mind – but their relationship was a lasting one, despite a period of suspension not long after he took over at Blackpool. Pontin's were having trouble with union penetration in the camps and Fred Pontin and Eric did not see eye to eye on a contentious matter, Eric taking the view that Fred's attitude was positively Victorian, even feudal as far as management–employee relationships were concerned.

All was soon well, however, and it is pleasing to report that Eric is now in happy and active retirement in Kendal after spending the whole of his working life in holiday camps where he worked in senior positions for the two major operators during a period in which the entire industry underwent massive changes.

What Pontin's did very successfully at Middleton Tower and at later large scale units was to combine the advantages of their two types of camp. Within a few years Middleton Tower had been completely rebuilt.

It had a magnificent theatre, named the *SS Berengaria* after the ship which foundered off the Lancashire coast. It was a favourite venue for entertaining the many thousands of visitors attracted to Middleton Tower each year. The theatre building contained many fittings salvaged from the wrecked ship and boasted a stage which would have been coveted by the manager of every provincial theatre in the land.

David Gwyn had a spell as general manager at Middleton Tower and recalls the necessity to improve the sound system which suffered from a poor arrangement of loud speakers in that the audience had difficulty in hearing the entertainers because of the noise from the bar. This was soon fixed and the Pontin's guests were now entertained for the very first time by a resident revue company, ably assisted by their own Bluecoats, who were also introduced to Pontin's in the early sixties.

Billy Butlin had his Red Coats for entertainment purposes but Fred Pontin's Bluecoats, in his opinion, fulfilled other, and to his mind, more important functions.

They acted as hosts and hostesses: they organised games, sports and entertainments and generally went out of their way to ensure that everyone would feel completely at home on arrival at one of the Pontin's centres. This remains the case, even more so today as a result of the introduction of new training techniques.

The management at Middleton Tower had been experiencing quite a large problem over the years. The site had tended to recruit staff from Glasgow and Liverpool, two cities which are said "not to get on".

Trouble usually arose after the bars closed when factions of the staff from the these cities clashed for reasons which could not always be fully explained other than by reference to tribalism. This could not be allowed to continue and the management switched their recruitment to towns in Lancashire.

This proved to be an admirable solution and David Gwyn went out of his way to consolidate the position by offering the staff better recreational facilities such as their own disco and organised football matches.

It has to be appreciated that employing seasonal staff is not the easiest of tasks and a happy camp, as far as the guests are concerned, depends heavily on being served and entertained by a willing, cheerful and well organised band of Pontin's employees. If a manager achieved this he was well on the way to producing figures which kept Head Office happy.

Keeping staff too happy, however, could bring quite different problems. They became reluctant to "migrate" to other centres when needed but where facilities are less generous and perhaps the general manager is not quite so cooperative and understanding. This makes life very difficult for a sensitive manager who, from time to time, finds it necessary to lay off people when bookings fall and less staff is required.

David Gwyn became quite disillusioned with this aspect of his duties, particularly at Middleton Tower and it seems certain that although this is an unavoidable facet of the holiday camp business the fact that it is a necessary task does not make it any easier.

In September 1976 Middleton Tower also acted as the venue for the Miss Great Britain finals which was considered to be a major publicity coup by Fred Pontin. The event was televised by Trident Television and after the contest was over Fred Pontin hosted a magnificent buffet dinner for 150 people including all of the judges, celebrities and contestants on the floor of the theatre with the TV cameras still in position.

This constituted quite a considerable logistics problem and posed a variety of risks which, if anything had gone wrong, could well have ruined what had been an enormously successful evening for the Pontin's organisation.

In the event, all went well and the guv'nor was well pleased but it is rather ironic to note that given the rather glamorous background history of this site the property was under serious consideration for use as one of HM prisons.

However, back in the sixties and seventies Pontin's customers were also enjoying the boom years as far as entertainment was concerned. But the exceedingly high quality of the Pontin's entertainment programme was not achieved without a great deal of work behind the scenes; work which required just as much talent as was being demonstrated on the stages and platforms of the camps, in the bars and on the floors of the ballrooms.

In those days there were 24 sites and it was necessary to recruit artistes and entertainers for two cabarets each night for seven nights a week. In addition, arrangements had to be made for appearances by nationally known names from snooker and soccer as well as other sports for coaching sessions at Pontin's camps.

Auditions for Bluecoats took place on an annual basis and although it might be thought that highly specialised people were recruited to pick out the people who possessed that certain flair, not to mention gift, for entertaining the campers from amongst the hundreds of applicants it is a little surprising to learn that in the sixties and seventies Fred Pontin came to rely on an ex-singer named Bridie Reid who stepped into the breach at very short notice. Although there was a break in her employment at Pontin's in this capacity, of which more later, she remained with the organisation and worked with Jim Kennedy, the former group entertainments manager who is mentioned elsewhere in this book, for many years.

Bridie developed her own brand of expertise in talent spotting or in her words "I developed a good eye for an act". There is a string of names who were in effect "discovered" by Jim Kennedy and Bridie Reid and who went on to make their names in show business on a big time basis, ever grateful to Pontin's for giving them that all-important first break in the entertainments industry.

Gary Wilmot, Brian Conley of "Jolson" and "Grimleys" fame, Peters and Lee, Jimmy Cricket, Iris Williams, Joe Longthorne and Tom O'Connor; all of these successful show business personalities were involved with Pontin's in the early days of their careers.

Some of the above were Pontin's Bluecoats and there were other Bluecoats who have also done well in show business. These include Shane Ritchie, the leading star of the West End musical "Grease", Gemma Craven who has played the part of "Calamity Jane" on the London stage and Roger de Courcy, the ventriloquist who is almost as famous as his dummy, "Nooky Bear".

The list does not stop there; you can also add Alex Bourne as "Buddy", Amanda Reddington of MTV fame, Carol Lee Scott ("Grotbags"), Andrew O'Connor as "Barnum", Stu Frances, Mick Miller and not forgetting Bradley Walsh who has become a very well known game show host and in 1998 was chosen to take the midweek National Lottery Show "On the road".

It might also be mentioned that prior to Fred Pontin acquiring the camp in Jersey the local entertainments manager was none other than the late Peter Sellers.

Shane Ritchie achieved the status of entertainments manager during his tenure of employment with Pontin's. Because of his special talent, which was readily apparent even in his early days, the company tolerated his extravagant appearance when other male Bluecoats, especially the new recruits, were expected to dress formally with neat hair styles and no obvious jewellery on view.

Shane had been know to turn up at a Bluecoats seminar with pink hair, a ring through his nose, ear studs and Teddy Boy gear. His superiors explained this non-conformity by stating that he had just got back from shooting a TV advertisement.

Shane was also famous for organising a party of fifty or so Pontin's guests to act as a welcome home party for the Canberra on her return to the port of Southampton from her tour of duty in the Falklands war.

This particular entertainments manager got his volunteer guests out of their beds at six o'clock in the morning and marched them down to the water side, near the Little Canada camp on the Isle of Wight.

You can imagine their disappointment to note when they got there that a thick fog had dropped down and nothing could be seen. Shane assured them that the weather forecast was for bright weather and they must be patient.

Some hours later, still shrouded in mist and feeling cold and hungry the guests pleaded to be allowed to get back to the camp. "No, you must stay and welcome the lads" was the response from Shane who had shown no particular patriotic fervour prior to this occasion. "We can't let them down".

About forty five minutes later Shane was relieved to hear the sound of engines. He led from the front by cheering and waving his flag and urging the guests to do the same.

The noise generated by this comparatively small party was really quite impressive but their enthusiasm turned to massive disappointment when out of the swirling mist steamed . . . the Isle of Wight ferry with the passengers mightily bemused by such an animated welcome from the shoreline.

It is not recorded how the guests dealt with Shane Ritchie, the future star of "Grease" on the West End stage, but he surely deserves full marks for enthusiasm.

Although Fred Pontin enjoyed the entertainment at his camps as much as his guests Bridie Reid recalls just how difficult it was to persuade him to hand out contracts for acts recommended by her at what he would describe as the exorbitant price of say £28 for a night's work. This could entail performing at two and maybe even three different Pontin's sites in one evening, if these sites were particularly close together, as some of them were in the West of England.

Bridie hated the ritual of having to get Fred's blessing to a contract before the act could be engaged. She felt that her success in securing top quality artistes should have justified more autonomy but Fred Pontin insisted upon controlling the purse strings and he was always determined not to exceed budgets which were running into millions of pounds annually by the end of the seventies.

As Bridie describes it; "Pontin's were not the cheapest, but they were the best". The entertainment was first class and the campers came to expect top class artistes. Under this heading Pontin's was undoubtedly the market leader. In Bridie's words "There was no one to touch Pontin's".

Peters and Lee were discovered by Bridie in an East End pub but by the time that they started their summer season with Pontin's in the early seventies they had a number one in the charts in the form of a popular ballad entitled "Welcome Home". Bridie signed up Peters and Lee for £28 for a night's work but according to their manager they were capable of earning £1000 a night after the record became a hit. His clients did, however, stick to their contract out of loyalty to Bridie who recognised their talent before they made it to the top.

Fred Pontin once turned down the chance to sign an undiscovered singer called Iris Williams, of whom Bridie had quite justifiable hopes of stardom. Fred thought that Bridie was offering too much to an unknown and returned the contract to her office torn in two with the words written in her employer's own hand, "I hate screaming women".

Not long after, Bridie presented an identical contract to Fred Pontin, after he had enjoyed a good lunch, and she was asked to describe the singer. "Oh, she's young, blond and beautiful sir" was Bridie's reply.

Fred signed the contract and asked Bridie where Iris would be performing. "Probably in Blackpool or Southport" was the reply.

"See she goes down to Devon" ordered her employer. Fred Pontin spent a lot of time at his West Country camps as his family connections were there.

Iris Williams also enjoyed a number one hit with "He was beautiful" before she joined Pontin's but she was distraught by a very unfortunate event when performing this song at Pontin's Bracklesham Bay.

Fred Pontin strode into the ballroom and hearing the ecstatic applause when the audience recognised the opening bars of Iris's hit song he made his way across to the startled singer, grabbed the microphone from her and announced "I'm Fred Pontin and I want you to know that Pontin's will always provide you with top class acts like this".

He then thrust the microphone back into her hands and swaggered away leaving a startled and bewildered Iris Williams virtually speechless. However, in the best show business tradition the show went on but Bridie Reid had to endure many moments such as these during her employment with Pontin's where, in her opinion, "That man, Fred Pontin thought himself to be bigger than the company".

It led to the break in her career with Pontin's as she decided at one stage that she had had enough. She didn't need this type of headache.

It was difficult enough to spot the acts and have them signed up without having further problems to deal with after the season had started.

After she left Bridie discovered that Fred Pontin had to employ no less than four men to replace her although this is hotly disputed by Sir Fred. After a while it was Miss Miller who persuaded Bridie to return on the promise of a "reformed" Fred Pontin. It didn't last long as she recalls that three months' later he was back to his old ways.

In the event Bridie stayed with Pontin's after the Coral and Bass takeovers and it was Bass who gave her the opportunity to engage acts for the Pontinental sites in the sun spots of Europe.

The Pontinental guests had been complaining that the sun was just not enough. They also wanted entertainment similar to that offered at the UK camps. This was not as easy as it sounds as work permits for the artistes were a constant problem.

This was subsequently solved by Pontinental offering the entertainers "working holidays" at Pontinental sites. They took advantage of this and their families also went along to enjoy the fun.

At one time in her career Bridie Reid worked for Butlin's, owned by Rank, and she, along with two other operators managed a budget of some £14 million when recruiting acts for the holiday centres and hotels.

In the late seventies Bridie had a spell as panellist on the popular TV programme *"New Faces"*. She loved these appearances and commenting on the acts was second nature to someone with her vast experience.

Bridie Reid became involved in introducing acts to TV producers and the artistes never forgot the start given them by Pontin's.

Although other members of Pontin's management team will be mentioned elsewhere in this book it is impossible to find enough space to mention all of the managerial staff with whom Fred Pontin had been privileged to work over all of the years. References already made to the work of Eric Bennett and certain of his colleagues will perhaps serve as a fitting tribute to everyone who had cause to suffer from the lashing of Fred's tongue and then came to appreciate that his bark had indeed always been much worse than his bite.

Fred often referred to the fact that if Rotweilers had been about in his day he could well have earned that particular nickname! As it was there were many others which came into common usage over the years, few of which bear repeating in this book.

Some managers felt that his methods and their success owed more to bullying than firm discipline and, as a consequence, found it very difficult to like their employer as a person. Maybe, this was deliberate policy on Fred's part as familiarity can be a barrier to extracting the high degree of professional competence that he demanded from his managers who he felt had the important responsibility of providing inspirational leadership to the entire staff, most of whom were seasonal and part time workers, not careerists.

A manager's job entailed more than keeping Fred Pontin and the customers happy. Quite apart from these onerous duties, as well as having to arrange to put right everything that went wrong, they had to implement the many changes which were being introduced.

Waitress service in dining rooms was another Pontin tradition which soon came under the microscope.

As time went by the tastes of Pontin's regular guests had become more sophisticated, so the company followed the latest trends. Some of the camps graduated to self-service dining rooms by introducing the "tray-and-away" systems, which were very cost-effective and brought in a wider choice of dishes. There were also carousels for the display of puddings and salad bars were introduced in order to cater for the people who were watching their weight and succumbing to the appeals for healthier eating.

Sister Elsie joined the main board in the late 1960s and she steered through this particular investment at six selected centres. The total capital cost was £250,000, a considerable sum of money in those days, but the payback period was little more than a year as a result of savings on staff as well as food. There was much less wastage. Fred always said that the only people to lose out were the pig-swill contractors.

Although the phased conversion to self-service commenced in the early 1960s some centres did not surrender their waiter/waitress service until 15 years or so later.

In 1977, David Gwyn, at his beloved Pakefield centre, confessed to be quite shocked to be informed by Sir Fred that the directors had decided that the self-service revolution would now extend to Suffolk. Knowing that he would have no say in the matter and that it would be hopeless to even try and oppose the decision David sought the views of John Hogg who was managing the local Warner's site. John mentioned to David that Warner's at Dovercourt, Essex had been working the self-service operation for years so David sent his catering manager, Ray Flook, to visit Dovercourt, the camp famous as the location for filming BBC's popular TV series *Hi-De-Hi*, and to report back. One wonders why David did not see fit to carry out a tour of inspection of Pontin's many centres at which the system had been working for many years but perhaps he had no wish for Ray Flook to be influenced by other Pontin's personnel!

In the event the report was favourable and Pakefield was converted successfully without any sign of opposition from its general manager. This particular transition is mentioned because the conversions to self-service, as well as self-catering, to which reference is made below, were not achieved without many problems, all of which were eventually overcome by what has been described as a lot of hard work and imagination.

These somewhat revolutionary developments in the holiday camp industry were not welcomed by all managers who did not readily appreciate the need for the board to adopt a corporate approach to the overall business. These managers saw no reason to change a system which had served them well for many years. They felt that their guests would resent the loss of personal service at their dining tables.

As with many other new developments in the business, they were proved wrong and they had to accept the inevitable.

Reservations were expressed about the vast amount of food which would be consumed if guests could help themselves to as much as they liked. They envisaged plates being piled high with the Pontin's version of nourishing grub.

However, it soon became known that for the first two or three days of their stay at a camp, guests would indeed "eat with their eyes". But as the week wore on experience demonstrated that appetites became less vigorous and costings of meals per person revealed that self-service resulted in lower expenditure than that for table service. Moreover, it was estimated by managers, who did not have the benefit of Head Office computers, that the payback period for the additional investment was no more than a season and a half.

As David Gwyn once described it "The guv'nor had won!" which does reveal his reluctance to accept the change but in later years and after more considered reflection he feels that without the transition to self-catering Pakefield would not have survived. Perhaps the same theory could be applied to other centres and thus to the overall size of the business as it is today.

By the early 1960's all of the Pontin's sites had been further modernised and extended in order to meet the growing demand for bigger, better and more comfortable facilities.

Self-catering and self-service were important departures from established patterns of the fully-inclusive nature of family holidays at around these times. These changes in policy for some of the larger centres were not to be accomplished without controversial debates both within and outside the organisation.

In those days Fred talked about the new image "Rent-a-Chalet" holidays, justifying the new approach by claiming that many of his guests were no longer prepared to be regimented to three meals a day taken only at set times. They wanted a change and a choice of their own.

The population of the United Kingdom had entered the age when many families were becoming owners of a motor car for the very first time in their lives. Not everyone wanted communal feeding and Fred was anxious to provide stiff competition for the caravan camps, which were growing in size and number. He was of the mind that providing organised entertainment in a self-catering environment might do the trick.

There are a number of alleged sources for the idea of converting selected camps to the self-catering concept.

Ann Miller claimed to have conceived the original notion from her continual irritation at the patched hole in the roof of each of the accommodation huts which were occupied by servicemen during the war. Osmington Bay had 120 very nice timber chalets, but when the army heating stoves were removed a small sheet of asbestos was used to cover the holes in the ceilings.

After two or three years of coping with temperamental and unpredictable chefs, she had joked about putting the coke burning stoves back into the units – thus allowing the guests to prepare their own meals.

She contended that this casual remark led to the policy of creating wholly self-catering holiday centres, which was looked upon in the early sixties as being quite a revolutionary concept for the industry.

An irony is that until the Osmington Bay camp was sold by the Pontin's organisation a few years ago it still offered full board accommodation and had never catered for children, mainly because of the undulating terrain of the cliff top site.

Brother Len has his own version. He attributes the origin of the idea to his bank manager, who introduced Pontin's to a caravan and camping site at St Mary's Bay, Brixham, as a potential acquisition. Seasonal occupation of caravans and tents is, of course, synonymous with self-catering and the property was referred to Fred as a possible conversion into a holiday camp. The site was duly purchased and converted into a fully self-catering holiday centre.

However, Sir Fred had always insisted that self-catering holi-days were his idea, because he was undoubtedly the first in the field as far as the larger holiday centres were concerned. This latter point is an established fact, because Wick Ferry was the first site to be converted in this manner.

In the winter of 1961/62 Fred consulted his old friend Billy Butlin on the subject and his somewhat Luddite response was that working wives had no wish to work in the kitchen when they were away on their hard-earned annual holidays. Fred's own view was that not all families wanted a cooked breakfast and could not afford a fully inclusive tariff which included a charge for something they had no wish to consume.

Some of Pontin's guests were making a habit of eating at restaurants outside of the holiday centres as a break from the normal routine. These were the type of people who would be attracted to self-catering holiday villages, which would continue to provide entertainment on an inclusive cost basis.

Whatever the source of the self-catering idea within the Pontin's organisation or otherwise, there is now much hard evidence that Pontin's took the initiative in providing self-catering holiday centres. Others followed much later, but it was not before Bobby Butlin had taken over from his father that Butlin's followed the trend.

There was initial opposition from the National Federation of Permanent Holiday Camps, whose members considered that the entire concept of holiday camps would be lost for ever. They were misguided in this approach and Sir Fred feels certain that this important change of policy on his part led to the boom in holiday centres for the remainder of 1960s and the early part of the 1970s.

Chapter Eight

SPORTING LIFE

Fred's booming business activities and his regular visits to Ireland once the Trabolgan camp had been opened in 1949 led to a keen interest in horse racing. Bill Smith, one of the original body of investors, was not only a close friend of Fred's but also a keen gambler, especially at the races.

It was, however, the chance meeting with emergent trainer Vincent O'Brien and his two brothers at a hunt ball, traditionally held in the main house at Trabolgan, that led Fred to achieving the status of being an owner of a racehorse. O'Brien did not open his world-famous training establishment on the 350 acre Ballydoyle estate until 1951. In those early days he had much more modest stables, comprising just eight boxes, in Mallow, Co. Cork.

He had taken out his first training licence in 1944, but it was 1948 before he started to achieve outstanding successes at Cheltenham with horses such as Cottage Rake, which won three successive Gold Cups, and Hatton's Grace, which won three successive Champion Hurdles. Vincent also trained three successive Grand National winners. He was still looking for customers in 1949, though, especially those who had the money to invest in horse racing, despite the austerity which was still in evidence after the war.

It was much too early for Fred to be thinking about attracting publicity from his horse racing activities. That was to come much later when television cameras were a regular feature at racecourses all over Great Britain, Northern Ireland and the Irish Republic. In those early days Fred Pontin was probably lured by the excitement and camaraderie of the racing fraternity.

In addition to the novelty of having some surplus cash in his pocket, he had the advantage of having access to Bill Smith's considerable knowledge of the sport and its intricate terminology. As far as betting was concerned, Fred had never been drawn to gambling for its own sake, probably because of his prewar activities as a book-maker. He was always very much aware that there is usually only one winner and that is very seldom the ordinary punter.

To have a direct interest in an *actual* runner was, however, quite a different matter. Fred was caught up by the stimulating atmosphere of race meetings, not only in the Republic of Ireland but also at Cheltenham's National Hunt Festival, which always has the support of a strong Irish contingent.

Fred's connection with Vincent O'Brien proved to be very profit-able, and not just because of the results produced from the training of the horses. Together with Bill Smith he attended every meeting at which they had a runner. Their young trainer, whose influence and reputation were increasing at a rapid rate, invariably seemed able to guide them in the direction of successful horses. It would not be correct to say that the bookies were taken for a ride on every occasion, but there is no doubt that they enjoyed many celebrations with their horse racing friends in those early days.

Although Sir Fred was not to know it at the time, his enthusiasm for the sport was to last over 20 years, during which period he achieved several spectacular successes, including appearances in the winner's enclosure at Newbury and Aintree. These were during the course of the most important annual meetings at these famous venues.

Bill Smith was a partner in Fred's early investments in the racing business. Vincent O'Brien bought two horses on their behalf. One was a complete failure, not even being placed, let alone winning, when it ran under their colours. Alberoni gave them their first taste of success, however, as well as some useful returns from the on-course book-makers. It was at a Phoenix Park, Dublin meeting which saw this horse romp home from a big field as the 6-4 odds-on favourite.

Alberoni went on to win several other races over the next twelve months under its new colours, but Vincent O'Brien and Bill Smith anticipated Fred's agreement to a sale of the horse at a worthwhile profit to someone who turned out to be Lord Derby's younger brother. As a new owner on the racing scene Fred felt that he had to accept the advice which had been given, but he was dismayed to learn at a later date that Alberoni not only continued to be successful but also won the Irish Grand National for its new owner.

There followed a few years of a routine but very enjoyable, interest in horse racing. Fred's relationship with Bill Smith became more distant when Bill went out to Kenya and retired from the board of Pontin's. However, this coincided with the time that the marketing and promotional advantages to be gained from horse racing became apparent as far as Fred's continually expanding business empire was concerned.

He bought a horse called Gay Navaree after he had made it known that he wanted to own a winner of the Grand National Steeplechase at Aintree. Bill Marshall, the Cheltenham trainer, was instrumental in buying the horse on Fred's behalf when he attended the Ascot sales.

This horse had twice been a finisher in the Grand National, but had then been taken out of training when the owner became mentally ill and was unable to attend to his affairs. The price was 2,700 guineas.

Fred was fortunate in being able to arrange for the name to be changed to Pontin-Go so that the company could cash in on the publicity generated by the horse's appearance at televised race meetings, including the 1964 Grand National. Earlier in the year Pontin-Go had a fourth place at Kempton Park and was second in a race at Newcastle.

It was felt that it was a good prospect for the big race at Aintree, which had no less than four favourites, starting at 100-7. Pontin-Go was a rank outsider with odds in excess of 66-1.

Prior to the race there was a tragic accident near the Canal Turn. A light aircraft crashed killing five passengers, one of whom was Nancy Spain, the well-known TV personality, author and journalist, who was to have been a guest of Mrs Mirabel Topham, the owner of the Aintree racecourse.

The race did, however, take place and Pontin-Go ridden by P. Jones finished in fifth place after being second over the last jump.

This result gave enormous encouragement, not only to Fred but also to his management and staff as well as his many guests who were starting to follow his racing activities with keen interest. Fred recalled that the jockey was exhausted at the end of the race, but Pontin-Go was in fine condition, with ears still pricked and probably ready for a few more jumps.

Team Spirit's was a popular victory that year, having won by half-a-length in a very exciting finish, being fifth over the last jump. It would have been even more popular as far as Fred was concerned if an offer to sell him this particular horse had been put into effect just a little earlier. Before he could take advantage of what was the favourable price of 5,000 guineas the American owner disposed of a half interest and Fred could only dream about what might have been.

Pontin-Go made another appearance in the same race the following year but fell at the Canal Turn. Fred then took the horse out of training into a new career in point-to-point steeplechasing, ridden by the daughter of one of his employees.

Another of Fred's Grand National prospects was foaled in France. The horse's name was identified with his latest venture in Europe. Go-Pontinental had a successful outing at the Yuletide Meeting in Liverpool on the fourth of December 1963, when it won the Santa Claus Juvenile Hurdle at 5-1. Bought on Fred's behalf as well as trained by Bill Marshall, it had no less than 22 outings over the next two seasons, but only one further appearance in the winner's enclosure.

The horse continued to mature, though not in a particularly spectacular way until it won The Canterbury Handicap Steeplechase at Folkestone in October 1968, when it was ridden by Josh Gifford. Whatever the results, the publicity was always useful for Fred Pontin and, of course, Pontin's.

This horse qualified for the Grand National, having finished second by half-a-length in the Topham Stakes when it was again ridden by Josh Gifford, but on the big day it was brought down by a loose horse called Peace Town.

Go-Pontin, by the famous horse Pinza, was another candidate for the fulfilment of Fred's racing ambitions. This horse carried high hopes as well as the name of the business, but after one or two unsuccessful outings, including a run in the company-sponsored Pontin Handicap Hurdle at Fontwell in 1963, it seemed clear that this specimen of horse flesh was not going to be a world-beater. A buyer was found. Fred didn't take too kindly to losers. His company wasn't a loser and it needed to be associated with success.

The horse continued to race under the name of Strapin, but with no first past the posts to be celebrated by the new owner, thus justifying Fred's decision. Once again, though, the company had enjoyed the benefit of the short-term publicity.

Fred was not to know it at the time, but it was to be a few years before the ultimate success was to be achieved. This was not without a great deal of hard work and dogged perseverance in pursuit of his ultimate goal. When it happened it was during the same horse racing season. 1971 was a year Fred would never forget but before the triumphant details are recounted it might be useful to explain his personal attitude to publicity and how he applied his theories to horse racing.

For obvious reasons, it can never be possible to arrange matters in a precise manner, otherwise Sir Fred would be a multi-millionaire on the strength of his winnings from the bookies. His instructions to the jockeys were to endeavour to keep a horse in the first three or four places. On this basis the television or radio commentator would be constantly naming a horse associated with the title of the company or one of the sites.

There would be what Sir Fred had always described as "the drip, drip, drip of publicity" directed at literally hundreds of thousands and, in the case of Eurovision coverage of the Grand National, millions of existing and potential clients of Pontin's and Pontinental.

Racehorses have always been an expensive luxury, but keeping them in training can always be justified if the resultant publicity results in substantial increases in annual turnover. Time and time again the results of market research demonstrated the worth of this form of activity. Who was Fred to complain if he was also enjoying the racing and all that went with the sport?

Unfortunately, he was not dealing with a bottomless pit as far as naming horses was concerned. The Jockey Club became aware of what was happening and they were not willing to see their sport exploited in this way. When George Wigg became chairman of the Horse Racing Levy Board he took a firm line against Fred renaming any further horses which came into his ownership.

Fred was to have the last laugh, as we shall see later, at the expense of the BBC television sports commentator and regular Grand National presenter, David Coleman.

But, for the time being, there are more facts to relate regarding Fred's most successful racehorses. Cala Mesquida was bought by Bill Marshall on a visit to France and Fred quickly named this latest acquisition after Pontin's very popular beach resort in Majorca. Trained by John Sutcliffe Senior this proved to be a horse of real quality and Fred rather enjoyed becoming accustomed to its success.

Its first season was 1969-1970. After a second place at Nottingham in October, Cala Mesquida succeeded in the Langley Handicap Hurdle at Windsor on 25 February 1970 at a price of 5-1. This was a memorable day for Fred, because not only did he win a substantial amount of money from a wager on Cala Mesquida, but at the same meeting he saw a horse called Specify brought home by Terry Biddlecombe as the 700th winner of his career in English racing.

The champagne had already been flowing and Fred was very much in the mood for a deal. Specify, which qualified for the Grand National by winning this race, was owned by Mr Paul Rackham, to whom Fred lost no time in introducing himself.

It is said that some people make their own luck. On that particular day Fred pushed his as far as it would go. He made it clear to Mr Rackham that he wanted to buy Specify, but the owner did not show any real interest in making a sale because he was also looking forward to having a runner in the big race at Aintree.

A few drinks and a happy atmosphere, however, soon produced some results. Paul Rackham named a figure of £15,000, which Fred felt was almost certainly on the high side and would be difficult to justify, his best offer having been £10,000. When Fred made what appeared to be an unsuccessful effort to split the difference at £12,500 he gained the impression that Paul Rackham wouldn't be averse to taking a flyer.

Fred persuaded him to agree to settle the price by the turn of a coin. If Fred won the price would be £12,500 but if Paul Rackham called correctly Fred would pay him his full asking figure of £15,000. Fred took a coin from his pocket and put it on the counter of the bar and invited the owner to make the call. In the event, he very kindly gave the honour to Fred who called "heads" – Specify was his for £12,500.

It has to be agreed that Sir W.S.Gilbert was close to the mark in his lyrics from *Iolanthe*:

> *Faint heart never won fair lady!*
> *Nothing venture, nothing win.*

Fred's purchase of Specify attracted some very useful publicity because a lot of people were aware of his ambition to win the Grand National. Fred recalls John Lawrence – later to become Lord Oaksey – writing that Fred had paid far too much money for the prospect and he was not alone in his opinion. Again, Fred was to have the last laugh.

Specify turned out to be quite a nervous horse, having broken a bone in its face when it fell in the 1968 Schweppes Gold Trophy. It had originally been raced hard on the flat as a two-year-old. When the horse became Fred's property he entrusted the brown gelding to John Sutcliffe to train alongside Cala Mesquida. Specify joined his stables at Ashtead, near Epsom, with instructions to prepare him for the 1970 Grand National.

This was not to be Specify's year. Critics of Fred's purchase felt that they had been vindicated. Although Specify was brought down at Beecher's Brook, the horse had performed well until this misfortune so Fred had no hesitation in entering, what he still maintained was a very good prospect, for the 1971 race. Fred had enormous faith in the horse and he tipped what he felt sure would be its victory to anyone who would listen, including what appeared to be his entire staff and a large proportion of his guests.

Fred Pontin could never be accused of lacking confidence in something he believed in. However, it is not just optimism which

drove Sir Fred. He had never been afraid of backing his own judgment in personal as well as business matters. Not all of his prospects
succeed but his positive approach to life had paid off more often than
not, particularly during the days he was responsible for running the
Pontin's organisation.

In the meantime, Cala Mesquida had went on to win hurdle races
at Folkestone and Nottingham at fairly short odds during the winter
of 1969/70, but was disappointingly unplaced in the Benson &
Hedges and Sovereign Handicap Hurdles at Sandown and Newbury
respectively in December and January 1971.

Although, as has already been stated, Fred Pontin could not be
denounced as a pessimist, it was not a supremely confident owner
who travelled to Newbury on 13 February 1971 when Cala
Mesquida was entered for the Schweppes Gold Trophy. This did not
prevent him from tipping the horse, so there were many very happy
people when it won a thrilling race on the last stride at a starting price
of 33-1 from a field of 23 runners.

The rider was John Cook, who was already booked to ride Specify
in the 1971 Grand National. The national Press and racing enthusiasts
then started talking about the prospect of a repeat success for the
"Winning Trio" – John Sutcliffe, John Cook and Fred Pontin. They
were not to be disappointed. They went on to produce a unique
double.

Fred even had his own horse tipped to him by a couple he met in
Miami, where he attended the Ali-Frazier fight in the company of the
late Jack Solomons. These tipsters had obtained odds of 40-1 after
getting their information from what they described as the horse's
mouth. They had been given the word by John Sutcliffe, but were not
aware that they were speaking to the owner. Fred had to wait to get
back to England before placing his bet when the best odds he was
able to obtain were 33-1.

The night before the big day Fred had dinner with the BBC's
David Coleman and his wife, Barbara. They knew each other from
their respective charitable activities with the Variety Club of Great
Britain. After a very convivial evening Fred had no hesitation in
recommending that Specify should be backed to win next day's big
race.

The future of the Grand National was then in some doubt. Mrs
Topham, had been considering retirement as owner of Aintree.
What should she do about a large area of freehold property which
produced worthwhile returns on only one day of the year? The
course was eventually bought by a property developer, Bill Davies,
but mercifully the land has never been covered in houses and the

most popular and most challenging steeplechase in the world is still a regular annual event despite recent problems with a false start leading to an abandoned race and terrorists' bomb scares.

The 1971 race was also distinguished by the fact that one of the jockeys was racing journalist John Lawrence, who was also a keen amateur rider. In his report on the race he wrote that no Epsom Derby could have produced a finer spectacle.

There was a desperate finish, with five horses together at the last fence. Specify produced what Lawrence described as "an extra gear as miraculously, like the Red Sea, a gap opened near the rails between Bongeeno and Black Secret". Apparently, John did not feel it fit to mention that Fred Pontin had bought himself a bargain after all.

To quote again from his report: "Specify went for the gap like a terrier at a rat hole". John Cook brought home what proved to be a very popular winner as far as Pontin's staff and guests were concerned.

This race was then described as one of the most exciting Grand Nationals on record and it is said that the entertainment provided on that day did much to preserve the future of this great sporting occasion. Someone wrote that after such "a glorious race" could the survival of the Grand National at Aintree ever be in doubt?

John Cook's performance in the race was described as a "hands and heels drive" and "one of the coolest examples of jockeyship ever seen". Fred Pontin would not argue with these comments. It was very sad that later that year John Cook suffered a broken leg, an injury which was to finish his racing career. He later went out to Australia and New Zealand where he became an assistant trainer.

Fred was unable to rename Specify as "Specify Pontin's" due to the efforts of George Wigg and the racing authorities, who subsequently made it illegal to change a horse's name after it had run as a two-year-old.

However, Fred made up for it when he was interviewed by David Coleman in the winner's enclosure after his famous Grand National victory. Eurovision took the live broadcast that year and, despite David's efforts to change the subject, Fred succeeded in broadcasting the message to millions of viewers that the win by Cala Mesquida in the Schweppes had "provided the deposit for the 1971 Pontin's holiday", and now Specify's win had added "the balance of the cost, plus some spending money". On that day the BBC afforded Pontin's thousands of pounds of free publicity.

Fred was somewhat overcome by the exuberance of the occasion, but he did not miss the chance to encourage the continuation of the drip, drip, drip of publicity, although on this particular occasion it was more of a deluge. Perhaps David Coleman forgave Fred because he revealed later that he had backed Specify to win the big race after Fred's tip over dinner on the night before.

The publicity did not stop there. Fred entered Specify for the same race in 1972 and the BBC obviously overlooked his blatant plug because they featured John Sutcliffe, his wife Claire, assistant trainer David Wilson, stable lad Ray McGhin and Fred Pontin himself along with Specify, on the front cover of the *Radio Times.*

The inside story stated that Fred had made no secret about why he was interested in racing, it being mainly for the publicity. They obviously felt that their viewers would be inspired to watch the race by publishing the picture and giving Fred and consequently Pontin's such a write-up.

Incidentally, Specify's 1971 starting price was a generous 28-1, so a "double" on Cala Mesquida and Specify would have produced incredible odds. Fred felt that it was a great pity that he hadn't thought of it at the time. But, as has already been explained, he had never really been a great gambler.

The value of such attendant publicity was particularly important because prize money in those days was very low, not much more than £15,000. By the time everyone had been paid there was not much available for lavish celebrations, yet the commercial benefits were very considerable. In modern times the winnings for the successful owner amount to well over £100,000 and are much more significant.

The 1972 race was not to produce another miracle, even though Fred felt that the gallant horse had an excellent chance. Specify, ridden by Bob Davies as a result of the injury to John Cook, ran a good race to finish sixth. This was before the days of Red Rum and until then no horse had ever won the race in two successive years.

Fred's magnificent brown gelding was then thirteen years old so he retired his victorious horse to the grounds of his hotel at Farringford on the Isle of Wight. This was once the home of Lord Tennyson. The poet's stables became the living quarters of Specify and his constant companion, an elderly donkey named Timber.

It seemed appropriate to have a retirement party for such a gallant racehorse so Specify was guest of honour at a celebration held at Farringford. Other guests were the training team, John Cook, who had by then announced his own retirement, Josh Gifford and Mirabel Topham.

When Specify eventually became too infirm he was put down by the local vet. Timber, by then 33 years of age, joined him on that same day in October 1982. Fred felt that it was only fitting that they should pass on to new pastures in each other's company.

After all this excitement, Fred started thinking in terms of winning a classic on the flat, so he bought a yearling. The horse was very well bred, but there were to be no more exhilarating successes. John Sutcliffe died from cancer in 1975 and Fred never looked around for another trainer.

He had achieved a great deal for himself and the company and he felt it best to rest on his laurels. John and Claire Sutcliffe were good friends and he used to enjoy driving down to the yard on Sunday mornings to have a yarn and see how the horses were getting on.

John Sutcliffe had taken out a licence in 1965, just two years after his son, John Junior was born. Specify and Cala Mesquida were counted as two of his three principal accomplishments in the horse racing business. These were happy years. Fred was very pleased that John found success with his horses.

An ironic footnote to this chapter is that in 1975 the Jockey Club amended their regulations so that owners could name their horses after a company's product or the company's name.

So far as Sir Fred is concerned, there were no hard feelings. He had got away with his little game – as did Sir Jack Cohen, founder of the Tesco supermarket chain. He had a horse called Tesco Boy, but he was not fortunate enough to emulate the achievements of his fellow East Ender, who had enjoyed a very good run for his money.

Once again, though, Fred Pontin had proved that he was a forward thinker. He loved to innovate and where he had experimented with success, others soon followed. In his eyes, there was no greater compliment.

Chapter Nine

THE GUV'NOR

Although Fred Pontin was an extremely dominant personality within the company, he had always been the first to appreciate that the foundations for success were built upon the "family" image. Not just in terms of the involvement of his wife, daughter, son-in-law, brothers and sister, but by the long periods of service from many employees, all of whom he also considered to be "family".

Research for this book has also confirmed that the long serving members of the staff still feel the same, often talking about how they "felt part of the family". It is really quite extraordinary bearing in mind the size of the business which was sold for some £56 million some twenty years ago.

It was not just the managers, but also catering, cleaning, entertainments and maintenance staff. Perhaps this is best illustrated by a quote from Wally Riglar, who was involved with the care and maintenance of Osmington Bay for over 40 years. He attributed the strength of Pontin's to the levels of hard work and dedication which were so much in evidence from all concerned in the early days.

"We all felt part of the team and one of the family," he said. "Mr Pontin always had time to discuss our problems and he and his family set an excellent example in terms of commitment to the success of the business."

Wally's loyalty is very touching, especially as he commenced his employment with Fred Pontin's company on wages as low as £6 a week. When he got married a few years later he was given a rise of £1.50 and he obtained a mortgage of £1,000 so he could purchase a bungalow at £1,850.

Fred recalled that Wally was very nervous about taking on this commitment so his employer was happy to set his mind at rest by telling him: "If you ever have a problem, come and see me". He never did, but Fred was very much aware that this assurance was enough for Wally. The bungalow is now valued probably in excess of £80,000 and Wally is enjoying a good pension as a result of the scheme which Fred introduced to the company in the early 1970s and subsequently improved by Coral and successive owners of Pontin's.

When Corals took over Pontin's in 1978 the salary scales were brought into line with the main group and Wally Riglar was given a rise of no less than 28%, which must represent some form of indictment in respect of the levels of remuneration which were in evidence when Fred Pontin was running the company, particularly as some staff received even higher increases.

It was not just the managers but also catering, entertainments and maintenance staff. Pay increases were not always foremost in Fred Pontin's mind when it came to looking after his staff.

However, his individual approach to remuneration was to offer some perks which he knew would be very much appreciated. These were not large cash bonuses, which had an adverse effect on profitability, but were nonetheless just as attractive and created much goodwill.

The gift of a week's free holiday at one of the Pontin's camps was a typical way of providing an extra reward for the more deserving members of the staff. When Fred was operating holidays abroad with Pontinental this created a new dimension, so large numbers of his employees took advantage of what appeared to be a very generous gesture on behalf of the management.

Perhaps it was but, in Fred Pontin's words, it was also cost-effective. Spare seats on a charter aircraft were being taken, usually at the last minute, by members of the staff and their families. When they arrived at the resort they were making use of vacant accommodation – so the direct cost to the company was limited to food, some additional cleaning, and the laundering of bed linen.

There was, however, more than adequate compensation, because the bars and gift shops enjoyed increased takings. These arrangements, that kept everybody happy, did not really differ from the concessionary travel allowed to employees of airlines. These seats were usually made available on a strict stand-by basis, without significant cost to the company.

On the subject of staff, Fred remembered a Yorkshireman named Danny Horrigan. This was in the early sixties and he claimed to be Britain's happiest man, even though his summer job was to wash up 3,000 plates at Pontin's Riviera every day. Danny had a change of employment each winter when he became a breakfast cook in a big commercial hotel.

He used to say, though: "Give me the life at Pontin's every time. I enjoy my work and when it's finished there's fresh air, sun and friendliness to spare". That's a good quote and serves to illustrate the phenomenon of staff dedication.

Another member of the staff, who started working for Fred Pontin in 1969 as a chalet porter and who became Operations Director of what was once known as Holiday Club Pontin's, is Jeff Mallinson. Incidentally, "Holiday Club" was introduced as a prefix to the Pontin's name for a period of time, no doubt in an effort to modernise the image but this terminology has now been dropped as a result of the changes which have taken place in the late nineties.

Jeff Mallinson knows of many stories about Sir Fred, some of which he says he would never disclose, but most of which are probably apocryphal. He once reminded Fred Pontin of an incident which took place in 1976, by which time his own dedication and potential had obviously been recognised because he had been promoted to general manager of Pontin's largest site, Prestatyn Sands Holiday Village.

Although he was the youngest executive ever to hold this post, Jeff had been told that his salary was to be regarded as provisional, pending the time when in Fred Pontin's typical words "you have proved your worth", hopefully within a period of say two to three months. This was Fred's preferred method of keeping his managerial staff on their toes by promising rewards only when their performance provided the necessary justification.

Over the last few months of 1975 Jeff and his team ran several special events at Prestatyn, which were followed by a very successful Christmas operation and he felt that he had earned his increase in basic salary.

At the beginning of January 1976 the North Wales coastline was devastated by hurricane force winds which ripped the roofs from eleven chalet blocks and caused tidal waters to flood the holiday village and adjacent Grand Hotel twice during a period of 48 hours.

The following weekend the centre and its buildings were hit again by similar storms, which destroyed five more roofs on the chalet blocks and again flooded the entire site. The damage ran into millions of pounds and insurance assessors were soon swarming all over the property.

Jeff led his team in the major task of reconstructing what remained of the holiday village and salvaging whatever was worth retaining for the coming season. Fred had kept in close touch with everything that had happened and he visited the site in early February to monitor progress for himself.

According to Jeff, his employer expressed much satisfaction at what had been achieved during what had been a comparatively short period of time and that everything appeared to be on course for the opening of the 1976 season. Jeff must have been anxious to ensure that all was to Fred Pontin's satisfaction. When he saw that the Chairman and Managing Director was pleased with what he had seen he tackled him about his rise just as Fred was about to climb into his car.

"I'm glad you are pleased with our achievements Mr Pontin. Can you now review my salary and give me my promised increase?" were Jeff's final remarks.

Fred turned round, faced him and roared: "You have half-destroyed this holiday village, flooded it on at least three occasions and have the nerve to ask for a raise? No way, I say, no way!" If Jeff's memory serves him correctly Fred then gave a half-smile and drove away down the roads, now cleared of sand and silt and leaving behind a much-chastened general manager.

There was a happy ending. Two months later he got his increase in salary, which is probably just as well – otherwise Pontin's would have had to look elsewhere for their future Operations Director.

Large numbers of purely seasonal workers were involved in the Pontin's business. For example, in the 1970's Blackpool employed about 500 people, but the staff turnover in the course of a 26 week season could be as high as twice this figure. This would be exceptional, however, and mainly because of the competition from other employers in such a popular seaside resort.

Eddie Stamper, one of Fred's longest-serving general managers, who joined Osmington as a catering manager in 1968, preferred to maintain that the hard-core of Pontin's staff return year after year because they had become truly infected with the "Pontin's disease", for which there is apparently no known cure.

He also talks of Fred Pontin attracting allegiances, but this is undoubtedly due to a way of life, not a personality. If anything, Fred was probably guilty of taking advantage of the job-dedication which had been shown over the years. If this is the case Fred could not possibly have held many regrets because the business is still there and it continues to provide pleasure for many thousands of guests each year.

The Chairman's site visits did not follow any set pattern, so the managers and staff were never given any advance warning from Head Office. If, however, there were two sites in fairly close proximity to each other the bush telegraph would work by means of a telephone call and the muttering of the password "coconuts".

Why this particular word should be used has never been revealed, and Fred could only only assume that it had something to do with the sound of the clatter of horses hooves. He never did ride a horse but perhaps they felt that he was the Lone Ranger with Albert "Maxie" Shirley as Tonto. Maxie was Fred's chauffeur during the winter months over a number of years, having completed "the knowledge" as a London taxi driver.

In the course of the season Maxie was activities organiser at Osmington, where he was very well known, as he is even today, for his Max Miller impersonations and entrepreneurial activities, ably assisted in those days by Wally Riglar.

Maxie appeared on Gerald Scarfe's BBC2 television programme for the *40 Minutes* series. He was shown doing his act at the Hackney Empire. He is now aged well over 80 and often takes winter cruises with his wife Penny, still unable to resist appearing on talent nights with his Max Miller scripts to which he adds his own special jokes and songs.

Fred counted Maxie as one of his old chums. He was a regular guest at Fred's Farringford Hotel on the Isle of Wight, where the genial host made a habit of having a party of special friends every Christmas. Maxie was the official Santa Claus and has also been known to respond to Fred's requests to travel down and entertain the children – often at very short notice – if there was a period of prolonged bad weather during the summer months and there was a need for someone to cheer things up a bit.

When Walter Rowley was manager at Osmington Bay in the early sixties and when Shortlake House, which is on the site, was the Chairman's home base, Fred made a habit of visiting every other camp during the course of the week, but usually returned to Osmington in time for dinner on Friday evenings.

After his meal Fred would enjoy a short rest and then go on a tour of the Osmington bars before ending up in the ballroom, where, just before the usual rendering of *Auld Lang Syne*, Walter would make a point of introducing the man who had founded the entire organisation to the guests. He liked to do this, but Fred had never thought that it was really necessary. The holidaymakers had usually had an opportunity to see Fred Pontin on his rounds; some had taken photographs and a number would even ask for his autograph. It should be added that if they were feeling generous and had enjoyed a good week, some of the guests would even go as far as to buy him a drink. These drinks were never refused and Fred usually responded by buying the odd round or two.

Just as the band had played their last piece of music Walter would take the stage and announce the Chairman's presence. The spotlights would switch from him to the balcony of what was known as the "Top Bar", where Fred would be standing, waving and smiling at everyone.

This became something of a ritual but Walter would not have stage-managed the operation if he did not feel that it was a worthwhile exercise. The response would not always be strictly complimentary. On one occasion, a guest nudged Walter and exclaimed: "Look at him! Just like Emperor Nero up there, isn't he?"

When this story was relayed to Fred he responded by saying that he trusted the comparison was not made in the literal sense because that particular historical figure had a reputation for cruelty and corruption and eventually committed suicide.

Regular site visits served the purpose of keeping Fred Pontin in close contact with his many guests, who appeared to appreciate that "the Guv'nor" was prepared to stay in one of the chalets and eat the same meals at the same tables as themselves.

At one such meal when he was eating breakfast with the camp management team Fred Pontin noticed that a shoe being worn by one of the waiters had its sole flapping, making an irritating noise as the young, probably part time, seasonal employee walked between the tables as he went about his duties.

The chairman called the waiter over to his table and drew attention to the footwear which was causing the problem. The lad looked a little puzzled, no doubt wondering why the great man should be so concerned about a rather trivial matter but his face brightened when his employer reached for his hip pocket and took out a wad of bank notes.

"Take this" said Fred Pontin, handing the waiter the elastic band which secured the fivers and tenners. "Put this around your shoe to stop that dreadful noise and make certain that you have a decent pair to wear in this restaurant tomorrow". At that, the chairman returned the money to his pocket, turned back to his companions and resumed the conversation.

As for the young waiter, his face registered embarrassment and then disappointment as he realised that he would not be getting the price of a new pair of shoes after all.

Fred Pontin has been known to be charitable in deserving cases but no doubt on this occasion the chairman wished only to make the point that he expected his staff to appear before the guests dressed in a clean and tidy manner. This rather bizarre gesture, although spontaneous, was quite typical of his approach to dealing with such matters; never conventional and always meaningful.

Fred enjoyed having drinks in the bar and there were many occasions when he demonstrated what appeared to be spontaneous generosity where it was felt that the situation warranted it. If, during any particular week, there had been justifiable grounds for complaint, this was a typically effective way of diffusing a possibly mutinous gathering. Fred wanted "last nights" to be happy and memorable so that the guests would take the opportunity to book up for next year before leaving for home. Everything could not be expected to go right the whole of the time, but the Pontin's staff and particularly their Chairman always did their best to make people happy and the enthusiasts continued to return year after year.

All these efforts resulted in Fred becoming very well known to his management, staff and guests. Michael Austin, the retired Marketing Director at Pontin's, when interviewed by a journalist, told him: "Mr Pontin is a hard man but fair, scrupulously fair". Fred liked to think that was an accurate description of how he was running the company in his day.

Fred was also impressed when an early sixties edition of *Investor's Chronicle* stated: "Fred Pontin is a dedicated man with no interest outside his family and his business". This was not strictly true, but it was the right thing to have written about you when you are anxious to impress investing institutions.

Tight control over expenditure was always being maintained. Whenever Fred visited the Pontin's overseas sites it became routine procedure for the local managers to seek his personal approval for any improvements or replacements they wished to undertake.

Together, the Chairman and the managers would go through each requirement, item by item, and the answers would come thick and fast – "Yes, no, agreed, defer or never". Before he left the premises Fred's decisions would be committed to paper and he would take a copy back to Head Office, where Ann Miller would be responsible for taking the necessary action.

The system in those days tended to be this informal, but it did work and everyone knew where they were.

Fred was not only looking for any readily apparent deficiencies, but also for signs of wastage. If he discovered something which might have been applicable to other camps he would issue a memorandum from the Chairman's office. He once decreed that 40 watt light bulbs should be used in the winter months in places where it was not essential for a higher wattage.

It can only be imagined what he would have to say on the subject if a subsequent site visit revealed that his orders had not been put into effect. Repeated transgressions would be followed by a Chairman's memorandum in vitriolic terminology with a copy circulated to every manager within the group.

Joe Rubido, one of Fred's managerial staff at Torremolinos, recalls him putting his hands to his head and shouting "My profits! My profits!" every time he heard a plate or a glass crash to the floor. This was all part of an act . . . he really wanted every member of the staff to know that any careless breakage or wastage was anathema to the Chairman.

However, it should be explained that Fred never complained about the size of the portions of food or how much wine was consumed at the lunch and dinner tables by his guests. It was waste that he hated and found abhorrent. Everyone knew it. Joe said that Fred's control was so tight that if his employer fell in the water he would never sink.

Despite Harry Warner once saying that Pontin, the newcomer, was ruining the holiday camp business, he found that before too many years had passed Fred Pontin had gained a nationwide reputation for driving the product forward.

This reputation is recognised too by Mike Austin, who joined the Pontin organisation as one of Fred's early protégés in the early 1960s. Mike has now retired from his position as Marketing Director of Pontin's, then part of the leisure division of the Scottish & Newcastle Breweries group of companies, alongside Center Parcs.

Mike has given Fred Pontin much cause for satisfaction when he readily conceded that his former employer's knowledge of the business has been second to none, and that Fred played a leading part in raising standards at a time when there was widespread complacency in the holiday camp industry.

With customers returning year after year in the sixties and seventies and most Pontin's centres fully booked, usually by early March, it needed a dedicated entrepreneur to continue to strive for higher standards in accommodation and facilities.

Fred made use of the regular meetings of the National Federation as a forum for the promotion of his ideas, such as introducing both indoor and outdoor heated swimming pools at some of the largest holiday centres.

He advocated the provision of more permanent forms of construction as far as units of accommodation were concerned . . . en-suite bath-room and toilet facilities . . . fitted kitchens in purpose-built chalets of bricks and mortar. All these improvements soon became the norm.

This was followed by the introduction of fitted carpets and even television sets. As the seasons became more extended Fred also made certain that heaters became a feature of the improved short-stay living quarters, which were now being offered to his increasing numbers of annual guests.

There was much scepticism about his determination to set new criteria in providing comfortable accommodation, not least from other members of the National Federation.

Mike Austin recalls that when Fred opened the newly acquired, and almost totally refurbished, holiday camp at Blackpool's Squires Gate, a local councillor remarked that Pontin's would be "ruining the business in the area" by offering bathrooms and toilets in the new chalets.

This fount of all wisdom emphasised his point by saying that working people "were content to have a good wash down when they left home and the same when they returned from their annual holiday".

Although this ludicrous philosophy seems difficult to comprehend – even for the 1960s – his point that working-class holidaymakers didn't need such luxuries was really concealing the fact that the traditional seaside landladies would be forced to effect similar improvements if they were to continue competing for the lucrative trade in family holidays.

The fact that standards have steadily improved since those days is surely a tribute to Fred Pontin's maxim that his company's reputation would be only as good as its worst accommodation. In the 1990s it was even known for Tory cabinet ministers to stay in bed and breakfast accommodation when attending the Conservatives' annual conference in Blackpool. Little did they know that Sir Fred Pontin had been first responsible for such an all round increase in standards.

Fred Pontin's policies were vindicated by the group results for 1963, which set another record. Net profits before tax came out at £661,760, with £271,792 being distributed to grateful shareholders by way of an annual dividend.

The number of Pontin's holiday centres in the United Kingdom increased to eighteen, following the acquisition of Broadreeds and Wick Ferry. Within ten years Pontin's had acquired six further sites, including Southport, Prestatyn, Camber Sands and Hemsby, Norfolk, which assisted in boosting annual profits to a shade under £2 million on a turnover of some £13 million.

Southport and Prestatyn were "green field" sites, which involved the construction of entirely new complexes of buildings. The majority of the work was entrusted to a young man, Trevor Hemmings, who was eventually to join the board of the main Pontin's company. Fred had come a very long way from the short season at Brean Sands in 1946, but he wanted to remain a man who wished to be seen to be closely identified with his family business.

It is worth pausing at this point in order to describe the innovative nature of Southport Holiday Village as far as Pontin's was concerned in that the size of the complex took the company away from the small family unit image. Even Southport was not intended to rival the massive camps built by Billy Butlin where 8,000 beds could be the norm but an Olympic size swimming pool, massive ballroom, supermarket, shops and miles of new carpet must have proved irresistible attractions to a total of over 4,000 guests which could be accommodated at any one time.

Several managers and senior staff at Southport have commented upon the early teething problems associated with such a large complex and experienced staff were drafted in to help from many outposts of the Pontin's empire. These trouble shooters had to work very hard in order to keep the guests happy but there were compensations.

The resident band was Joe Daniels and his Hotshots and the warm and colourful Ainsdale Bar served as a welcoming venue for entertaining local footballing celebrities from Liverpool and Everton. In those days these famous clubs were managed by Bill Shankly and Harry Catterick and the many star players included Steve Heighway and Kevin Keegan.

At least one general manager, who served his time during the early days at Southport, described it as the eighth wonder of the world. Obviously an overstatement but this site became a very firm favourite with Pontin's most loyal customers, including, of course, the Sharples family mentioned during the opening paragraphs of this book.

Although the Pontin's head office was in London and the business empire had its roots in the West Country it was the north west of England which saw significant growth as the larger sites were acquired and redeveloped.

As usual Fred Pontin was a regular visitor and after a day's work he liked to be entertained alongside his guests in the ballrooms, bars and theatres of his camps.

On one occasion the Chairman rang the camp at Morecambe from his London office in Oxford Street and asked who was appearing in cabaret that evening. He was told that it was Charlie Chester. Sir Fred replied "Charlie is it; he's a good friend of mine. I'll try and be there."

Because time was short Sir Fred decided on travelling by British Rail and he joined a train bound for Glasgow and which would be stopping at Preston en route. His secretary arranged for a company driver to pick him up for the onward journey.

On his arrival at Preston the Chairman was met by Tiny, a huge mountain of a man who knew his employer well. He greeted Sir Fred and asked where he was to take him.

The reply was "I'm going to Morecambe to see my old friend Charlie Chester".

"Right, Sir Fred" said Tiny. "Why not sit in the back, have a bit of a kip? I'll have you there in no time". The driver knew his chairman well and he was accustomed to see him sound asleep in the back of the car during the course of his driving duties, particularly towards the end of a hard day. He was aware that his employer worked long hours.

After about an hour Sir Fred woke up from his dozing and failed to recognise his surroundings. "Where on earth are we?" he shouted above the noise of the engine.

"We are on our way to Chester Sir Fred" replied Tiny.

"Chester?" boomed the Chairman. "I don't want to go to Chester. What on earth are you playing at? I'm due in Morecambe to see Charlie Chester's cabaret act."

Tiny slammed on the brakes and the car drew to a halt. He turned round and faced his angry employer. "I thought you said that you were going to Chester to see Eric Morecambe."

How Sir Fred responded to this news is best left to the imagination.

With the continuing growth of his holiday camp empire, Pontin's United Kingdom operations by the end of the 1977 season consisted of thirteen holiday camps with fully inclusive tariffs, eleven self-catering holiday centres and a chalet hotel in Jersey, Channel Islands. Overseas there were hotels and holiday clubs in Sardinia, Ibiza, Morocco, Spain and Majorca, where there was also a holiday village.

By this time group annual turnover had risen to approximately £39 million, of which over £10 million was from overseas activities. Pretax net profits were running at some £6,600,000 and shareholders were continuing to enjoy generous dividends.

Success in business inevitably leads to a thirst for achievement in other walks of life and over the years Sir Fred Pontin was very fortunate to be able to indulge himself by participating in activities which not only gave him enormous pleasure, but also helped others less fortunate than himself.

Fred Pontin had never forgotten his roots, but at the same time he had never had any inhibitions regarding an acceptance of a lifestyle which soon became second nature to the lad from the East End of London.

Chapter Ten

COSTA DEL PONTIN'S

Fred Pontin must have been working at intense pressure, but he cannot recall that he was unduly conscious of any strain. Despite the article in *Investor's Chronicle*, he did have outside interests.

He had his horse racing, the occasional night at a greyhound track, his charitable and social activities with the Variety Club and he liked to enjoy a drink and a meal at well-known West End nightclubs.

All of these pursuits were an escape from the business, as was his membership of Jack Solomons' World Sporting Club. Fred had enjoyed boxing from his school days and he loved to attend Jack's many promotions. Pontin's often got involved with sponsorship at these events and part of the purse would often be a free holiday for two at a Pontinental holiday resort. The company received the publicity and Fred got the enjoyment.

Pontinental was yet another "first" for the innovative Chairman, and what follows is a short introduction to the concept.

The impressive trading results were starting to include revenue from Fred Pontin's incursion into what the travel writers then described as the sun-drenched beaches of Continental Europe under the banner of Pontinental Holidays.

It was Fred who thought of this rather obvious name and this soon brought an exceptional degree of free publicity in the popular press. Holiday camps for foreigners? Has Fred Pontin gone mad? The journalists were, of course, missing the point.

Fred was intent upon exploiting cheap air travel by introducing his customers to the much more reliable weather conditions in the holiday resorts of southern Europe, not in selling holidays to the locals. In the event, a useful proportion of Pontinental's non-UK guests were to emanate from these sources.

In the early sixties not all of Fred Pontin's fellow directors shared his enthusiasm for taking their successful formula for family holidays to the beaches of the Mediterranean. Yet the weather was far more reliable and the sun shone for much longer periods of time and over an extended summer season.

It was also clear that Fred's people liked getting sun-tanned in order to let everyone know that they had been away.

Ann Miller's first reaction was that she felt that the Continentals would not be attracted to what she felt was a peculiarly British-type of holiday. This was one of the very few occasions, though, when Fred did not accept her advice.

She soon admitted that she had also missed the point as far as Fred's original plans were concerned, because it was always his clear intention to offer Pontin's existing guests an even wider choice of holiday venue.

This was the time of cheap charter flights and Fred calculated that he could offer two weeks in Sardinia or Majorca for approximately the same cost as a fortnight at Barton Hall.

Without elaborating on the economics of the operation in any great detail, the land was cheap as were the building costs, providing they were carefully controlled. Fred also planned to take advantage of some cheap loans from the Spanish Government, who were keen to promote tourism.

As for catering costs, these were very competitive and Fred soon realised that, at his chosen locations, the local staff looked upon their work in the kitchens and restaurants as rewarding and satisfying employment in which they took pride. This did not always prove to be the case at his sites in the United Kingdom. An important plus factor on the marketing side was, of course, cheap liquor and plenty of it.

Fred's plans for Pontinental were not brought to fruition without a fair proportion of problems. His board of directors felt that the United Kingdom business was producing very good returns and most held the view that there seemed little justification for any speculative investment overseas.

Needless to say, Fred was not to be deterred and he found support from not only loyal members of his staff, including Walter Rowley, his family and close friends, but also from City merchant bankers, M. Samuel and also from American Express.

At one time Fred had set up some deals with Spanish partners, and their tastes proved to be over extravagant. He was accustomed to watching every penny with his British operation, but exercising the same elements of constraint on overseas expenditure was far more difficult. There were also exchange control problems and the necessity to obtain permission from the Bank of England for all foreign currency transactions.

In retrospect, it must have been his legendary energy which carried him through. He enjoyed his overseas visits which was a major compensation and he relished the thrill of finding suitable locations, which in those days were often derelict tracts of land with no infrastructure. Yet they had the glorious advantage of being right on a beach with a clear blue sea just waiting for his first visitors.

Flights in unpressurised aircraft and landing on grass runways where there are now international airports also stand out in his memory. Not everyone appreciates just what a pioneer of package holidays Fred Pontin proved to be and it is certainly not known just how difficult it was to convince his own board of directors, let alone the financiers that his Pontinental project was a worthwhile exercise which justified the initial investment.

As Pontin's original involvement was confined to merely a right to subscribe for up to £750,000 of share capital in Pontinental Limited at par out of the first £1,500,000 to be issued by that company, this was looked upon as very much Fred's personal venture.

Although he was disappointed by the lack of faith being shown by the majority of his fellow board members at Pontin's Fred was realistic enough to be aware that there were shareholders to consider, and he had to live with the fact that he could not always rely upon his intuitive judgment being backed by the company's hard cash.

Fred's personal stake was roughly equivalent to the money put up by each of the corporate investors. The publicity created by this new venture quickly seized upon the fact that it was Fred Pontin, not the public company which bore his name, that was taking the risk inherent in such new developments. This did nothing to harm Fred's image as something of a corporate buccaneer as far as his regular customers were concerned. Perhaps Fred Pontin could be looked upon as the Richard Branson of his day. There's a thought!

Pontinental was never a public company, but Fred's reputation in the City of London was sufficient to persuade certain members of the Stock Exchange to create a very limited, but active market in the shares. Before very long the one shilling (5p) shares were changing hands at prices up to 13 shillings (65p), which caused Fred to issue a statement to the effect that he deplored the practice. What a far cry from his days with Martin Coles Harman when the main concern would have been how much money could be made in a single day, based upon a bubble which was quite capable of bursting at any time.

Fred Pontin's statement was his personal attempt to restore an element of realism to the trading in the shares of Pontinental. The early results could not possibly justify such capital appreciation and, if matters were not checked, he felt that there could be a ticklish, and possibly a damaging sequel, to these transactions.

Fortunately, the Council of the Stock Exchange took their own action and barred all further dealings in the company's shares. The grounds for this were that there could not be a truly free market in shares of a company whose membership is limited to 50, as was the case with private companies at that time.

It would be quite impossible for similar events to take place in the early 2000s and it is to his credit that in the much less disciplined days of the early sixties Fred Pontin was prudent enough to take what remedial action he was able before matters got out of hand. He was, of course, flattered by the success of Pontin's earlier capital issues, but the speculation in Pontinental was embarrassing for him, especially in the light of what was to transpire in due course.

Sardinia, the second largest island in the Mediterranean, was the chosen location for the first Pontinental resort. The Pineta Beach Hotel at Platamona opened for business in 1963.

This was not to be without some fun and games on the day, when Fred's first guests arrived by charter flight from the United Kingdom. It was a very important, if not an historic, occasion, as far as Fred was concerned, so he was determined to be there to meet them.

He also had to think quickly because he knew only too well that the building contractors were still laying the concrete in the main drive when he set off to the airport to welcome the new arrivals. There were many last minute jobs being done, so the longer the arrival of guests could be delayed the better as far as his somewhat frantic hotel manager was concerned.

Pineta Beach had a fine white beach backed by scented pine groves and is situated on the north-west coast, only 20 miles from the airport at Alghero. Strictly speaking, there would normally have been little delay in getting everyone to their holiday destination. Some quick thinking was called for. Fred decided to greet everyone by announcing that as they were the first of his guests to Sardinia it seemed only fitting to arrange for the coach driver to show them all just how attractive the island was. He was also prompted to give them a taste of the local wine.

They set off on what was to prove to be an prolonged and rather extensive tour. Because of the difficulties back at the Alghero site of Fred gave instructions to the coach driver to proceed around the island until such time as the order was given to head for the hotel.

One sharp-eyed client spotted a building he had already seen and exclaimed: "We're going round in circles, we've been here before".

Fred reassured him by stating that he must be mistaken and added: "All these foreign places look the same". As usual, his charm allowed him to get away with it.

However, there had to be a time when matters could be delayed no longer. As a result, when the new arrivals, anxious to get on with their Sardinian holiday, climbed out of the coach at the new hotel they left footprints in the concrete, though they found a warm welcome when they got inside the premises.

They all knew that they were Pontinental's first clients and took the many teething problems in their stride. Fred did not try to cover all of the inadequacies and did his best to offer a measure of compensation by ordering several rounds of free drinks.

After Pineta Beach became an efficient operation and had earned a good reputation it enjoyed many visits from celebrities from the world of sport. Amongst many others the resort became a firm favourite of heavy weight boxing champion, Jack London and Coventry City football club's manager, Joe Mercer who went on to become very distinguished in the higher levels of our national game.

Ann Miller always had a special affection for Pineta Beach and she took a special administrative interest in the resort.

Sir Fred Pontin reflected that it must have been the challenge of making a success of the entire concept of Pontinental in the face of the opposition which really fascinated him. However, it was very hard work and many mistakes were made.

There were great difficulties in recruiting the right people and also in comprehending the local issues. Solving – even ignoring – planning problems, dealing with errant building contractors, pure naïvety and tolerating bureaucratic nightmares were part of his daily life in the early part of the 1960s.

He must have been a glutton for punishment, especially as he did not have the customary consolation of the unanimous support of the board, the main opposition being led by Tim Moorcroft, who was previously with Butlin's and may have remembered Billy's unfortunate experience in the Bahamas where a Butlin's investment came unstuck.

Each member of the board of directors could see that Fred was spending a great deal of his time in dealing with all of these matters, but, despite this, they did not attempt to curtail his activities. On the other hand, they saw no attraction in exercising Pontin's option to subscribe for new capital in Pontinental. It was, however, arranged for the necessary date to be extended, mainly on Fred's recommendation and certain parties expressed optimism that one day all would come good.

Pontin's did not become financially involved with the overseas operation until the end of 1964, when they loaned up to £350,000 on a short term basis to cover Pontinental's capital commitments for developments already in progress. This cash flow problem came at a worrying time for Fred personally. He could not have been expected to take on the entire burden and everyone knows that early building estimates are always exceeded before construction finally comes to an end. The building of the Channel Tunnel is an excellent example of this.

He gave his personal guarantee that this money would be repaid by 31 March 1965, which was somewhat out of character, because he was not too keen to set this type of precedent in connection with an investment he did not absolutely control.

In the Chairman's annual statement to Pontin's shareholders Fred undertook to supply the latest trading results for Pontinental in early 1965 and also promised to convene a special meeting before any decision was taken in respect of the exercise of the option.

By that time Pineta Beach was operational and the 1965 brochure was also offering the newly-constructed hotel S'Agamassa at Santa Eulalia del Rio, Ibiza, which was managed by Fred's son-in-law, Peter Hopper and his daughter Patricia. The holiday village in Cala Mesquida, Majorca, had also opened in 1964.

As Pontinental expanded and became an important profit earner for the group Peter Hopper was given increased responsibilities, taking over the duties but not the position of Tony De Candamo who resigned his position as managing director of Pontinental at the end of 1965. In 1972 Peter was not only appointed joint managing director of Pontinental alongside Fred Pontin but also appointed to the main board of Pontin's. In Peter's words "I put my heart and soul into the business" and he is extremely proud of his role in contributing to Pontinental's success. It must also be acknowledged that at that time Fred Pontin must have had high regard for his son-in-law's capabilities and achievements.

The stage was soon reached where Pontin's needed to extend the scope of its booking facilities, which were traditionally handled at the site of each operational unit. Their advertising budget was growing in each successive year and the results of this increased exposure on TV, in national newspapers and various journals led to the public demanding easier access for enquiries and booking.

Fred opened an information and retail travel office adjoining Oxford Circus in the West End of London and a similar bureau opposite Liverpool Street Station in the City. These premises also undertook all manner of travel business, as well as receiving bookings for Pontin's own centres, which again was a new departure for the company.

The Oxford Street building also had the benefit of a private cinema. This was used to show colour films of the activities at UK and Mediterranean holiday resorts. The screenings took place on a daily basis throughout the booking season and proved to be a great success.

In the lates sixties Pontin's customers were making use of the Oxford Street premises for instant bookings and Sir Fred recalls the packed waiting lists of fans waiting for cancellations. He was giving them what they really wanted but it really frustrated him when he could not find enough "beds" to satisfy the demand.

The Oxford Street facilities were also of great assistance to Fred when he was seeking to impress stockbrokers, institutional investors and the company bankers. Pontin's image was being transformed and was analogous to their growth. Pontin's were approaching the time when they would be matching Butlin's virtually bed for bed, whilst their smaller units were still proving to be very attractive to their long-term guests.

Overseas, however, Fred still had a lot to do. His problems were by no means over. Despite his earlier assurances to the board and the shareholders, Pontinental was not coming good, though he was not losing faith and continued to back his judgment by further personal commitments.

Further comment upon the effect of the lack of confidence by Fred's colleagues will be covered a little later, but it did not please him to have to report in his annual statement that the Pontin's loan to Pontinental had been increased to £500,000 and repayment delayed to 30 June 1966. This extra money would not have been made available without his own personal guarantee, so he gave it on the basis that it served to increase his determination to succeed.

Business at home was going from strength to strength meanwhile, and annual profits were approaching the magic total of £1 million following a period of sustained investment and expansion.

Pontin's option to subscribe for shares in Pontinental was extended again because the board would not sanction a permanent investment in their Chairman's overseas adventures.

It must be stated, though, that Pontinental would not have survived this period without the support of administrative staff at Pontin's UK head office. Apart from the loan arrangement, which was necessary to safeguard the capital already invested by the shareholders, the administrative back-up may not have been strictly official, but it was readily forthcoming in terms of logistical support.

The situation could not continue on this basis forever, and in June 1966 Pontin's acquired the entire share capital of Pontinental against the issue of 4,200,000 deferred ordinary shares . . . the equivalent to a price per share of seven pence ha'penny in old money or 3.125p in decimal currency. This was at a discount on the original par value of one shilling (5p), but trading results could not possibly justify a higher figure.

Part of the deal was for Pontinental to rid itself of the Spanish partners, so the transaction involved the division of assets, although Fred was successful in retaining the best sites for Pontinental. He had always been an excellent negotiator and he served his UK shareholders well in completing this particular deal on a project in which he had invested so much time and effort.

The decision on Pontinental was more or less inevitable, given Fred's personal commitment to do all that he could to justify the basis of the original investment, and he deeply regretted that at the time Pontin's came in with their subscription for the deferred ordinary shares the founder shareholders lost money on the deal. Those Pontinental shareholders, including senior management at Pontin's, who decided to retain their shares in Pontin's, however, eventually had a good run for their money when the group provided excellent returns. The deferred shares were converted to ordinary shares in April 1969.

It seems clear that Sir Fred's image was not unduly tarnished by these matters, because it was soon proved that his original policies were to be vindicated. In terms of his own investment, he also took a "paper" loss, which he attributed to under-capitalisation for what was really a long term project.

It was too much to expect that Pontinental would produce immediate profits and – not for the first time – Fred Pontin learned from the experience.

In an effort to promote Pontinental he coined the phrase for the overseas holidays as "Blackpool with the sun", but this did not really catch on. Mike Austin's view is that although the overseas trading activities were an initial drain on domestic profitability, taking a long term view the parent company benefited enormously. It changed the Pontin's image in terms of public view and perception of a company which was then known for holiday camps that carried a down-market cachet.

Pontinental proved to be an exciting name, eminently marketable when package holidays were becoming more and more popular with the British public. Fred Pontin was undoubtedly ahead of the market and with the benefit of hindsight it now seems clear that if he had been successful in receiving the full support of his board, right from the outset, Pontinental would not have suffered from being under-capitalised and success would have been theirs that much earlier.

Relieved of his personal obligations, and with the somewhat belated whole-hearted backing of his board and shareholders, Fred set about achieving a level of popularity for continental holidays which he felt sure would guarantee success for the overseas holiday centres.

It must be remembered that in the mid-sixties package holidays in Europe were still somewhat of a novelty as far as the mass market was concerned. Pontin's regular guests were inclined to be rather timorous about unorganised holidays abroad, but Fred was able to convince them that Pontinental was an entirely different matter.

They had learned to trust him at home and it was not long before they were displaying judgment in his favour for places farther afield.

The UK business was by no means suffering from the competition offered by Pontinental. If people were intent on going abroad, they would have been lost to Pontin's, anyway, so it made sense to offer the overseas alternative as part of the "family" operation. Market research also showed that the public were reacting more favourably to Pontin's on the basis that by having such attractive and exotic places abroad their sites at home must also have a lot to offer.

Although Pontinental had separate advertising material, the UK brochure also featured the overseas locations, which made it a much more attractive proposition. Pontin's obtained new business, especially from families with young children, and it was not long before the fuller range of their attractions was being translated into higher profits, although even when Pontinental became profitable the margins were below those of the domestic business.

At a time of currency restrictions Pontin's holidays abroad were looked upon as being cheap and competitive. Fred calculated that visitors to Pontinental hotels and holiday villages would still have an adequate amount of spending money to take with them.

Nothing in the risk taking world of commerce can go completely smoothly, though. They had operational problems at Cala Mesquida on Majorca. This was formerly a camping site, operated and mainly frequented by Germans. Before Fred Pontin transformed it by adding 142 brick-built double chalets, shower blocks, dining room, kitchen and bar the resort was totally lacking in any modern facilities and services.

The approach road was nothing more than a rough track, but it was the lovely bay, clear blue water and wide beach which always captivated the new arrivals. Accommodation in those early days was pretty basic, though there were already plans to offer far superior apartments with en-suite facilities. It was absolutely essential that Pontinental should generate a high level of popularity.

There were no less than three managers, all of them English, during the 1964 season and Fred was wondering how he was going to face the summer of 1965 when Walter Rowley came to the rescue.

At the end of the 1964 season Fred Pontin arranged for all of Pontin's managers to be given a complimentary holiday at the Hotel S'Agamassa in Ibiza. He was later told that this event was looked upon as a gathering of the clans and a good time was had by all.

Walter Rowley had heard the gossip about a disastrous summer at Cala Mesquida and he volunteered to go and have a look with a view to taking over the manager's position for 1965. Fred was pleased to make the arrangements for him to take his family across on the ferry. Despite a rough crossing and a stay in an hotel with no electricity, Walter liked what he saw and decided to take up the challenge.

It was typical of Walter that during the winter he studied the Spanish language to overcome any problems in communicating with the large numbers of local staff. This was in addition to his duties in supervising the building programme.

He did a marvellous job and the new holiday village was ready when the first guests arrived. Before long guests from the UK were turning up in very large numbers and Fred recalled that in the 1965 season Pontinental were offering a return flight from Luton or Gatwick, two weeks full board, accommodation and free wine with lunch and dinner, as well as the organised entertainment for just £49 per person. In 1999 values this is £541 and a comparable, all-inclusive holiday in the Airtours brochure for the last year of the twentieth century is offered in the range of £489–£799, depending on the date of travel. This appears to indicate that not too much has changed, although there is no mention of free wine at meals.

The drinks in the Cala Mesquida bar were also very cheap, again as a matter of policy. Walter Rowley proved to be an excellent manager and he stayed in the position for eight years, during which period Pontinental further improved the resort and also added the nearby Cala Mesquida hotel to accommodate a further 180 guests in this increasingly popular location.

Walter always made a point of helping his guests to ensure that they got plenty of food by teaching them the Spanish word for more which is "mas', pronounced "mass". He always got a laugh on the final night when he announced that he had received his usual weekly letter from the Pope which confirmed that there had been "more masses said in Cala Mesquida than in all the churches in Spain".

Walter liked to tell the story of the seaweed and how genial Fred Pontin worked a miracle!

The bay at Cala Mesquida was prone to regular inundation by a particularly obnoxious type of seaweed, which seemed to be influenced by wind and tide. One moment the beach and surf would be clear, but in no time at all the whole bay could be covered by a dreadful substance. It could hang around for days and sometimes weeks on end, quietly rotting on the shoreline and creating a dreadful odour.

The locals could offer no explanation for the phenomenon, but, as it tended to disappear as quickly as it arrived, everyone learned to accept a temporary inconvenience.

On one particular occasion, however, the weed arrived and considerably outstayed its welcome. Fred Pontin arrived at Palma airport on one of his regular visits and Walter met him by announcing that the guests knew that the Chairman was coming and were "gunning" for him because they were furious that their holiday was being ruined by the state of the beach.

They felt that the management should be doing something, such as importing special equipment for a big clean-up operation – an impossible requirement for such a remote location on a comparatively small island in those days.

Fred told his manager that he would meet a deputation after dinner and would do his best to calm matters, probably by offering a round of drinks but he added "What in the hell am I supposed to do about clearing up something for which Mother nature is responsible?"

Fred didn't get a chance to put his plan into effect. They were waiting for him as soon as he entered the bar.

Their spokesman came up and asked: "Are you Fred Pontin?"

Fred replied that he was, and he was then asked what he was going to do about the seaweed. Speaking completely off the cuff he rejoined:

"Why do you think I'm here? I've arrived specially to deal with the matter. I've arranged for all the necessary labour and machinery to clear the beach".

He added "The weed will be gone by the time you get up tomorrow morning."

Walter looked at his Chairman in a very critical manner. He knew that Fred was booked out on a very early flight and it would be the site manager who would have to face the music the next day.

"Do you mean that Mr Pontin?" asked the guest.

"Of course I do" was the instant reply.

Fred was given not only a round of applause, but several drinks by guests who seemed absolutely convinced that all would be well if the Chairman said so.

There has to be a happy sequel, otherwise the story would not be worth telling. A storm blew up that night and Walter remembered hearing the noise of the tide and surf growing louder every minute. The next morning the beach and bay were clear.

Fred could not wait to confront the spokesman from the night before and bask in the glory of his "miracle". Unfortunately, the person concerned couldn't be found and Fred had to be on his way to Madrid, en route to Heathrow, safe in the knowledge that poor old Walter didn't have to make any excuses on his behalf.

The guests soon became aware that nature had come to the rescue, but they were very impressed that Fred could be so certain that it would happen on that particular night. Walter did nothing to break the spell, so it was "Good Old Fred" for the remainder of their holiday.

Pontin's expanded the site quite considerably during the three years or so following the original acquisition of Cala Mesquida and even Walter Rowley, who always "ran a good ship" if such a military gentleman will forgive a naval metaphor, needed experienced assistance during these times.

Tim Moorcroft, the Group Controller and a main board director of Pontin's, sounded out David Gwyn, who had been getting a little bored at Pakefield and needed a change, with a view to his travelling out to Majorca in order to give Walter Rowley a hand.

After first getting his instructions from Fred Pontin at the Oxford Street offices David was soon aboard an afternoon flight out of Gatwick and was met off the coach from Palma airport by Walter Rowley. It was a two hour, and rather bumpy journey by road to Cala Mesquida but there was no time to relax.

Even Walter's local knowledge and the respect he had earned from the Spanish people did not prove sufficient to ensure the smoothest of starts to the season. David recalls how Walter was faced with 25 babies all needing cots and baby food and parents who were far from happy by the lack of such necessities.

It took time to organise the cots so the solution was to improvise by making use of drawers which were intended for storing holiday clothing in the guests' bedrooms. A form of baby food "came from somewhere" and Majorca, then rather new to the package holiday business, has been well stocked with such essentials ever since.

Walter had been a very special colleague to Fred Pontin. The one he turned to when he received his knighthood. Fred felt a need to share the aura which affected him at that rather auspicious time. Fred chose this special friend and loyal colleague, who joined Pontin's as a trainee manager in 1961 on leaving the army, where he had served as a Lieutenant-Colonel.

Walter had been told by an army chaplain, who had previously attended a Butlin's camp in an official capacity, that running a holiday camp was just like organising an army unit, so Walter responded to an advertisement in the *Daily Telegraph* and applied for a managerial position with Pontin's.

Fred Pontin took an instant liking to this new recruit and, after a short period of induction at Sand Bay, Walter decided to stay. He was involved with the company in one capacity or another for many years after. When in retirement, living just a stone's throw from Pontin's Brean Sands centre, he spent some of his latter years writing books.

Walter was manager at Osmington Bay for three years, taking over from Ann Miller, who was appointed a director of the parent company. He then worked from the Bournemouth office on Pontinental matters before going to Majorca. He had also undertaken duties as a public relations executive and until comparatively recently he had continued to keep his hand in by acting as a company consultant on special events, where his experience was invaluable.

As a most reliable colleague, Fred had no hesitation in asking him to travel up from Somerset to deliver his employer's formal acceptance of the knighthood to number 10 Downing Street. Fred didn't go as far as to inform Walter of the contents of the envelope, which he had kept locked in the safe. Fred feels that Walter knew what it was all about and he was not surprised when the list was published on the Queen's Official Birthday.

The future Sir Fred Pontin wanted Walter to be associated with the event and the visit to the inner sanctum of the Prime Minister was his way of achieving this aim.

Walter Rowley's success in Majorca has been highlighted in order to illustrate that efficient and friendly management was an absolutely essential ingredient for a successful site, whether it was in the United Kingdom or abroad. Pontinental was fortunate in having some outstanding general managers and managers, all of whom made important contributions to the eventual success of the company in its overseas operations.

Fred treated each Continental resort on the same basis as the centres in the UK. They all had regular visits from "the guv'nor" and the local staff became accustomed to his "lookee, lookee" tours of inspection.

Fred Pontin's empire was now very widespread. Because he liked to travel light, he made arrangements for several changes of his personal clothing to be available at each resort. He enjoyed until the end of his life a reputation for being smartly dressed but this could not be done if one was forced to wear a crumpled suit. He found that he needed only a briefcase when travelling abroad so he did not have to put up with regular baggage delays.

If Fred was going on his own it was usually necessary for him to travel on scheduled flights, but on frequent occasions he took any available opportunity to join his clients on charter aircraft if this did not prove to be too inconvenient.

Fred liked to think that his Pontinental guests appreciated the boss travelling with them, eating the same food in the dining room and joining them for a drink in the bar both before and after the evening entertainment. The chairman found himself joining in the fun and it all helped to promote the "family" image which became the Pontin's hallmark over the years.

Another important personality in the development of Pontinental was Fred's old friend Joe Rubido, who comes from north-west Spain. He used to run a pub in Hyde Park Square where Fred was a regular visitor in the mid-sixties. At the time Pontinental was undergoing an important transitional period from trading losses and operational problems to the creation of a viable undertaking.

It was only natural that Fred and Joe should talk about the Spanish resorts which were under Pontinental's control and the new development which was planned in Torremolinos. Joe took some persuading, but he joined the staff of the new hotel as bar manager.

Joe recalls that he arrived to find what he described as a "building site", even though he maintains that Fred had assured him that the hotel was ready to welcome its guests. Perhaps Fred had done so, but Joe always knew that the guv'nor had a reputation for being an optimist. When Joe gave the address of the hotel to the taxi driver he was told that he must have "booked too early" because it was clearly unfinished.

Even then he was not totally prepared for the chaos which was causing Fred's brother Len, who was supervising the building contractors, so many sleepless nights.

Nevertheless, the hotel opened on July 4 1970, when 500 guests arrived at what Joe continued to insist upon describing as a half-finished hotel. Fred was there at the time and reluctantly conceded that the first guests had a lot to put up with, although he assured everyone that this was down to the building contractors, not Pontinental.

On one occasion Fred became so frustrated at the lack of urgency which was being shown by the construction work force that, when he saw a man filling a wheelbarrow with soil while another man watched with his hands in his pockets, he went over, grabbed a shovel, thrust it in the hands of the onlooker and ordered him to get on with the job.

The man didn't argue and started working immediately, but you can imagine Fred's surprise when that evening the same man went up to him in the bar and told Fred that he felt that he was owed a drink. He turned out to be a guest and had taken the orders from Pontinental's Chairman quite literally, no doubt with his tongue planted firmly in his cheek. He got more than one drink for being such a good sport and they both had a laugh about Spanish construction workers.

Fred soon discovered that most of his overseas visitors were Pontin's clients of very long standing. They even described their hotel rooms as chalets!

Their loyalty to him and the company came to the fore when Pontinental experienced a strike by the local labour force. It was not just their establishment; most of the coastal hotels were similarly affected. Almost all of Pontinental's guests set to work, made their own beds and, with the assistance of Joe Rubido and other managerial staff, a rota was set up. The hotel continued to operate on a virtually normal basis.

When the meals had been prepared by the chef, who was not one of the strikers, the meals and drinks were served by a party of guests, who would later join the others on the beach and around the swimming pool, continuing with their holidays as if nothing was amiss.

One client insisted upon taking control of the Hobart dishwasher in the kitchen and would let no one else near it. By way of sustenance he was supplied with a case of wine, and he kept the machine going for hours on end until the strike was settled after a few days.

Pontinental's guests manned the bars, supervised entry into the dining room, cleaned the bedrooms, changed the linen and one particularly gifted engineer even fixed the lifts which had ceased to operate.

Fred Pontin was only too thankful that there were not many strikes, but the one to which reference has just been made was followed by a shorter one in the following year. It is perhaps difficult to accept this as a true story but the previous year's expert on the Hobart dishwasher just happened to be there. He again came to the rescue without a word of complaint and was duly rewarded with ample supplies of the local wine.

Fred puts this type of response down to team spirit created by people such as Joe Rubido, who seemed to have an incredible knack of getting people to do what he wanted. If there was any sign of trouble Fred would try to be there in order to take the brunt of the complaints or criticisms, but it was Joe who created the atmosphere which made the Chairman's task that much easier.

Joe did go too far one evening, however, when he took the microphone to thank everyone for their assistance and co-operation. He went on to joke about the Spanish unions and said that they had caught the British disease by creating so many strikes.

One guest, who was a staunch trade unionist, took great exception to Joe's remarks and behaved in a very threatening manner. The situation was saved when another guest came to the rescue, took a swing at the complainant and shouted, to great applause: "Don't you be rude to our Joe!"

After these strikes Fred thought it only right and proper that his guests should be compensated for the inconvenience. Each was given a £50 voucher towards the following year's holiday.

He took a similar line in rewarding the UK staff with "free" Pontinental holidays if he became aware that there were some empty seats on the chartered aircraft to the various resorts. This was not unusual in the off-peak season and the staff appreciated the gesture although it is also fair to say that they probably spent all of the Summer bonuses from their employer at his overseas centres.

Such largesse by the guv'nor was also extended to VIP's, Fleet Street journalists and stars of the the worlds of sport and entertainment. Pontin's sponsored the annual Miss Great Britain Beauty Contest in those days and winners and contestants alike were treated to holidays at Pontinental centres. These personalities were very well received by Fred's paying guests, particularly when he would often accompany them on a flight, and the presence of these stars and celebrities, not to mention the gorgeous girls, added to the excitement of what was for many, their first holiday abroad.

This particular scheme was Fred's method of spreading the word about his Pontinental sites and was a very efficient way of making use of empty seats. Much goodwill was created in this manner and it cannot be denied that Fred Pontin's name was synonymous with good and usually quite free publicity.

Joe and Fred once travelled to Malaga to purchase a set of drums for one of the hotel's entertainments staff called Vic Bickers, who was marvellous at his job of entertaining the children. He had been pressing to be supplied with drums for some considerable time. He said that the guests could then enjoy him accompanying the very talented pianist who performed every night in the main bar.

Joe was certain that Vic had no idea how to play the drums, but Fred became so bored with the constant lobbying that he agreed to supply what was needed and, in any event, it would make a pleasant day out with his old friend.

Joe was right. When they got back to the hotel Vic could not even set up the newly-purchased instruments of percussion and, when he eventually succeeded in creating some form of structure, it was clear that his talents lay elsewhere.

He was going through the motions without making a sound and in the meantime the pianist ignored him. Fred and Joe were making catcalls from the bar "Come on Vic, let's be having you", but not even a whisper was heard. Vic never touched the drums again and they became somewhat of a white elephant, but at least it stopped his continual pleading.

People remarked that Fred been too soft in dealing with that type of case, but, if certain individuals were good at their jobs, and Vic certainly came into this category, he saw no reason why they should not be allowed to indulge themselves on the odd occasion, especially if it did no one any harm.

These were, however, impulsive gestures on Fred's part and no member of the staff could be absolutely sure how he would respond to any similar requests.

Joe's first season at Torremolinos was intended to be his last as far as he was concerned. The hotel closed at the end of October and the winter was spent in finishing it off properly. He told Fred that he had had enough, he was worn out, it was too hot and he found difficulty in understanding the southern Spanish dialect.

He had been in the UK a long time, but it still seemed peculiar that he appeared to dislike his native country. He once complained that he had a severe attack of "Montezuma's revenge" when he went back to spend a short holiday in his home region.

Fred Pontin had a job on his hands in persuading him to return to Torremolinos. It took many pints at the Highland Bar in Hyde Park Square before Mike Austin and his Chairman persuaded Joe to go back at the start of the following season. He said that this was very much against his will, but Fred was absolutely delighted when he stayed for no less than eleven years and played a great part in making the Torremolinos into a very successful hotel. So successful was this venue that the street alongside the hotel was renamed Cala Pontinental.

By owning the Pontinental resorts, Pontin's had created an extra dimension to its business. By the early 1970s the demand was exceeding supply as far as the overseas sites were concerned.

Fred had planned to double the occupancy at Torremolinos to over 1,000 beds and, in due course, he even went as far as to anticipate formal planning permission because of frustrating delays in obtaining official written approval from the local authorities. New attractions included an indoor heated swimming pool, grill room and conference facilities, because Fred was convinced there was business to be had during the winter months.

He built extra accommodation for 120 guests at the Cala Mesquida Hotel, which was renamed Hotel Pontinental and subsequently became an important and successful adjunct to the holiday village centred around the ever popular bay. Sardinia had also been the subject of expansion, but it was not until 1972 that Fred negotiated a deal which succeeded in providing the Pontinental operation with an additional 4,200 beds at one stroke.

Pontinental acquired S.A. Holiday Club, a Belgian group operating six holiday villages in Majorca, Spain's Costa del Sol, Morocco and Greece. This timely acquisition not only gave Pontinental the extra beds and improved their range of sites for Pontinental's British market, but also put them in a position of considerable strength as far as the overseas holiday market was concerned.

Over half of the additional beds were being sold through Belgian, German, French and other European tour operators. This deal put the Pontin's group of companies into the major league and well ahead of the British competition – and any other European operator for that matter.

Fred Pontin now felt confident that his dreams of creating a truly international holiday empire had been realised. Moreover, he was able to emphasise that his company's overseas investments provided financial security to the British holiday-maker, allied with complete control of accommodation and service. Their customers knew what to expect and they were not disappointed.

No one now talked about Pontinental's "problems" – only their successes. Fred was beginning to ask himself if there were any new mountains worth climbing?

As a postscript to the Pontinental story it has to be reported that Pontin's have not featured overseas holidays since the early 1980s. When Bass took over the company rationalisation took place and the Pontinental resorts were transferred to their Horizon subsidiary and were subsequently sold elsewhere in the travel industry. This was truly the end of a special part of the Pontin's story and the name Pontinental no longer exists.

It was not long before City Editors and financial journalists in the national Press were speculating about the future of Pontin's, but not because there were doubts concerning its stability or its long term prospects. It was really the line of succession which seemed to provide the fascination.

Sir Fred Pontin, had now passed his seventieth year and, although he had never mentioned the word "retirement", it was inevitable that there would be talk about the likely candidates for taking over a business with annual profits of around £7 million, earned from a turnover which was then approaching £50 million.

Sir Fred did not deny that he had let it be known that a bid would be successful if the price was right, but he also had his own views on the type of company which would be best-suited to safeguard the interests of a loyal staff and to take Pontin's into the 1980s.

Even when he was into his nineties Sir Fred was flattered and sometimes embarrassed by the fact that many of Pontin's guests were still under the impression that he had remained at the helm of the company. This may, or may not be due to the fact that when Trevor Hemmings and his team succeeded in negotiating the biggest ever management buy-out in the history of the travel industry when they acquired Pontin's from Bass in 1987 they were kind enough to appoint Sir Fred to the strictly non-executive post of Honorary President of the company.

This was a touchingly generous gesture, which served as a form of compensation for Fred's previous disappointments.

By the early 1990s only three general managers had survived Fred's regime at Pontin's: Eddie Stamper at Osmington Bay, David Gwyn at Pakefield and Pat Braiden of Plemont Bay in Jersey, who started out as a Bluecoat.

It is fitting that it is this particular trio which had remained with the business when they saw it change hands several times. Each typifies the special breed of men who become what can only be described as "infected with the fascination" such a career provides.

Pat Braiden has many stories concerning Sir Fred and has kept many of his Chairman's memoranda from head office as he feels that these can perhaps be regarded as collectors' items from a memorable era of "hands on" management in the holiday camp industry. A selection of these communications appears elsewhere in this book.

On one occasion Pat recalls that his camp in Jersey was experiencing some problems with the food; not serious problems but from time to time most camps suffered from a group of campers who lost no opportunity to complain about what were rather trivial and quite understandable shortcomings in food presentation and content.

Unfortunately the press had got hold of stories about trouble in the Pontin's catering arrangements and some rather fanciful reports had appeared in the newspapers.

Fred Pontin decided to visit Jersey in order to supervise what the management and staff were doing about the situation and perhaps to add his weight to any reassurances being given to the campers.

On his arrival he got heavily involved with the local management, catering staff as well as the grumbling guests and decided after hearing both sides of the story that matters had been blown up out of all proportion by people whom he really regarded as professional troublemakers, looking for some unwarranted compensation.

He had come across this sort of difficulty on many such occasions and knew how to deal with it without causing offence to anyone. When such an episode demanded soothing tones and making any necessary amends the Chairman's authority and presence worked wonders.

With the trouble over and as far as Fred Pontin was concerned, everybody happy and enjoying themselves he sat down at a table in the dining room for a meal with Pat Braiden before going on to the ballroom to watch the evening performance from the Bluecoats.

Suddenly Fred felt a hand on his shoulder. A man had come up behind his chair and the Chairman felt the pressure of the firm grip.

He didn't think about who it was or what it was all about. He leapt up and turned around and faced one of his guests. It felt to him as though he was the proverbial camel with the final straw having come to rest on his back.

"I don't give a damn if you don't like the food. If it's good enough for me it's good enough for anyone." He paused for breath. "I'm sick and tired of all these unjustified complaints. If you don't like the food pack your bags and go home now. Take your bloody complaints with you."

What was quite astonishing was that the man said nothing. He turned on his heel and did just that. He left the camp within a very short while but the disturbance in the ballroom was leaked to the press and on arrival at his home airport the guest was met by some reporters demanding to have the details of the latest scandal from Pontin's.

"There was no problem" replied the man who showed little concern at his surprise reception. "I went up to Fred Pontin in order to thank him for a great holiday and he told me to clear off back home. And here I am. Thank you and good night."

Sir Fred's personal authority knew no bounds and Pat Braiden swears that this story is true.

As a footnote to this episode it was reported that Plemont Bay, Jersey was earmarked for closure after the 1999 season and it looked as though this site commenced the next millennium as a yet another housing estate.

As President of the company Sir Fred still kept in touch with the group's activities, but his visits to individual centres were very rare, unless there was some special occasion, such as the fiftieth anniversary celebrations in 1996 when he returned to his first site at Brean Sands in order to officially open a new access road.

A few years earlier he was also invited to a rather special celebration; the twenty-first anniversary of the British Red Cross Society week in Pakefield. Sir Fred was also present when Trabolgan was brought back into the fold. Nowadays this centre caters mainly for the Irish market which is in sharp contrast to the earlier trading experiences at this site.

Sir Fred had never been too surprised by his popularity with the guests, because he had gone out of his way to create a high profile within the business. Appearances in the dining room, ballroom, and, more popularly the bar, were commonplace both at home and abroad. In that respect he could never be compared with that fictitious, but always absent proprietor of holiday camps, Joe Maplin, in the already-mentioned popular BBC TV programme *Hi-De-Hi*.

To Sir Fred it was rather satisfying that he seemed to occupy a modest place in the treasured memories of at least a cross-section of the hundreds of thousands of his guests over the years. He knew this because when he was at the helm at Pontin's he was accustomed to receiving sacks full of letters telling him so.

Chapter Eleven

ARISE SIR FRED

The citation indicated that Fred Pontin's knighthood, which was announced in Her Majesty the Queen's 1976 Birthday Honours List, was awarded for charitable services.

Although he had been personally active in this field of activity for many years, his main energies in this respect had been channelled through his membership of the Variety Club of Great Britain, a children's charity into which – on the introduction of Albert Stevenson – he was admitted as a Barker in 1966.

The next year Fred was both pleased and delighted to be asked to join the "Crew", in other words the organising committee. In the following year he was astonished and then proud to be nominated for Chief Barker by the late Jimmy Carreras, Variety's International Chairman, who also received a knighthood for similar charitable services.

Fred was then elected to succeed Sefton Myers, who was a tower of strength in his year of office during which the Variety Club raised an all-time record sum of £685,000 under his leadership.

Variety in this country is known especially for its world-famous Sunshine Coach Scheme, which supplies vehicles to charitable organisations connected with the welfare of handicapped and under-privileged children throughout Great Britain. These vehicles can be high-top mini-coaches or even larger passenger carrying vehicles, which cost more than twice as much to supply in a fully equipped manner in order to cater for children with physical handicaps.

The coaches are delivered to such grateful recipients as hospitals, children's homes, boys' clubs, spastics societies, Dr. Barnardo's Homes, special schools and to branches of the British Red Cross Society.

The Club also responds to countless requests for other forms of charitable contributions to literally thousands of children who are short of warm clothing and toys at appropriate times during each year.

There are various funds and campaigns within the organisation, such as the Heart Fund and the Christmas Toy Campaign. The full nature of the Club's entire range of activities are strongly supported by many members of the show business fraternity as well as business tycoons and entrepreneurs such as Sir Fred Pontin.

Almost countless social and fund-raising functions took place throughout Fred Pontin's year as Chief Barker. It was through Variety Club activities that Fred became acquainted with members of the Royal Family, such as His Royal Highness the Duke of Edinburgh, the late Earl Mountbatten of Burma, both of whom were awarded gold card life memberships, Her Royal Highness Princess Alexandra and the Hon. Angus Ogilvy.

The role of the Chief Barker is to spearhead the Variety Club's efforts to raise the money needed for its work and Fred set about his task with even more energy than he was accustomed to generating for his business activities. He travelled all over the United Kingdom attending as many functions as he possibly could.

During his year of office there were celebrations marking the 50th Anniversary of the Royal Air Force and the 25th Anniversary of the Royal Air Force Association. One of the highlights was a Variety Club luncheon at the Savoy Hotel, where Prince Philip was Guest of Honour. This event was covered by BBC TV, ITN, Pathe News and the BBC Overseas Service, as well as the national newspapers, which ensured generous publicity for the work of Variety.

Nineteen-Sixty-Eight was a year that always remained within Fred's memory. His life was one long round of travelling and meeting people. With his holiday camps spread around the country the "coconuts" password would not have been needed if his managers had been fortunate enough to have had access to the itinerary for his duties with Variety Club.

If Fred was in the West of England he took the opportunity to pay what he was amused to hear were termed as promiscuous visits to as many of his centres as he could fit in to a usually overcrowded schedule. Everyone was kept on their toes.

The various managements were aware of the fact that this was a very special year for "the Guv'nor", so their regular efforts towards charitable fund raising among staff and guests became more intense throughout the peak holiday periods and special weekends.

Among the more memorable functions was a Sports Celebrities' Luncheon attended by forty of Britain's most famous sportsmen, including Josh Gifford (National Hunt), Henry Cooper (boxing), Sir

Alf Ramsey (football) Noel Murless (turf), Henry Cotton (golf), Stirling Moss (motor racing), and Roger Taylor (lawn tennis).

On March 12 Fred also chaired a luncheon at the Savoy Hotel which honoured eleven personalities selected for their outstanding achievements during 1967 in films, on TV, the stage, radio and records. Among the most notable recipients of Variety Silver Hearts were Irene Worth (Stage Actress), Warren Mitchell (BBC TV Personality), Dame Edith Evans (Film Actress) Kenneth Horne (BBC Sound Radio Personality) and a Special Award for that distinguished actress of the British theatre, Dame Gladys Cooper.

The Variety Club still holds an annual awards ceremony as part of what is often termed "the congratulatory back-slapping season" for the entertainments industry. It is an excellent method of raising money and brings enormous publicity because the ceremonies have been known to be televised on one of the national networks.

The host celebrity, almost invariably Terry Wogan in later years, makes a point of featuring a generous plug for one of Variety's most deserving causes. This assists in the never-ending attempt to perpetuate public awareness when so many other charities are also competing for generous donations. These times were well before the days of the National Lottery.

Members of the British public have always responded magnificently to appeal after appeal, and none more so than the hundreds of thousands of guests at Pontin's holiday centres over the last half century or so.

Variety's annual Members' Derby Sweepstake grossed an all-time record total of £87,600 at the Derby "Stag" Dinner held in the Savoy on May 22nd 1968 and Fred Pontin played a prominent part in the draw. Variety's seventh annual Gala Greyhound Race Meeting at the White City stadium on the following Saturday attracted such stars as Diana Dors, Charlie Drake, Eric Sykes, and Roy Hudd.

Pontin's sponsored two races that night and the records show that Prince Philip, a keen supporter of the Club's charitable activities, arranged for his own dog, Camira Flash, to compete in the Sir Billy Butlin Stakes. Unfortunately for H.R.H., it was beaten by Yellow Printer, which set up a new course record for the distance.

Fred Pontin has had many an enjoyable night at the "dogs", and none more so than when he was privileged to be accompanied by Prince Philip at Clapton Stadium during that same year. This was shortly after Fred and the Queen's Consort had attended a tea party and commissioning ceremony at the London Hospital, where Fred had presented a new heart machine in gratitude for his recovery from a serious motor car accident. This was the hospital's first heart machine and it is understood that it is still in use today, although there have been modifications and improvements over the years.

It is not recorded if Prince Philip had never been to a no-frills grey-hound meeting before, but he did not surprise Fred Pontin when he responded to the latter's suggestion in such a positive manner. Fred was aware that his Royal guest on that particular evening was fond of taking a break from his normal routine.

The Royal Family is known for not carrying any money, but there was no problem on this particular occasion as Fred Pontin recalls that Prince Philip showed no inclination to have a bet, even though Fred had two of his own dogs running that evening. Prince Philip was more interested in savouring the atmosphere.

This memorable year continued with Variety's 15th annual Star Gala at Battersea Park Festival Gardens. The event was sponsored by the *News of the World* to benefit the Heart Fund. Despite occasional showers of rain, the fans turned out in their thousands to meet their favourites from screen, stage, television and discs, including Tony Blackburn, Judith Chalmers, Liz Fraser, Dickie Henderson, Richard Todd, Robert Morley and band leader Joe Loss.

Variety was honoured during May by the presence of Bob Hope at the tribute luncheon to the record industry held at the Savoy. Bob sat on Fred's right-hand side and the Chief Barker for that year recalls that the comedian seemed desperately tired after an all-night flight to London. However, Variety's American visitor was still voted an absolute "wow" by the 480 assembled guests, who included a then-bearded Harry Secombe, Sandie Shaw, Jimmy Tarbuck, Victor Silvester, Max Bygraves, a regular performer at Pontin's centres and Jimmy Young.

It was Fred's duty to chair the luncheon, though you can imagine how relieved he was not to have to follow Bob Hope. Announcing him was nevertheless a daunting task because any joke would appear inadequate in front of such a master, but Fred managed to survive the ordeal and hopefully raised the odd smile.

Bob cracked a couple of jokes about Harry Secombe's weight and went on to allege that he himself had tried to cash in on the pop record market, but instead of winning a golden disc for selling a million records he was given "a golden hole for selling none". He was being modest – everyone knows that *Thanks For the Memory* has sold hundreds of thousands, if not millions of copies and is known throughout the Western world. Bob's address was preceded by Norrie Paramour giving his own piano rendition of the comedian's theme song.

Sir Fred had never been a natural public speaker, though with many company annual general meetings behind him not to mention his annual "spot" at the Pontin reunions, he had been getting in plenty of practice. Fred found that starting "cold" was always a problem, but after the odd drink he managed to get into some form of stride and people were always very kind, even if he had an "off day".

He was sometimes disconcerted to see his speech referred to as a "charming address". In estate agent's parlance this is a euphemism for something entirely the opposite, but Fred learned to concentrate on putting on a good show and not to let the side down.

Representing Variety in distinguished company was an undoubted honour and Sir Fred was pleased to recall that fellow members were kind enough to remark that his natural confidence and never failing smile played a significant part in his successful year in office.

His biggest test at speech-making came when Prince Philip was guest of honour at a private dinner-party given by the Executive Board and Crew at the Dorchester Hotel on Thursday, February 29th 1968.

It fell to Fred Pontin to propose the toast to their Royal guest . . . he is too modest to sing his own praises over-much regarding that special occasion other to say that he hoped that he carried it off to everyone's satisfaction, including H.R.H.

Other features of his "Variety Year", were Royal World Premieres of two films which are still regularly shown on TV some 30 years later. These were *Chitty Chitty Bang Bang* and Lionel Bart's *Oliver*. Fred felt overwhelmed by the splendour of these occasions. *Chitty* "the most fantasmagorical musical entertainment in the history of everything" was screened in the presence of Her Majesty The Queen at the Odeon Leicester Square. The premiere of *Oliver* had earlier received the endorsement of H.R.H. Princess Margaret and her then husband, the Earl of Snowdon, who were accompanied by the Prime Minister, the Rt. Hon. Harold Wilson and his wife Mary.

The numbers of famous film stars attending these spectacular occasions were enormous. Fred recalled that he found that it was difficult to keep up with what was going on because his eyes were wandering in several different directions at the same time.

Chitty was also part of a quite breathtaking feat of organisation. Arrangements were made for the simultaneous twelve-city World Premiere of Albert R. Broccoli's temporary diversification from his James Bond movie productions, but even Fred could not have been present at all of the venues at the same time.

All were held on the same day as the London showing – December 16th 1968 – and the film was exhibited to distinguished audiences from every principal town and city in the United Kingdom from

Glasgow to Brighton. Variety was to benefit from every triumphant performance.

It is fitting to mention that this mammoth project, the most ambitious of its kind ever undertaken in the UK at that time, was initiated by Variety Crewman Kenneth Winckles, who was then Managing Director of United Artists, but formerly with the Rank Organisation, whose Odeon theatres were an essential element in the operation. Star interviews from the Odeon Leicester Square were relayed nationwide by closed circuit television.

Fred Pontin's year of office as Chief Barker created a new record in terms of raising money. The figure comfortably passed the £1 million mark (almost £10 million in 1999 values) for a single calendar year, but he was the first to concede that it was the teamwork which produced such exceptional results. He was also fortunate to be involved with such a tremendous programme of activities.

Even at the age of 93 Sir Fred remained a member of the executive board of the Variety Club in recognition of his enormous contribution to fund raising during the period when he was able to exploit the massive amount of power at his disposal for the benefit of the show business charity when Chairman of Pontin's. However, it will be understood that this was no longer an active position as far as Sir Fred was concerned. He left the onerous duties to people who had perhaps inherited some of his legendary energy.

Bernard, now the late Lord Delfont, succeeded Fred Pontin as Chief Barker in 1969, when Fred was honoured with the title of Elder Statesman and presented with a gold life membership card, which he always cherished. "Bernie's" year in office started with a bang at the annual dinner-ball at Grosvenor House, Park Lane, when the proceeds grossed yet another all-time record of £60,000 – overtaking Fred's own figure from the previous year.

Bernard was also awarded his peerage in the Birthday Honours List of 1976, which was a nice "double" for Variety, as well as for the Grand Order of Water Rats of which both were Companion Members. Other notable Companion Rats are their Royal Highnesses Prince Philip, the Prince of Wales and Prince Michael of Kent.

The work of the Grand Order, of which the late Bud Flanagan was a founder-member, is very much associated with charitable causes closely linked to the entertainments industry. Membership is very exclusive and Sir Fred is extremely proud to have been a member for many years.

Also that year a fellow-member of Saints and Sinners – another exclusive club, where membership is limited to 100 members – Group

Frederick Pontin, Sir Fred's father who was a cabinet maker of some distinction. Some items of fine furniture crafted by him are still in use in the Pontin family today.

Sir Fred Pontin's mother, Elizabeth who later appeared with her son in an episode of BBC TV's Dixon of Dock Green which was filmed at Pontin's Barton Hall and starred the late Jack Warner as PC Dixon.

Elizabeth Pontin with children; Stanley (left), Harry in the middle with Fred on the right hand side.

An early celebration at Brean Sands, Fred Pontin's first holiday camp. He acquired it from Leslie Dean who is pictured wearing a black tie in the centre of front row with his wife, Audrey to his left. On the far right of the same row is their daughter Valerie who first answered the door of the family home to Fred Pontin when he called in the Spring of 1946 on a mission to persuade Leslie Dean to part with the Brean Sands site.

Sir Fred having a night out with his daughter Patricia when the Pontin's empire was enjoying its heyday.

A happy family Christmas for the Pontin family. On Sir Fred's left is his first wife Dorothy who lived well into her nineties. Behind Dorothy are Peter Hopper and his wife Pat, the only child of Sir Fred and Lady Pontin. The grandchildren are also much in evidence.

The enormous bar and entertainment complexes at present day Pontin's holiday camps cannot compare with the cozy living room atmosphere at Brean Sands in the very early 1950s when a TV set was still a novelty.

Happy campers posing for a publicity photograph for an early fifties Pontin's brochure.

So this is how the Bracklesham Bay bar/lounge looked in the late forties! There are no prizes for identifying a rolled-up-sleeved Fred Pontin at the far right of the bar counter.

An early 1960s river scene at Wick Ferry, Christchurch, the first Pontin's holiday camp to be converted to what was then a revolutionary self-catering concept for the industry.

A late forties aerial view of Trabolgan in Ireland, the former home of Lord Fermoy and until quite recently an important feature in the Pontin's portfolio of holiday resorts.

A happy 'family' picture of the staff at Osmington Bay in the late forties with Fred Pontin and Miss Ann Miller in the centre of the front row. In those days Osmington Bay was a home base for Fred Pontin. Others pictured include Molly Posnett, Patricia Scott, Maureen Power, Paul Warner, Reg Whittaker, Harry Vernon and Mary Read.

Bob Monkhouse certainly had an eye (and both hands) for the ladies at the final of this Miss Pontin beauty competition in November 1956. However, perhaps his earnings in those days did not extend to an investment in white tie and tails as sported by the ebullient Fred Pontin and the other competition judge.

Fred Pontin telling Max Bygraves a story for a change.

A moment that always terrified Sir Fred - walking alone into the spotlight at a Royal Albert Hall Pontin's Reunion.

Fred Pontin crooning? Probably not but he looks the part.

Fred Pontin appreciating Max Miller's patter at a Pontin's Annual Reunion in the late fifties.

Fred Pontin enjoying one of the perks of his job; interviewing Miss Pontin at the 1956 Annual Reunion where the final of the beauty competitions was held.

Pakefield manager, David Gwyn with his 1988 'Pontin's Manager of the Year' trophy presented by Trevor Hemmings (r) and Graham Parr (l) when they were leading lights on the Pontin's board. Trevor Hemmings now has an enormous leisure empire and owns a controlling shareholding in Arena Leisure plc, a company once capitalised at over £500 million on the London Stock Exchange. Graham Parr was the company's Managing Director.

Billy Butlin and Fred Pontin enjoying a friendly drink in between bouts of bidding for each other's customers in a highly competitive market.

Holiday camp 'Kings' (left to right) Sir Billy Butlin, Alan Warner, Sir Fred Pontin and Bill Warner with a ready supply of the finest wines in the background.

Fred Pontin's racing triumph; he is seen leading in the victorious Specify, winner of the 1971 Grand National, on a day he would never forget.

Nat Cohen introduces HRH Princess Margaret to Sir Fred Pontin at a Variety Club event.

They are all 'Royals' in this picture. Two holiday camp 'Kings', Billy Butlin and Fred Pontin having a laugh over some of HRH Prince Philip's holiday snaps.

Sir Fred greeting one of his heroes, Lord Louis Mountbatten at a Variety Club function. Lord Mountbatten was a frequent visitor to Sir Fred's Farringford Hotel on the Isle of Wight where they enjoyed the odd cup of tea or coffee together.

HRH Princess Alexandra appears to be saying 'Are you really the Fred Pontin'. Actor, Richard Todd confirms that he is indeed the great man.

Sir Fred's precious souvenir of a unique occasion, Lord (Manny) Shinwell's silver salver with the engraved signatures of so many British Prime Ministers and other leading politicians.

Sir Fred engaged in a non-political discussion with Lord (Manny) Shinwell and Lord (George) Wigg at a World Sporting Club event.

Fred Pontin enjoying a glass with comedian Jimmy Edwards and no doubt wondering if such a moustache would be good for his image.

Lord (Bernard) Delfont and TV personality Peter Haigh with Sir Fred at a Variety Club function.

Sir Fred Pontin enjoying a happy moment with Jack Cohen, the founder of the Tesco's supermarket empire, at a Sportsman's Club event.

Boxing, holiday camps and politics; an unlikely combination. Jack Solomons, Sir Fred Pontin and Lord (Manny) Shinwell, all pals together at Buckingham Palace when the boxing promoter received his OBE.

Captain Douglas Bader received his knighthood, so Fred Pontin was in distinguished company.

Although the Saints and Sinners Club was not formed as a charitable organisation, over the years it has donated many tens of thousands of pounds for good causes. Co-founders were Percy Hoskins, former chief crime reporter of the *Daily Express*, and Jack Hylton, the famous impresario. Jimmy Tarbuck was the 1998 chairman and one of the vacancies in the early nineties was filled by Sir Denis Thatcher. Lady Thatcher has been known to be a guest speaker at a club luncheon event.

Arthur Lewis MP put Fred's name forward for his knighthood and Fred was rather flattered when the parliamentarian told him that he had performed this service for only two other people: Sir Charles Clore and Sir Isaac Wolfson, both of whom were well-known benefactors on a very large scale, especially to Jewish charities. Fred knew Arthur through his membership of Jack Solomons' World Sporting Club.

Another political friend who joined Fred Pontin in his love for boxing was the late Lord "Manny" Shinwell, Companion of Honour and a long-serving and very distinguished Member of Parliament, who was elevated to the House of Lords after being a member of the House of Commons for almost fifty years, being a junior minister as early as 1924.

It was Fred Pontin who took the chair at the celebration of Manny's 90th birthday, when a dinner was held in his honour at the Grosvenor House Hotel under the auspices of the World Sporting Club on 21st October 1974.

If Fred was ever to be overawed by a distinguished gathering, this had to be it. This spectacular occasion was attended by no less than five former British prime ministers, four of whom are no longer with us. These eminent guests were Lord Avon (formerly Sir Anthony Eden), Harold Macmillan, Sir Alec Douglas-Home, Harold Wilson and Edward Heath. Other noteworthy parliamentarians included Selwyn Lloyd, the then Speaker Elect of the House of Commons, who gave the first speech in honour of a most warm-hearted and genial friend.

The best speech was given by Harold Wilson, who, after addressing the holiday camp entrepreneur as "Chairman Fred", as opposed to the "more formidable Chairman Mao", struck just the right note. Fred remembered his quip that in the knowledge that Manny had married again just the year before and at the age of 88, many of his friends who knew him had come to the conclusion that he "probably had to". This brought the house down, with much table-thumping and Manny laughing more heartily than the rest of the guests.

Harold Wilson presented Lord Shinwell with a silver salver, which was engraved with the signatures of many of the distinguished guests, including that of each prime minister alongside Fred Pontin's own. Some time later Fred received a telephone call from Manny, who said that he would like him to buy the salver for the sum of £5,000. He wanted Fred Pontin, who was well known for his generosity, to send the money to a list of his nominated Jewish charities.

It was impossible to argue with such a personality and on such a delicate subject. Manny was determined not to keep the gift on a shelf or in a cupboard. He wanted it to be associated with acts of benevolence and compassion to others.

Fred Pontin readily agreed to purchase the silverware and sent off a number of cheques, each in the name of Manny Shinwell, to his favourite charities. It is not generally known that this was the fate of the commemorative gift given with such great affection on behalf of all present on that great occasion. Sir Fred retained the salver and its future will have to be considered.

Manny was a unique character, who more than deserved the tributes made on that memorable evening. He did, of course, live to be one hundred and one years of age. When he achieved this significant milestone he spent nearly two hours in shaking the hands of one thousand admirers at a Parliamentary reception. Many there had been his political opponents yet counted him as a lovable adversary, never as an enemy. Sir Fred recalled being with him just a day or so before he died and found his vigorous character very much in evidence to the every end.

The late George Brown is also a character to be remembered. Sir Fred met him at that celebratory lunch. There was some light-hearted banter between Fred, Manny and George and the former was flattered by George Brown's remark that he felt that Fred should have been in the House of Lords, where his knowledge and experience would have been very useful.

Nobody took the hint . . . but it is probably just as well because Sir Fred is not sure that "Baron Pontin of Bracklesham Bay" would have gone down too well with his guests! The knighthood raised more than a few eyebrows in the bars of the Pontin's camps. Perhaps his image as a man of the people was slightly dented.

Looking again at charitable activities, the British Red Cross Society had always been one of Sir Fred's favourites. He regarded the international organisation, of which it forms part, as the leading charity of the world.

It had been his privilege to support many good causes and appeals over the years, but the Red Cross always figured prominently as recipients for what he had been fortunate enough to be able to contribute on a personal basis, as well as through the company.

Fred Pontin, whose assistance was sought in 1960 by the Director of the Dorset branch of the British Red Cross Society, the late Miss Norah Branigan, OBE, and the writer is indebted to this lady for being able to place on record some of the history of Pontin's association with such a worthwhile cause.

Norah and her committee hit upon the idea of organising a brief holiday for disabled young people as well as residents in hospitals for the elderly. She started out in 1954 by persuading Dorset County Council to lend her a former Children's Home in Dorchester, which she furnished and equipped by exploiting every conceivable source of goodwill from friends and colleagues.

Only very small numbers could be accommodated on this basis. After continuing the process for five successive years she decided that the results were so worthwhile that efforts should be made to repeat the exercise on a national basis.

She went to see Fred Pontin and he readily agreed to make the entire accommodation at Pontin's Riviera chalet hotel in Weymouth available to the Red Cross completely free of charge. For two years this Weymouth venue became a holiday resort for disabled people from all over the country until, as a result of a change in policy, future guests were from Dorset only.

These weeks were such a great success that in 1963 Red Cross National Headquarters contacted Norah to see if she would sound Fred out on the subject of running a National Camp for disabled people. Representatives of Pontin's, led by their Chairman, had a meeting with national officials and it was agreed that Pontin's Blackpool camp would be an ideal venue for up to a thousand disabled people, accompanied by sufficient numbers of helpers.

This inaugural national week took place in October 1963, not in the best of weather conditions but everyone was thrilled by a visit from Princess Alice. Another venue for the Red Cross has since been Pakefield in Suffolk. These weeks started in 1971 with David Gwyn, the now retired manager and his successor, catering for some 800 visitors and helpers each year.

The Dorset holidays at Riviera continued for many years. From 1968 Fred was able to arrange for Pontin's to waive all charges, thus releasing branch funds for other equally worthwhile causes. All the Red Cross had to do was to cover the cost of travelling and the transfer of equipment. Everything else was free, and it is pleasing to report that successive owners of Pontin's continued their support by heavily subsidising these annual events until as recently as 1997. Their largesse was then brought to an end on the basis that Pontin's felt that they were not getting enough publicity from these annual events. This is surely an excellent example of corporate hard-headedness in a cruelly commercial world.

The British Red Cross Society has always had a tireless body of workers without whom these weeks could never take place. Sir Fred is aware that as far as Dorset was concerned Norah Branigan was anxious to single out Heather Walters, who was associated with the Riviera holidays from the outset. Ann Miller must also be mentioned in this context, because over a period of many years she bore the brunt of the close liaison that was absolutely essential for the success of these rewarding occasions.

Fred Pontin did not support these very worthwhile causes in order to obtain rewards, but he was immensely honoured to receive what Norah had described as the "highest grade" of the British Red Cross Society's Badge of Honour. He treasured this for the remainder of his days. He also remained Honorary Vice President of the Dorset Branch of the British Red Cross.

They say that charity begins at home. Bearing in mind that the Borough of Christchurch is very close to Bournemouth, where Pontin's maintained its head office for many years, it should not be surprising that there were occasions when Fred Pontin did his best to help the odd local cause throughout the 1960s.

Pontin's started a long association with the town in 1962, when they received planning permission, at the third time of asking, for the holiday camp at Wick Ferry. Over the years Fred was able to associate himself and the business with a wide range of local charitable activities.

It was a chance remark in 1968 by the Mayor, the late William Bridge, that led Fred Pontin to donate an official coat of arms to the Borough.

The mayor had remarked that the item suspended from his chain of office was merely a replica of the old borough seal and not a coat of arms, because none existed. Fred saw an opportunity to make a popular gesture, offering to pay for what would be necessary to produce the armorial ensigns by the Richmond Herald. There followed a long period of local consultation until a final design and the motto *Fidelity and Freedom* were agreed.

Fred Pontin was presented with a fine painting of the armorial ensigns in January 1971, when he was amused to read a report in the local paper reporting that King Alfred had never thought of giving a coat of arms to his Royal Borough: this was left to Fred Pontin, "which must be classed as a singular piece of one-upmanship!"

The painting was once displayed in the reception area of Wick Ferry Holiday Village, but it was then restored to Fred's personal possession. Fred was more than pleased that Ann Miller accompanied him when the borough presented him with the painting, because she did so much to assist Fred in achieving a particular level of status three years later.

Fred had no idea that all of this would lead to him being admitted as an Honorary Freeman of the Borough of Christchurch. But it did, and the ceremony took place on February 5th 1974, when he was presented with a casket containing the Scroll recording the admission. There was no doubt that he was overwhelmed by the honour and it did not escape his notice a direct connection with the earlier event when he spotted that the Scroll, illuminated on vellum, included a colour reproduction of the Coat of Arms of the Borough.

Chapter Twelve

POTTING BLACK

The success of any business is linked to input and cash flow. It doesn't matter how good you consider your product to be; if no one buys it you have no business.

Once it has been established that the customers are there and that demand can be satisfied, the next aim must be to ensure that the operational revenues are not too cyclical and become evenly spread throughout each financial year.

In some concerns this is not possible. Fireworks and Christmas crackers are good examples and the same has to be said about certain elements in the leisure industry. Way back in 1946 a season at Brean Sands was no longer than twelve weeks or so, but over the next three years this term was extended to cover a period of six months from Easter to October. It was the peak periods of the school holidays, though, which really ensured maximum occupancy.

With land and buildings remaining idle for six months, and with no appreciable revenue – advance deposits being the only form of cash return – it will be appreciated that Fred Pontin's energies and those of his staff were being devoted to every conceivable form of innovation to prolong the operational season.

Some managers proved to be much better than others at this task. One or two eventually assumed roles which would rival the achievements of the more prosperous impresarios in the West End of London. This is not an exaggeration when describing this aspect of their managerial activities, as will be illustrated later.

Fred Pontin himself, came up with the odd idea or two, but he would not take the credit for the majority of the suggestions which were put forward any more than he would confirm that all received his immediate blessing. Bob Chapple and the ubiquitous Walter Rowley, in his new role as a public relations executive, were in the habit of using their Chairman as their sounding-board for what became known as Special Events. These were designed to be held at Pontin's various holiday centres during the off-peak seasonal periods.

Other holiday camp operators made efforts in the same direction: Ladbrokes, for example, specialised in conferences. Pontin's had an advantage in the overall exercise by having smaller-sized units and a wide geographical spread of the sites.

Ballroom dancing was an obvious activity that could be exploited to its full potential because this was one of the leading forms of entertainment in holiday camps just after the war. Ballrooms were invariably the first additional facilities after bars and restaurants had been constructed.

Pontin's guests loved to dance to local and sometimes resident bands and they still do. It was, therefore, a natural progression to promote competitions leading to area and regional finals, then to the grand finals staged at Pontin's annual reunions. The reunions were first held at London's Seymour Hall; then, as the company grew in terms of volume of business, at the Royal Albert Hall in London.

It all started at Osmington Bay on the initiative of Ann Miller. The dancing festival organiser was the late Frank Mayne, who, with his partner Gladys Christopher, ran the Mayne Schools of Ballroom Dancing in Dorchester. In the business of promoting ballroom dancing he was known as the "Quiet Man" and was held in the greatest respect. He received a well-deserved award from his peers in 1982.

These dancing competitions, over which presided the top adjudicators in the United Kingdom, were always treated very seriously. When the later stages were reached it was absolutely essential to employ some of the leading orchestras in the country.

National Finals almost invariably featured names such as Joe Loss, Ted Heath or Victor Silvester and to the present day these events still attract well-known musical ensembles, thus maintaining the highest possible standards.

The finals were held at the excellent ballroom at Osmington Bay as well as at Southport where they were also very popular. Some of the greatest names in British ballroom dancing have appeared, or taken part, in Pontin's Dance Festivals, including Bill and Bobbie Irvine, thirteen times world champions, who often gave demonstrations.

Some of the more successful contestants, many of whom had started serious dancing only as a result of a holiday at Pontin's, went on to turn professional and even become world champions. Many such people commenced their dancing careers by joining the more experienced couples on the floor and, after gaining in confidence, by subsequently competing in the regular novice competitions staged at the Pontin's camps.

Included in this select group are Stephen Hillier and Lindsey Tate. Others who turned professional were Keith Clifton with partner Judith Alston and Vic and Terry Marsden, who now live and teach in Spain.

From a pecuniary point of view it is pleasing to record that all of these events were attended by groups of loyal supporters, as well as the enthusiastic dancers, ensuring maximum use of the company's accommodation, bars and restaurants. On the other hand, it gave Sir Fred enormous personal satisfaction to know that this purely commercial enterprise has led to the lives of a significant number of people being considerably enhanced. They, in their turn, have given so much pleasure to thousands of others.

Although dance festivals still figure in Pontin's activities these are now featured at various centres rather than just one and take into account modern trends in dancing styles.

It has been said that Fred Pontin was a pioneer as far as special events are concerned . . . and that others followed where Pontin's took the lead. This is undoubtedly true, but all the company was doing was to discover the identities of leading enthusiasts for any given popular activity and offering them the best possible facilities for increasing the scope of their pursuits with the benefit of accommodation in order to provide an excellent atmosphere for improved social relationships amongst the various memberships. Nowadays, some experts call this bonding.

Pontin's now describe what Fred Pontin knew as Special Events as Special Interest Breaks. These are advertised to include new features such as Murder Mystery Weekends, Psychic events, Cockney Celebrations, Health and Fitness and even Christmas Crackers where enthusiasts can enjoy Christmas and New Year breaks starting in September!

A good example of one of Fred Pontin's special events was a model-making and handicrafts week, a suggestion which gave rise to great scepticism as far as his initial reaction was concerned. He described it as "kids stuff" when the proposal was first discussed. He had no time for such hobbies but he was persuaded to give it a trial and Brean Sands for many years hosted the "World's biggest residential festival for model and craft enthusiasts". However, fashions as well as enthusiasms come and go and this particular special event has become extinct as far as Pontin's is concerned. One of the replacement Special Interest Breaks is one which offers enthusiasts an Antiques Workshop and fayre "for those who treasure their past".

Pakefield took advantage of its favourable position on the east coast and its close proximity to the port of Lowestoft by arranging with the local angling club an annual event which became known as the Pakefield Fishing Week. This is as popular today as it was when it was created on the initiative of David Gwyn, with the full support of Sir Fred Pontin, as far back as 1978.

The popularity of professional snooker was undoubtedly created by colour television and BBC TV's programme *Pot Black*. In the early seventies Pontin's hit upon the idea of sponsoring a Pro-Am Snooker Festival held in May of each year at their Prestatyn Sands Holiday Centre, just after the World Championship had been decided.

Mike Austin was responsible for its promotion and he formed a Pontin's snooker committee, whose first members included the then World Champion, Ray Reardon, and Ted Lowe, the TV commentator.

The festival, which carried the incentive of big prizes, had two parts: a competition between eight invited professionals, who were all paid appearance money; and the Pontin's Open in which professionals took part in the closing stages against the amateurs, who had reached the last twenty-four after coming through five or six preliminary rounds.

The professionals were subjected to a handicap system devised by Ray Reardon and Ted Lowe. Each amateur was initially given thirty points in each frame, later reduced to twenty-one, the value of three blacks, when it became clear that the standard of the amateurs was higher than at first thought.

In 1974 the festival attracted, in addition to Ray Reardon, who won the professional tournament, such well-known names as John Spencer, John Pulman, Eddie Charlton, Graham Miles and Fred Davis. It was a great success. During the next two years the professional competition was won by Alex "Hurricane" Higgins and Welshman Terry Griffiths respectively. In addition to the eight invited professionals, other "pros" could take part as long as they were prepared to pay their own way.

The first winner of the Pontin's Open was a youngish amateur, also from Wales, called Doug Mountjoy, who beat Ray Reardon in the semi-final and John Spencer in the final round. He never looked back after that remarkable victory even though he was to later confess that it was all he could do just to afford the cost of the holiday to compete in the tournament. It was obviously the best investment he had ever made in the whole of his life and Doug Mountjoy is now part of the Pontin's story.

The attraction, as far as the holidaymakers were concerned, was that snooker enthusiasts were able to mix with these great players, not only in competition on twenty-four top quality tables but also socially. All the well-known professionals were Fred Pontin's special guests for that particular week at the Grand Hotel, Prestatyn, just across the road from the camp, which Joyce Hey, a long time and very dear friend and personal assistant of Fred's, managed for two years. Joyce, an ex-Butlin's employee was also general manager at Southport in addition to undertaking similar positions of responsibility within Pontin's. In later years she became Sir Fred Pontin's partner and more latterly his wife and he recognises an enormous debt to her love, loyalty and devotion.

Fred Pontin, needless to say, was an enthusiastic visitor to these popular snooker festivals, and not just to watch the flow of cash. Play was on a twenty-four-hour round-the-clock basis. Pontin's attracted maximum occupancy of 3,600 guests and had to turn many way because of the lack of space.

Fred enjoyed watching the matches and mixing with the players, both amateur and professional. It gave him great pleasure in later years when he saw how some of the young and gifted enthusiasts graduated to become not merely very successful but also world champions. Steve Davis, with long ginger hair, won on his first visit to Prestatyn and John Parrott and Neal Foulds progressed from Pontin's Junior and Open tournaments to even greater rewards elsewhere.

Darts Festivals were also an obvious attraction. These were organised in association with the *News of the World* in the early days. This form of excitement took up no less than three tremendous weeks in each year. It all started at Brean Sands, but Camber Sands and Prestatyn were soon drawn into the new concept.

Very attractive prizes were on offer for men's, ladies and mixed competitions. Eric Bristow won his first major tournament at one of Fred Pontin's camps long before he became world champion. Other companies have followed Pontin's with this type of event, but Pontin's were the first – much to the Chairman's great satisfaction.

Fred had played darts on only one occasion in his long life. It was the day that he bought the camp at Bracklesham Bay in 1947 and Fred can only put it down to beginner's luck. He was playing a game in the local pub with the vendor, Joe Lyons, along with Leslie Dean and George Harrison.

They were playing a game of 501 against four of the locals. Towards the end of the game, with the locals needing only double one, it came to Fred's turn to throw and the score needed was 157. His "team" had to finish on a double and with just three successive darts Fred scored a treble 20, treble 19 and a double top!

They were all flabbergasted, but he protested that it was a complete fluke. The regulars, who had thought they were on an easy wicket, wouldn't play any more, money having changed hands on the initial challenge. Fred was never tempted to enter any of his tournaments – on the basis that it's always best to quit when you're ahead.

Pontin's were also pioneers in advertising at football grounds, Blackpool having the foresight to allow the company to have boards behind each goal mouth, bearing the slogans "Go Pontin's" and "Go Pontinental". Because of Fred's local connections, he tried to persuade the board of directors to put their ground, which had development potential, up for sale. The facilities, particularly car-parking, were rather inadequate.

He thought that they would be well advised to apply the sale proceeds in building a modern, out-of-town stadium, preferably near the motorway, thus attracting larger crowds. They were in the First Division in those days, had won the FA Cup and had players of the calibre of Sir Stanley Matthews and Stan Mortenson.

Unfortunately they did not take Fred's advice, but he enjoyed his early connections with the club, at one time being asked to join the board of directors. He also tried to persuade them to raise money by a public flotation on the basis that he would underwrite the issue but nothing ever came of Fred's early initiatives. Once again, he can be said to have been ahead of the times, bearing in mind the number of football clubs which have now become public companies with their shares quoted on the London Stock Exchange.

These football connections came to the fore in the early 1970s, when Fred Pontin came up with a scheme for organising Football Weeks. For an initial period of three years Pontin's brought together genuine supporters of famous football clubs in a friendly but competitive atmosphere, well away from the hooliganism which was already being experienced at some of the matches on Saturday afternoons.

Again, they had a success on their hands and the concept was extended in 1976 to a six-a-side football competition for junior players from the supporters clubs. With the help of Jimmy Hill, Pontin's negotiated a £90,000 deal with Ted Croker, Secretary of the Football Association, for a three-year sponsorship of the FA Charity Shield. This match, played at Wembley at the start of each season, was between the winners of the previous season's First Division championship and the FA Cup.

These matches were always televised, so Pontin's gained very valuable publicity as well as generous measures of goodwill.

Immediately prior to this annual fixture, which still takes place today, albeit under different sponsorship, the company staged the final of the Pontin's Holidays six-a-side competition. What a thrill it was for these young players to play their match on the famous turf at Wembley Stadium. They seemed to be oblivious of the crowd growing bigger for the main event of the day. Fred felt very proud of all of them, especially those who went on to become full internationals.

Pontin's were assisted in all of the work which went on behind the scenes by some of the great names from the world of football, such as Bertie Mee, Bob Wilson, Lawrie McMenemy and Sir Geoff Hurst.

Fred's keen interest in the game dated back, of course, to the prewar days at Walthamstow Avenue, but his connections with the Football Association usually resulted in some tickets for the big games, including the FA Cup Final. He became accustomed to watching this ever popular fixture from a table in the restaurant, his usual companion being Joe Rubido, who is also a great fan. Having regard to Pontin's major sponsorship of football at youth and national levels, Fred was disappointed when tickets ceased to become available in later years.

Football coaching seemed to be a good idea in the early 1960s, so he engaged soccer stars of the calibre of Jimmy Armfield, now a successful radio commentator and pundit on the sport, Dave Mackay and John White, formerly of Spurs, as well as Ron Flowers of Chelsea, to undertake coaching sessions at camps in Devon, Suffolk, Sussex and on the Isle of Wight.

Former England captain, Billy Wright was in charge of the operation and he did a great job on behalf of Pontin's. Stan Mortenson was also involved with coaching the national game at the northern sites. It was not just the young lads who enrolled for these courses – there was also the occasional balding head, not to mention growing paunch, to be seen on the playing field.

Pontin's have also enjoyed playing a leading role in the world of brass bands and Fred Pontin had no hesitation in claiming credit for this innovation which is now in its twenty ninth highly successful year at Pontin's.

It all started on a Sunday afternoon at Southport Holiday Village in 1974, when Fred Pontin was surprised to see several hundred guests ignoring the beautiful weather by sitting in the ballroom listening to the Prescot Brass Band. He felt that if the music was so popular there must be scope for a special event.

On that particular day Fred did not need a lot of persuasion by Christina Lawton, secretary of the Prescot band, and David Gwyn, who was the Southport manager at the time, to put up prizes for a competition. Matters developed further when he met none other than the legendary brass band figure Harry Mortimer, CBE, at a Derby County football match and the Pontin's Brass Band Committee was formed with "H.M." as musical consultant.

Fred had always felt that brass bands and Pontin's would be good for each other because Pontin's had perfect facilities for the annual championships, which are still taking place with well over £15,000 at stake in terms of prize money and holiday vouchers.

There are senior and youth sections. Bands qualify at three regional venues over the Easter holidays before going forward to the Grand Finals at Prestatyn Sands in the last weekend in October. Approximately two hundred bands compete throughout the Pontin's Brass Band Championship, all accompanied by thousands of supporters.

During the course of the first ever brass band competition at Pontin's there was a near disaster. The calculations on the amount of booze likely to be consumed proved to be a gross underestimate on quantities and the bars ran dry. The site's management were forced to borrow from local bars and clubs. This was never to happen again.

Fred Pontin knew such competitions would be good for business, as well as the popularity of brass bands, and this has certainly proved to be the case. Moreover, he had always considered the people involved to be the most warm-hearted and generous anyone could ever wish to meet and he had always felt honoured to have been involved with the movement. Wearing his commercial hat, Fred knew very well that they were also good drinkers and that was always very good for business as far as he was concerned. No doubt, Colin Homer, the present managing director of Pontin's thinks so too and has this in mind when he writes a welcoming greeting in the souvenir programme for the Grand Finals.

However, the brass band movement suffered a great loss when Harry Mortimer died in 1992. He was undoubtedly a legend and many well deserved tributes were paid to his brilliant and distinguished career. The Prestatyn finals weekend now stages as its top competition, in terms of prize money and calibre of band, the Harry Mortimer Memorial Championship which was won by Tredegar Brass Band in 1997.

In 1998 Prestatyn was the venue for the 25th anniversary brass band championships. As always, this was a special occasion and a tremendous weekend for brass bands' many supporters.

To his final day Sir Fred's past services to brass band music were recognised by his life membership of the Prescot Band.

On the subject of music, Bob Chapple's great love was Country and Western, so festivals were started at several locations. These not only attract top artists, but give a chance for everyone to make the grade at properly organised auditions.

Eddie Grundy of *The Archers* could well have achieved his ambition to have been a big star if he could have persuaded his father to allow him some time off from Grange Farm to appear at Pakefield, Southport, Barton Hall or even Brean Sands, which is not too far away from Ambridge.

These popular events always attract large numbers of fans and maximum occupancy is virtually guaranteed.

This subject leads to the "impresario element" in the ranks of some of the more enterprising managers of Pontin's holiday centres. This particular form of creative activity has taken people such as David Gwyn, who started as an office junior and who is now the retired general manager at Pakefield, into show business in quite a big way.

His promotions featured jazz, *Sounds of the Sixties* and the *Big Bands*, all of which have more than a hint of nostalgia for his loyal fans. He attracted jazz bands with huge reputations, such as Mr Acker Bilk, Monty Sunshine, Ken Colyer and Kenny Ball and pop groups from the sixties who are still going strong to-day.

The Searchers, Fortunes, Swinging Blue Jeans and the Rockin' Berries are names even Fred Pontin had heard of, and dance orchestras led by Ray McVay, Eric Delaney and Chris Dean who took over after the death of Syd Lawrence are still firm favourites at Pakefield. These musical extravaganzas in the months of April, May, October and November have always been extremely well-supported, making important contributions to Pontin's out-of-season turnover.

David revels in the description "Mr Big Band of Europe" and his enthusiasm continued to grow as each year passed. He is an unashamedly passionate devotee of derivative musical style, especially that of the late and much revered Glenn Miller and he judged, quite correctly, that amongst the Pontin's guests and their friends and relations there were a great number of similarly-minded people.

Now in very active retirement, David continues these activities under the banner of David Gwyn Leisure with a base in his home town of Lowestoft. In tribute to what was described as David's outstanding support and encouragement for big bands and all forms of live music, in 1992 he was appointed an Honorary Member of the Musicians' Union. David regarded this honour as one of the highlights of his career.

Nowadays, special events at Pontin's have followed the latest trends and fashions. Most of the old stalwarts are still going strong but new ideas have come into play such as line dancing which has been phenomenally successful, Salsa dancing from South America, tap dancing, petanque, classic cars, bridge and as already mentioned breaks for antiques enthusiasts.

At least one Pop Festival also featured in the Pontin's programme for 1999. A three day event was organised at Camber Sands where habitués of the muddy fields of Glastonbury were offered chalet accommodation on the initiative of a singer in a Glaswegian group who once worked in a holiday camp. Backed by the impressive organisational skills of impresario Harvey Goldsmith, Pontin's Bluecoats were on duty to ensure that everything went with a swing. Rumour has it that there was also a guest appearance from Paul Shane who appeared in the long-running comedy series *Hi-De-Hi*.

It is impossible to write about special events without mentioning Christmas festivities at Pontin's. Certain of their sites were opened up for the Christmas and New Year periods from the early 1970s. From the outset these events seemed to hit the right chord with their clients because the camps were always full. Mothers had no worries about having to cook the traditional fare if they wanted some time off from the kitchen, and there was no need to be involved with any drink-driving.

Entertainments staff and Bluecoats always arranged a very full programme of events to include music, carol concerts, dancing (ballroom and disco) and a range of professional cabaret acts to suit every taste. Any gaps were occupied by wrestling bouts, film shows, bingo, snooker tournaments and whist drives.

There was just about everything the guests were accustomed to enjoying in the summer season but with more time to savour what was on offer.

At the end of the twentieth century virtually all of the Pontin's centres opened for the Christmas and New Year celebrations with a packed programme of entertainments for all members of the family. The company was rewarded with near one hundred per cent occupancy throughout the group.

All of this is a far cry from that very first time that a Pontin's camp opened for the yule-tide festivities back in 1946 when the "Blood Wagon" conveyed the Christmas poultry from Brean Sands to Osmington.

Chapter Thirteen

END OF A DREAM

Any objective commentator on the life and times of Sir Fred Pontin would find it difficult to come to any conclusion other than that 1978, 1979 and 1980 were three of the most confusing and hectic years of his entire life. Sir Fred, when in his nineties, described it as a bitter and very sad period for him and the company he had worked so hard to build up.

Ownership of Pontin's changed twice in this time . . . first to the Coral Leisure Group and then to the brewing giant Bass, with other interested parties hovering around.

The company first merged in 1978 with the Coral Leisure Group, which included the Joe Coral betting shop business. In common with Ladbroke's, who had been buying up independent holiday camps since the early 1970s, Coral were to fall foul of the gaming laws in 1980, when they found their depleted cash flow could not service their heavy borrowings.

As the entire Pontin's operation, let alone the Blackpool centre, had often been described as the "biggest free house in the United Kingdom", it seemed perfectly logical also that ownership should pass to a leading brewer. It was Bass which eventually moved in with an unconditional offer to acquire from the Coral group a business Sir Fred had held so dear for many years.

In those days Pontin's could no longer be truly described as a "family" company in the strict sense of the word. Although the business continued to operate much as normal, given the continuity of middle management, the sale of the enterprise had suffered the loss of its national figurehead, just at a time when the holiday camp industry entered a phase of difficult trading conditions.

Fred Pontin had undoubtedly entered the business at an opportune time and, despite his all-too-often- expressed misgivings regarding the circumstances in which he relinquished managerial control of the company that still bears his family name, he probably left at the right time. In his later years he would have found it very difficult to countenance the radical changes which needed to be introduced to his business empire.

The terms of the acquisition by Coral left Sir Fred a rich man by any standards, but he was by no means ready for retirement. Until he died he had never really understood the meaning of the word, because he considered business as something to be enjoyed. The thrill of manipulating assets, whatever form they may take, was an activity which always attracted his interest, even in his advanced years. The thrill of the chase never failed to capture his imagination.

But, after the Coral involvement, it seems clear that he never really felt happy in the way "his company" was going. In particular, he was feeling responsible for his former close colleagues.

Sir Fred Pontin found himself bidding farewell to his personal staff at the Oxford Street offices. Eileen Langridge had been his private secretary since 1975 and had performed the rather demanding duties in a highly competent manner.

They had their differences over punctuality, as she will readily admit, but she was always very loyal and could see that Sir Fred was very unhappy with the turn of events. At the time he had felt that everyone, including the majority of his own board of directors and Trevor Hemmings in particular, had turned away from him by becoming so closely associated with, and supportive of, Coral's managerial methods.

Sir Fred had said that with the benefit of hindsight he appreciated that this was inevitable. The management could not serve two masters and Coral represented the future of the enterprise. The "King" was certainly dead and he could not have expected any significant influence over what was happening during the post takeover period.

It became very clear that Sir Fred could never have tolerated any long term relationship with Coral in control of what he had always felt was his company. He had no wish to be on the sidelines, so his mind turned to the immediate future. He would have liked to have retained the services of Eileen, but he could not justify her employment on a full time basis and Sir Fred advised her to remain with Coral. She did not stay for too long, however.

After a period as a temporary secretary when she left Pontin's she applied for a job as secretary/personal assistant with an old friend of Sir Fred's, the veteran boxing promoter Mickey Duff, and her former employer was more than happy to give her an unqualified letter of recommendation. Mickey told her: "If you were good enough for Fred Pontin, you are certainly good enough for me".

Eileen was a virtually indispensable member of his organisation for some twenty years. Mickey, himself a former boxer and with a career in the business approaching half a century, has now staged what looks like his final promotion, typically in the East End of London. Eileen must be experiencing a sense of déjà vu, in that she had now seen out two stalwarts with national as well as international reputations in their respective fields.

Both she and her husband John have become fanatical boxing fans, having first become interested as a result of Fred Pontin's association with Jack Solomons and the World Sporting Club. This is probably just as well, bearing in mind that Eileen probably spent more than half of her waking hours in handling Mickey's extensive business affairs.

Eileen has said that she is very proud to have Sir Fred Pontin on her curriculum vitae. He returned the compliment by paying tribute to the way she looked after him at Oxford Street over a very stressful period of his life. She had been there when he received his knighthood and had seen how he had presided over increasing company profitability, only to see him get involved with a sale which Sir Fred came to bitterly regret.

Sir Fred felt sure that Eileen's time with him was a valuable experience and who could argue with that? Sir Fred had said that he could only hope that her next employer would not follow a similar path to his. If Mickey Duff had shown any signs of doing so Sir Fred felt sure that Eileen would have persuaded him see the error of his ways.

To say that Sir Fred was disappointed by the outcome of the events which took place in the early part of 1978 would be a considerable understatement. However, he was realistic enough to appreciate that he was in no position to exercise absolute control over the series of circumstances at the time; events and decisions that led to the relinquishment of his influence over the affairs of a business that had transformed the lives of so many people over thirty years and more.

Sir Fred, in recounting the events of late seventies and not wishing to rely too heavily on the benefits of hindsight, had, from time to time, sought to come to terms with his attitude to some of the after-effects of the takeover of Pontin's. At the same time, he had also endeavoured to impart a degree of circumspection when giving his personal account of the course of events which led up to the sale in March 1978 of his company. It must be remembered that lot of important people were involved and not all of them would agree that Sir Fred's recollections were strictly in accordance with the facts. But this could be said by anyone of their own personal experiences, especially after a period of over twenty years have passed.

It would be misleading to give any indication that Sir Fred was becoming increasingly lethargic in his approach to a business which was then firmly established, both at home and abroad, with an extremely loyal band of guests. On the other hand, anyone in their eighth decade of life could be forgiven for becoming a little listless. After all, he had accomplished so much to the acclaim of so many and one is tempted to ask what was left for him to do?

There was still plenty to occupy Sir Fred's mind, even if it was not like the old days. He confessed that he was more than a little irritated, though, when two members of his board, Bob Whitehead and Tim Moorcroft, sounded out the possibility of placing him on the sidelines not long after his seventieth birthday.

Their idea was for him to become "President" of Pontin's with Whitehead as chairman and Moorcroft, of whom Sir Fred had already thought of in terms of coming to the end of his career with the company, being appointed sole managing director, having held this position jointly with Sir Fred for some time. The guv'nor's instant reaction was to tell them: "You must be joking!"

At a later date he came to appreciate that this was probably the time when the seeds were being sown for changes in future control.

On that occasion Sir Fred felt it fitting that he should remind them that he had control of the board through his family and loyal ally, Ann Miller. It should be said that he appeared to hear no more talk on those particular lines, although his trusting nature was undoubtedly being put under a little pressure as a result of this incident. He had no idea what might be going on behind the scenes.

Perhaps this is why Sir Fred approached Peter Hopper during the late summer of 1977 when, according to his son-in-law and during the course of a visit to the Hopper home in Cranbrook, he asked Peter if he would join him as joint managing director following Tim Moorcroft's retirement due to ill health. Peter expressed himself as being very pleased to accept and regarded it as recognition of his abilities and in appreciation of all of his hard work for the company since he joined Pontin's in 1964.

Unfortunately for Peter Hopper and no doubt due to Sir Fred's somewhat mercurial reputation for impromptu statements and decisions the appointment was never consummated and Sir Fred was soon in negotiations to sell his business to Coral.

To this day Peter Hopper is of the opinion that if he had joined his father-in-law as joint managing director Sir Fred's wishes for succession would have been realised and, who know's? at least one or two of the Hopper boys could well have joined the company. But this is, of course, pure speculation. Instead, Peter Hopper is of the opinion that Sir Fred, by his often expressed views on the lack of interest in his business by the Hopper family, had made his daughter and son-in-law scapegoats for his unforced sale of the company.

When all of this was happening, Trevor Hemmings, had made his presence felt in more ways than one. He assisted in slimming down the operation where it was necessary and took part in negotiations with the unions. He reviewed the many sites and also examined other possibilities for expansion by acquisition. Sir Fred had gathered together a very professional team of managers over the years, but as far as the board were concerned he had retained "family control"; yet the board minutes disclose there were never any serious disagreements among the directors so if there was opposition to the family control element it did not rise to the surface on a formal basis.

Sir Fred felt that there would not be too many raised eyebrows by these explanations, especially as research had revealed more than a little Press speculation in the mid-Seventies on the future of Pontin's and the intentions of their Chairman.

The *Sunday Times* was rating the shares as a firm "buy" and a good takeover prospect in November 1975. It made the point that the company was more than likely to fall into a corporate lap when the time came for the Chairman to retire. Derek Porter wrote in his column in the *Evening News* of the takeover rumours so often sweeping around Fred's holiday camp empire and was astute enough to link these to Sir Fred's consultancy agreement with the company.

Another national newspaper went as far as to list some of the starters in the Pontin's stakes at a time when the company's shares were changing hands at 27p. Allied Breweries, Bass, Thomas Cook and one or two of the so-called tobacco giants looking for diversification into leisure, were brought into the frame, but if market rumours were to be believed Sir Fred was seeking a price of at least 40p for each share.

It is interesting to note that Bass were mentioned as long ago as 1976, but it was not until 1980 that they finally took the plunge and acquired Coral, which included Pontin's. That was after Grand Metropolitan had withdrawn from the fray, following a reference of their intended purchase of Coral to the Monopolies and Mergers Commission.

It is difficult to comprehend why the breweries were so hesitant to place their accrued surpluses into family holidays, especially having regard to the added benefits of being able to sell their beers to what could be described as a captive population of holidaymakers. Although it is true to say that Grand Metropolitan, whose interests included the Watney breweries, had already acquired the late Harry Warner's group of camps.

Scottish & Newcastle Breweries, a group with a market capitalisation of well over £3 billion, were once heavily invested in Pontin's and Center Parcs.

In the event, there had been a series of approaches to the Pontin's company – the most serious being from the Ladbroke Group. Sir Fred never took Ladbroke's Cyril Stein's intentions too seriously and, as he told George Ross Goobey at the time, he was not attracted to leaving Pontin's in the hands of an amusement machine and betting shop organisation. Ladbrokes have changed quite considerably since those days; their market capitalisation is over £3.5 billion and are now heavily invested in hotels.

It is, therefore, all the more extraordinary that it was Coral, whose core business, as Sir Fred was well aware, was in betting shops and casinos who were to be successful with their £56 million bid for Pontin's in January 1978. Having regard to the passage of time, Sir Fred was not sure that he was able to provide a definitive answer to what must appear to be an intriguing question, especially in view of his feelings of regret, even remorse, which arose from the biggest financial transaction of his entire business career.

At twelve minutes past three on the afternoon of 4 January, 1978 Pontin's shares were suspended at 38p "pending an announcement", when the final stages of negotiations were taking place between Sir Fred and Nicholas Coral, chairman of Coral Leisure Group. There had been abundant rumours concerning the identity of the bidder. Trust House Forte, EMI and Trafalgar House were among names mentioned, it being felt that Pontin's were too big for Coral to digest, even though they were capitalised at some £75 million before the acquisition.

The offer price, represented by a mixture of cash and Coral shares, valued each Pontin's share at 49p, thus putting a price tag of £56 million on Sir Fred's company. Some commentators felt that this was on the high side and that the deal might be resisted by Coral's shareholders.

On the strength of these comments the price of Coral shares fell by over ten per cent, thus devaluing the bid to a certain extent as far as Pontin's shareholders were concerned, but the matter proceeded to completion . . . not without many serious misgivings and second thoughts on Sir Fred's part.

However, the deal came as a real surprise to those directors of Pontin's who were "not in the know" as negotiations were in the advanced stages. Peter Hopper recalls that it was not until 5 January 1978 that he received a telephone call from a stockbroker friend who wished to know why Pontin's shares had been suspended on the previous day. Peter had to confess that it was all news to him and it was only when he contacted Sir Fred that he was informed of the deal with Coral. Peter telephoned his wife Pat with the sad news who responded by saying "There goes all our futures".

According to Peter, all of Sir Fred's close family and associates were excluded from the secret negotiations. Peter Hopper maintains that his father-in-law could have been saved from what Sir Fred has described as a disastrous deal if only he had consulted them on whatever was troubling him and which had led to the negotiations with Coral. This again must be treated as speculation in the absence of any clear evidence of what Sir Fred Pontin's true intentions were in late 1977.

In accordance with the merger arrangements Sir Fred joined the board of Coral Leisure, together with Bob Whitehead, Trevor Hemmings and Peter Hopper, the latter mainly as a result of his Pontinental responsibilities. All of Pontin's board of directors retained their positions either on a fixed term basis or with provision for periods of notice.

In Sir Fred's case it was specifically stated that he would remain as Chairman of Pontin's only until 31 March 1980 and his appointment as Managing Director would expire after just twelve months.

It was Sir Fred's original intention not to have his name connected with the casino and bookmaking side of Coral, but his own directors insisted that he should join their management team to reassure Pontin's shareholders as well as the employees. Sir Fred also signified his intention to stay in executive control of Pontin's for the full two years, with Coral not being in a position to interfere with the running of the company for at least twelve months. This, however, was not to be the case. Sir Fred's suggestion that the merged group should be named Coral Pontin Leisure Group Limited also fell on deaf ears as far as Coral were concerned.

It was further stated in the offer document that a new managing director of Pontin's would be appointed when Sir Fred relinquished the post, on the basis that Coral would by then have assessed what changes in management structure and style would be needed.

These arrangements should have persuaded Sir Fred that his life was about to undergo a sea change of some considerable significance, but at the time he had other things on his mind, not least the continued doubts and uncertainties about the rationale of the entire transaction.

To complete the management structure for the merged businesses, Nicholas Coral and David Spencer, respectively chairman and financial director of Coral Leisure Group, joined the board of Pontin's and Bob Whitehead and Sir Fred were also appointed to what was known as the management board of Coral.

Coral, already sensitive to its heavy reliance on earnings from gambling operations, had previously acquired control of Centre Hotels at a cost of some £17 million. The Pontin's purchase was considered as a move to take them into a much bigger league. This was achieved only by the doubling of their reliance on borrowed money to some £35 million, which left them in a state of some vulnerability when they eventually ran into trouble with their casino licences.

Sir Fred was reluctant to reminisce too much on his past association with Coral. The deal was officially represented as a merger between the companies, but was really a full scale takeover of Pontin's, a fact which is unlikely to be denied by anyone.

These were not particularly happy times for Sir Fred Pontin. He felt uncomfortable. It was inevitable that he would resent the foreshadowed changes in managerial style and control. A lot of paper was flowing about, all from Coral's head office. The more he saw of it the more he regretted the so-called merger.

Something had to give. Following rather stilted negotiations with Michael Hoare, Coral's Managing Director, it was announced in October 1978, just a few days after Sir Fred's 72nd birthday, that he intended to resign as Chairman and Managing Director of Pontin's and as a director of Coral Leisure Group at the end of March in the following year. His sister Elsie and Ann Miller came to similar arrangements at the same time with their new masters. Fred's son-in-law Peter Hopper also joined this mini-exodus from the merged companies.

Because at that time Sir Fred Pontin was still firmly ensconced in the offices at 240 Oxford Street, Michael Hoare found it necessary to obtain Sir Fred's personal assurance that he would be able to establish a line of communication with Pontin's management. There is no doubt that this fact alone speaks volumes on the atmosphere which was prevailing during the first season of operations after the takeover.

Arrangements for succession were being put in place, and Sir Fred's overall influence was diminishing by the day as far as the attitude of the Coral management was concerned.

News of his impending departure was not greeted with a great deal of surprise, bearing in mind the arrangements disclosed at the time of the merger. On the other hand it signalled the end of his close personal association with a business which, according to a quote given to Melvyn Marckus, then of the *Sunday Telegraph*, Sir Fred Pontin had "always nurtured, like a child".

Bearing in mind that he was of an age when most people would be content to leave the scene peacefully it was thought that he might well retire to the country and put his feet up. This was never in his mind, but the shock of leaving when the following April came around was more than he had bargained for.

He lost his private office, his administrative back-up, his loyal staff and colleagues – but most of all his personal empire, bailiwick, call it what you will. For over thirty years Sir Fred had been touring his sites, meeting his staff, taking his decisions, chatting with his guests and above all counting his successes. It had now gone.

Sir Fred recalled just how empty his life felt when he realised that everything had come to an end. The fact that he was a wealthy man did not come into the equation: it was a sense of loss or even bereavement which had brought his world to what seemed to be such an abrupt conclusion. He should have known what was going to happen but Sir Fred had been an optimist all of his life.

Negative thoughts were never part of his business philosophy, but this experience had a devastating effect on his outlook on life. To make matters worse – the wound was entirely self-inflicted. There were statements in the Press that the initiative for the Coral bid had come from Sir Fred. According to him, this was not strictly the case.

He had been introduced to Coral by Sidney Jenkins, a jobber whom he had known from his days in the City in the early 1920's. Sidney had his own firm, which was responsible for floating what was then John Bairstow's Moat House Hotel group. Sidney had good connections in the leisure industry and it was on his introduction that Sir Fred commenced talks with Nicholas Coral.

Whatever Sir Fred's motives at the time, the fact is that he didn't have to make the sale. The company was in good shape. According to him, there just seemed to be some form of momentum taking over which he felt powerless to bring to an end. Perhaps he wanted someone else to covet what was his own creation. There are many areas of speculation and most of Sir Fred's former colleagues have their own views on the subject. It is clear, however, that not all of these views and opinions would have been shared by the former Chairman and Managing Director of Pontin's.

Quite apart from substantial interests in the holiday industry at home and overseas, Sir Fred had taken Pontin's into solar energy after encouraging results from the use of panels in heating their swimming pools. He had also diversified into building and construction, when Ambrose Builders Limited was acquired in June 1977.

This company had been formed by Trevor Hemmings, who had been responsible for the major part of a £2.5 million contract to build Pontin's new holiday village in the sand dunes at Ainsdale, near Southport in 1968. He followed this a year or so later by similar work at Prestatyn on an even larger scale.

Trevor had been a successful house-builder and when the Southport contract neared completion, he sold this part of his business to Christian Salvesen for the sum of £1.7 million. Ambrose made an important contribution to group profits and Trevor became a large shareholder in Pontin's, having received 2,500,000 shares for his personal holding in the construction company.

It will be seen, therefore, that there was some justification for Sir Fred's view that a corporate acquisition of Pontin's would be an excellent investment with a view to long term growth by any company wishing to become involved in an important sector of the leisure industry. Pontin's could be considered as having a degree of protection by the diversification into separate markets.

Another important factor was the fact that Pontin's had secured a more even cash flow as a result of the extended season, special events and the continued operation of centres in the Mediterranean.

Looking back, Sir Fred is willing to concede that he could well have been affected by a degree of frustration. Not only was there no logical and uncontroversial successor to be recruited from the ranks of his own board of management, but there had been a distinct lack of interest from what he would have called a bidder of some quality.

In retrospect, it is difficult for any independent observer to understand why Sir Fred did not look upon Trevor Hemmings, who has since distinguished himself in an outstanding manner, as a logical successor. On the other hand, Sir Fred has been known to refer to "that builder? . . . he was shovelling cement when I first came across him". Given that attitude, it is not difficult to appreciate why Sir Fred failed to recognise or went as far as to deliberately ignore Trevor's since more than realised potential.

Fred Pontin knew that, despite the considerable efforts undertaken by the company's stockbrokers, Pontin's shares had never got near to attracting a triple "A" rating from the City. Financial journalists were never short of a story during the days of their rapid expansion, but had then written that Pontin's was a share that had failed to inspire investors.

Sir Fred, who by his own conduct, had become so closely identified with the successful enterprise, and was all too well aware of the growth in value of the original investment, had always found it difficult to comprehend the attitude of the investing institutions. It appeared that, despite the Pontin's profits record and sound asset-backing, the company would never have achieved the status of the so-called glamour stocks. Pontin's seemed destined to remain among the "also-rans" as far as the investors on the London Stock Exchange were concerned.

The company had its supporters, but in the City it was perceived that the holiday camp image would never lead to Pontin's becoming a "Rolls-Royce" stock. But look what happened to that company!

In the circumstances, it appeared that Coral's genuine and enthusiastic interest was considered as a welcome development as far as Sir Fred was concerned. When the final price was agreed he felt that, notwithstanding the reservations of Pontin's stockbrokers, Simon and Coates, he had obtained a good deal for his shareholders. This view was shared by the board, although there were some dissenting comments from members of his own family, as well as Ann Miller, once full details of the merger had been given to them on a deliberately belated basis.

Peter Hopper recalls that it was a somewhat shattering experience for him to read in the Daily Telegraph during the course of his train journey to London on the morning of 6 January 1978 that the Pontin board had voted unanimously to accept the offer from Coral for their own shares and had recommended the bid to all shareholders. This was news to Peter who maintains that he had not been aware of any board meeting taking place on this particular basis.

There was considerable anger at the board meeting which took place on the day Peter Hopper had read the article in the Daily Telegraph. It soon became clear that Sir Fred had committed the family's and other private share holdings to a deal upon which they had not even been consulted. However, it was felt that any news of boardroom dissension would have been damaging to both companies and it was agreed that there was no way out other than to let matters take the course agreed by their Chairman. Their loyalty to the man who had created the business was paramount.

It became clear that ignoring a company director's duty of fidelity, other than Sidney Jenkins, Sir Fred had consulted no one about the very early stages of the Coral negotiations, not even Ann Miller. He did take Bob Whitehead and Trevor Hemmings into his confidence though, once he was satisfied that a deal could be done. He asked them to join him at a meeting in his apartment at 55 Park Lane where they were introduced to Nicholas Coral, Michael Hoare and David Spencer, all members of the board of management of the Coral Group.

Bob and Trevor were sworn to secrecy. Once the price had been agreed even Sir Fred found it necessary to inform the other members of the board and call in the professional advisers. It would be accurate to say that when he made the announcement at the meeting of the directors shock waves could be felt around the room. He was very much aware that members of his family and Ann Miller could hardly believe what was happening.

A discussion took place during which it became clear that there was to be no unqualified support for the deal with Coral. Some members felt that an association with their gambling interests would not be good for the image of Pontin's. Ann Miller certainly made it clear that she felt that the merger would not be to the advantage of the company, and it was not too long before Sir Fred started to share her thoughts. Very real doubts began to creep in and they never really left him.

Just a few days later, on 10 January 1978, a further meeting of the directors was held in order to finalise certain matters to be included in the formal offer document. In addition to finalising a profit forecast, a most important element as far as the final price for the shares was concerned, there were other considerations: such as what was thought to be the company's rather generous non-contributory pension scheme and the possibility of the Office of Fair Trading becoming involved.

The minutes of this meeting clearly record that Sir Fred was not satisfied with the terms of the deal, particularly as the value of Coral shares had fallen quite considerably since the terms were first announced. It was also clearly recorded that at that stage he was not prepared to be persuaded to declare his intentions in respect of the offer as far as his personal holding of nearly four million Pontin's shares was concerned. This was a surprise to some members of the board as they understood that he was already committed as far as his holding was concerned. It had been announced as such and had been reported in the press.

It was stated at the meeting that his attitude was causing ill feeling at Coral, but this was to have no effect on the stance Sir Fred was taking at that time.

It is interesting to record that these same minutes made it very clear that Trevor Hemmings and Bob Whitehead did not share their

Chairman's misgivings, the former going out of his way to reassure Sir Fred and, presumably, everyone else present that all would be well and that the market in Coral shares would recover from the over-reaction to the merger of the two companies.

Bob Whitehead registered his concern that Sir Fred's attitude might have some adverse effect on the relationship with Coral. The Chairman's second thoughts were, therefore, being resisted by colleagues on the board who were not members of his own family and close supporters. Sir Fred had often asked himself why this should have been the case. An independent observer might link their attitude to what had happened when it was suggested that Sir Fred should step down and become President of Pontin's on that previous occasion. Sir Fred's autocratic style was clearly not universally appreciated and perhaps some members of his loyal board were not so loyal after all.

Just ten days before the offer document was posted, a further meeting of the board was held and the minutes of this meeting clearly record that Sir Fred commented on what he thought were omissions from the minutes of the previous meeting held eight days earlier. At *that* meeting he had continued to express his serious reservations on what was happening with the company.

A tape recording was played. After it had been heard by all concerned, Bob Whitehead felt it necessary to comment that, whether the directors liked it or not, Pontin's was being sold to another company and the new owners would be in ultimate control. He went on to say that the members of the board of Pontin's would not be able to do as they pleased, as had been the case in the past. He added, to deepening gloom on Sir Fred's part, that these facts had to be accepted.

Fred's misgivings were again discussed and the minutes record that Bob Whitehead, the Vice-Chairman, even commented on the fact that the Chairman's letter to Pontin's shareholders seemed to be "lacking in enthusiasm" for the deal. Sir Fred was persuaded to think again on this point.

The momentum for the deal was undoubtedly there and the board was firmly enmeshed in the wealth of detail which accompany merger transactions of such magnitude. The combined group was to be capitalised at a figure in excess of £130 million, thus placing it in the forefront of the British leisure industry in those days.

It was not a deal which could be easily cast aside, given that it was already a long way down the line and was receiving strong support from the non-family elements on the board.

It was significant that this latest meeting of the directors had not included the presence of Fred's brother Harry, sister Elsie or Ann Miller. Sir Fred was lacking in his usual personal support from these quarters. He was particularly upset that his old friend Jack Bishop, from whom he had acquired Seacroft Holiday Village at Hemsby-on-Sea in Norfolk some years previously, had sided with those who were enthusiastically supporting the Coral deal.

Jack Bishop later confided to Sir Fred that he bitterly regretted that he had not appreciated that his Chairman was so very unhappy about the way matters were evolving. Otherwise Jack may well have acted differently. He remarked to Sir Fred that it would always be on his conscience but he also knew that the person who had bought his holiday village all those years previously and who had contrived to afford him a seat on the Pontin's board had never sought fit to hold anything against him in this respect. Jack Bishop died a few years ago but Seacroft remained part of Pontin's until late 1997.

The time came for the final meeting at the Berkeley Square offices of Coral Leisure. Those present included Sir Fred's colleagues from Pontin's, representatives from the purchasers, merchant bankers, chartered accountants and solicitors. Sir Fred recalls that he confided his even more belated second thoughts to Percy Cansdale, whose firm had been auditors to the company for over thirty years.

Sir Fred's latter day recollection was that he told Percy that he wanted to pull out of the deal, but Percy responded that matters had gone much too far. Percy added that if Sir Fred reneged on the sale of Pontin's he would never again be able to show his face in the City.

Over ensuing years, Sir Fred had found it very difficult to forgive Percy Cansdale's lack of support at that admittedly very late stage as he felt that he could have avoided what he had still considered was a disastrous sale. But, on the other hand, Sir Fred's feelings had the benefit of hindsight. In other words he was then very much aware of how subsequent dealings with the ownership of Pontin's were responsible for setting Trevor Hemmings on the road to becoming a multimillionaire with reported assets approaching £500 million but with some people, including Sir Fred Pontin, estimating his total wealth at some £750 million.

After the sale of Pontin's to Scottish & Newcastle Breweries in 1989 for the sum of £61 million Trevor Hemmings was regarded as the largest individual shareholder in the group and in December 1999 *The Times* was reporting that Trevor's name had once again appeared on the shareholders' register with a 3.79% stake valued at £104 million.

Trevor has proved himself to be a remarkably astute businessman and by no means an individual who could possibly be described with

any justification as "that builder" and "a shoveller of cement". Sir
Fred Pontin emerged from humble beginnings and it is difficult to
comprehend how he could have resented such commercial success by
a former colleague, unless it was felt that there remained a feeling of
real or possibly imagined grievance.

Sir Fred further recalled that Vice-Chairman Whitehead, who
was a partner in solicitors Clifford Turner and Co., agreed with
Percy Cansdale's view and confirmed that everyone would be placed
in an impossibly embarrassing position if Sir Fred decided to with-
draw from the deal.

By that time the board had, of course, recommended the deal in an
official notification to the Pontin's shareholders. Members of the
board had accepted the offer in respect of their own share holdings,
and the investing institutions had done likewise. The papers were in
their final form. Everyone now felt that Sir Fred had negotiated a
good price and the interests of the Pontin's shareholders would be
best served if the takeover was completed in accordance with the
agreed arrangements.

This reference to the Pontin's shareholders was telling as far as
Sir Fred was concerned. He had been very proud of the fact that his
company's shareholders were so numerous. He wasn't aware if the
vast were all ordinary people who had perhaps enjoyed his hospitality
at the Pontin's camps but he had always looked upon them as *his*
shareholders and he had an undoubted loyalty towards them.

There arrived a time when even someone as powerful as Sir Fred
Pontin felt, even at that late stage, that he must accept the will of the
majority. He had no option other than to suppress any further
thoughts of overturning the deal. Percy and Bob's advice was profes-
sionally sound and so, despite his deeply-held misgivings, the papers
were signed and control of Pontin's passed to Coral Leisure.

Sir Fred was aware that Percy Cansdale, who died in 1998, felt
that the Chairman had always resented the fact that he followed his
recommendation and not his own judgment – however remiss – but
Sir Fred was willing to concede that that would be overstating the
case. It was only after a long period of time and thoughts of what
might have been that gave rise to feelings of regret. But that's life and
life had to go on.

Sir Fred's brother, Harry died suddenly only a few weeks later and
not long after the offer became unconditional. This fact had not left
Sir Fred with anything but sad memories of that particular period of
his life. It has not been easy for him to provide an account of what
was, after all is said and done, an ill-fated series of events as far as he
was concerned.

Perhaps "Thirteen" is an appropriate number for this unhappy chapter in his life . . .

Mention has already been made of the Pontin's Annual Reunions, which were held in London and sometimes at Belle Vue, Manchester and date back to the 1950s. At first these operated on a camp basis, with perhaps Little Canada or Pakefield having their own functions, but Sir Fred soon recognised the value of getting everyone together; management, staff, regular guests, journalists and trade connections in the course of one spectacular night of entertainment each year. In any event, perhaps these events fed upon his show business ambitions. He was very much in the entertainment business and the annual reunions gave him a wonderful opportunity to perform amongst his colleagues and friends, the paying public, and the people who publicised and supplied his business.

This Gala Reunion was always billed as "Pontin's Night of the Year" and in 1967 the company graduated from the less glamorous Seymour or Porchester halls to the Royal Albert Hall, where excellent use was made of the many boxes and licensed bars.

Group entertainments manager, Jim Kennedy who was a regular compère on these occasions describes the regular annual event at the Royal Albert Hall as a magical occasion, always oversubscribed in terms of selling tickets and with no expense spared regarding the quality of the music and also the cabaret.

Various competitions were taking place at all of the Pontin's sites during the season, such as the Miss Pontin Beauty Contest, Miss Max Factor, the amateur dancing events, donkey derbies, talent competitions, various indoor and outdoor sports and even the heats leading up to the Most Elegant Grandmother award. The prizes were always presented at the Royal Albert Hall, the venue for the national finals, and Pontin's also arranged for various celebrities to collect cheques on behalf of the charities which had been supported by guests at their sites.

There have been many well-known names over the years, including visits from Dame Vera Lynn, Bob Monkhouse, Charlie Drake (an ex-Butlin's Redcoat), Bernard Bresslaw and the late Diana Dors, Dennis Price and Ben Lyon.

The evening's activities at every reunion were such that there was always something exciting taking place. The organisation was in the capable hands of David Lever, Pontin's Chief Entertainments Executive in association with Albert Stevenson, fellow member of the Grand Order of Water Rats and of the BBC.

Fred Pontin's prime function was to act as host on these occasions. His private party always occupied the Royal Box, by special
permission, and his very close friends had their own boxes on each
side, so that he could pop in and out during the course of the
evening.

Each Pontin's centre had its own licensed bar in this world-
renowned building, each of which Fred Pontin would visit during the
course of the evening. This is where the real reunions took place, with
guests mixing with their special holiday friends and exchanging
memories with the staff. Most of Fred's clients met each other on just
two occasions throughout the year: on their summer holidays and at
the annual reunion.

Although being the host and having a high profile, Fred Pontin
never ceased to be terrified of having to walk down the stairway on
to the floor of the hall. There would be a fanfare of trumpets, the
auditorium would be in darkness and the only illumination was the
group of spotlights which were focused on his entrance.

He recalls, quite vividly, that the effect of this was to inflict virtually
total blindness upon him. He was also quite horrified at the thought
of tripping head-over-heels, thus destroying the entire effect. But
somehow he never did, though he feels that he would have been
challenging the law of averages if the event had continued for many
more years.

The Chairman's speech was intended to tell everyone what was
going on in the group by way of improvements and new attractions
and he took the opportunity put across his thanks to the large
numbers of his management and staff, to whom the annual reunion
was the high spot of the year.

Sir Fred knew that 1978, though, would be his last as official host.
He never forgot the poignancy of the occasion. Fortunately it was
not really appreciated at the time that it would be the last Pontin's
spectacular at the Albert Hall, so matters did not become too
emotional from that particular aspect.

But it had led him to reflect that the decision to bring an end to the
long sequence of annual reunions and gala occasions was linked to
the loss of the "family figurehead" He trusted that no one would
disillusion him in this respect, because that is the way in which he
liked to feel the matter was handled by the new owners of what had,
after all, been "his" family business for a period of over thirty years.

It was undoubtedly the end of an era. Sir Fred left the scene with
a heavy heart.

He also recalled just one more aspect of that last night at the
Albert Hall. In his speech he paid a moving tribute to Ann Miller

and the enormous contribution which she had made to the success of Pontin's over that period of thirty years.

He disclosed to the audience that, although he was the one who was always up front and took all the bows, she had been involved with every decision he had ever taken in the business, with the exception of one – the acceptance of terms from Coral.

Sir Fred went on to say, with Nicholas Coral standing at his side, that he felt that not consulting her had been the biggest mistake of his life. Thousands of his loyal clients, members of staff, colleagues and close friends were listening to these remarks and although Sir Fred claimed not have been aware of it at the time he was told that Ann was in tears.

It could be said that April 1979 was the start of a fresh phase in Sir Fred's active life. He had an arrangement with Coral to retain the flat at 55 Park Lane for a given period of time, so he made this the base for his future activities. He still retained the office premises in Pine Grange, Bournemouth, where Ann Miller continued to look after his affairs.

There was no question of retirement. It wasn't too long before he was talking to other people in the leisure industry.

Chapter Fourteen

PRESIDENT FRED

Before Sir Fred Pontin finally relinquished his executive duties with Pontin's there was a very pleasant interlude.

One of his former entertainments' managers, Danny Bowshall had emigrated to Australia and settled down in Queensland, from where he had kept in touch. He persuaded Sir Fred that there could be some attractive opportunities for setting up Pontinental-type holiday villages in one or two of the Eastern States.

Arrangements were made for the Chairman to pay a visit Down Under, so, in February 1979, he left with a very full itinerary, taking in a visit to Singapore on the outward journey and a stopover in Hong Kong on the return flight.

Danny had carried out some useful preparatory work and he made arrangements for his former employer to meet the premiers of Queensland and New South Wales, who expressed a great deal of willingness and enthusiasm for Sir Fred's type of leisure project. They offered incentives, such as a grant-aid and low interest bearing loans, which would have left Pontin's with all of the equity in any new enterprises.

They were very keen to promote tourism on the Gold Coast, with a view to attracting visitors from Japan, Malaysia and Hong Kong, and felt that Pontinental-style villages would be ideal for this purpose.

Sir Fred attended civic receptions, and was interviewed on TV and radio, as well as by the Press. All-in-all he was very impressed with the prospect of yet another sphere of operations.

A twin series of Test Matches was just coming to an end, Australia being host to both England and the West Indies after the resumption of "peace" in the cricket world following the dispute with Kerry Packer's World Series organisation. Australia were in the process of achieving a clean sweep in the series against England, thus regaining the Ashes following England's five wins to one defeat on home ground in 1977, but all was not doom and gloom.

Sir Fred remembered attending a very lively birthday party for Fred Trueman, at which he was fortunate enough to meet some of the best-known names in post-war cricket, as well as the famous "Fiery Fred": Richie Benaud, Sir Gary Sobers, who was knighted in 1975, and England and Essex cricketer of considerable distinction, Trevor "Barnacle Bill" Bailey, who was also a star performer for Walthamstow Avenue's post-war football team.

Sir Fred gained access to this rather select celebration because he had met Trevor and his wife, Greta, while flying out to Australia. Fred was travelling first-class and could find no one interesting to talk to, so he carried out a recce towards the rear of the aircraft and came across Trevor and Greta, together with two of their friends, Frank and Celia Wilson. He rather attached himself to them and he recalled having some excellent times together both in Australia and on the return journey.

Whilst Sir Fred was carrying out his business activities, Trevor and Greta moved on to Tasmania to visit friends and Frank and Celia carried out a similar mission in New Zealand. They all agreed to meet again in Sydney for the Test Match before flying home via Hong Kong, where they spent three nights and enjoyed some wonderful meals.

Fred was very excited at what proved to be his only opportunity to see test cricket at such a famous venue as Sydney, and his new friends used their influence by arranging for him to join them in the members' stand.

Fred had purchased a movie camera the day before so that he could record some highlights of this fight for the Ashes. With this in mind he moved down to the front row of the stand which had been taken over by the Press photographers. These hard-nosed Antipodeans did not make things too easy for him, but he managed to shoot some footage of the players leaving the pavilion as well as some of the action on the field of play

Unfortunately, he had no record of this important sporting occasion; he had left the lens cap on the camera! This caused him much embarrassment and frustration but Celia Wilson still recalls the episode with considerable merriment because it provided everyone with a very good laugh.

In the course of their return stopover in Hong Kong Sir Fred remembered visiting a shop where Frank bought Celia a most magnificent handbag. Sir Fred felt that he wanted to repay some of the kindness which had been shown to him on that memorable trip, so he decided to purchase an identical item for Greta Bailey. He was not sure sure whether or not it would have been her own choice of accessory, but, at least, it provided her with a memento of what was undoubtedly a pleasant trip, and which had afforded Fred Pontin a measure of escape from his stresses in the UK.

The pressures were soon there again. Within only a few weeks of his return Sir Fred found himself bidding farewell to his personal staff and having to rearrange his business life. The prospect of any future investment in Australia was forgotten.

He recalled that it was a strange and considerably unnerving experience to find himself with the proverbial empty in-tray after many years of continual and sometimes frenzied activity; it was as if the world of commerce had come to an end as far as he was concerned. He likened it to being in outer space, away from everything which had been so important to him over a considerable period of time

To pursue this analogy even further, the camps, villages and holiday centres were literally on another planet so far as Sir Fred was concerned. Whatever was happening in the world of Pontin's, one factor was for sure – they had no further need for his guiding hand.

If decisions needed to be made – there was someone else to make them.

Negative thinking had never been part of Sir Fred's make-up or temperament, however. The immediate task was to find himself something to do. This could mean only one thing: he needed another business. Not one to be started from scratch but perhaps some promising enterprise which could benefit from his rich vein of experience in the leisure industry.

He had a number of exploratory meetings with a number of leisure industry tycoons, but he could never come to the right sort of agreement and formula where he felt that he could really commit himself.

He continued to look around for other propositions. He was amused to discover, quite by chance, that his birthday on 24 October was shared by broadcaster Sir Robin Day and Rolling Stone Bill Wyman, but the star sign of Scorpio appears to be the only thing they have in common. It may well be, as the *Evening Standard* put it in an article in October 1979, that they have shared Fred Pontin's special talent of putting into effect a unique formula of combining business with pleasure.

He applied this philosophy when he invested £300,000 in purchasing a thatched hotel-pub-restaurant known as The Fisherman's Cot situated in a well-known beauty spot on the banks of the River Exe, near Tiverton in Devon.

There were only fourteen bedrooms, but there was planning permission for a further twenty three chalet-style bedrooms at this favourite retreat for anglers wishing to enjoy the fine salmon and trout fishing in the area.

Sister Elsie was living not too far away at Stoke Gabriel, near Totnes, and she agreed to help her brother in supervising the new business. This was Sir Fred's second hotel. He had owned the Farringford Hotel at Freshwater since 1968, when he purchased it for the second time, having bought and sold it eight years previously.

Farringford – former home of Alfred, Lord Tennyson – occupies a superb site with a swimming pool, croquet lawn, tennis courts and a nine-hole golf course designed by Clive Clark. Sir Fred continued to make regular visits to the hotel and enjoyed entertaining his friends and close colleagues there, especially at Christmas although not so much in his later years.

This hotel featured in one or two "paper" transactions in the 1980s and again in the early nineties, but until relatively recently he had never relinquished an interest in a property which he had regarded with a great deal of affection for a number of reasons.

His most successful racehorse, Specify, did, of course, spend the last of its days at Farringford and he also remembered the frequent visits of Lord Mountbatten when he was Governor of the Isle of Wight. He would make a habit of calling in for morning coffee or afternoon tea and Sir Fred got to know him quite well.

He once stayed at Lord Mountbatten's home and drove him up to London the next morning in his much-cherished Bentley. He also visited Fred Pontin's holiday camp at Little Canada – as part of his official duties, not as a paying customer!

Sir Fred recalled that in the year of Lord Mountbatten's appallingly tragic assassination by the I.R.A. he had asked him if he was able to be present at a charitable function with which Sir Fred was involved. Lord Louis explained that he had to decline the invitation because each July was reserved for a family holiday in Galway on the West Coast of Ireland.

When Sir Fred remarked upon the security aspects of such a sensitive visit, Lord Mountbatten dismissed the risks by saying that he was "very well known locally", had been going there for many years, and "always enjoyed the company of the people of Galway". Lord Louis never returned from his visit in that particular year. His brutal death shocked the whole of the civilised world.

Because of the Farringford connection with Lord Louis Mountbatten, a local resident, Mrs Gertrude Gilchrist, ably assisted by Ann Miller, organised a floral festival at the hotel as a tribute to the dead hero. The premises were taken over by superb displays of flowers provided by members of local flower clubs. The arrangements reflected the national colours of countries in which Lord Mountbatten had served during his long and distinguished career.

Pontin's was never far from Sir Fred's mind, however in the months that followed his departure from the Coral Group. During 1979 he had kept in touch with what had been going on, even ringing up some of his former managers, who were undoubtedly suffering from split loyalties as a result of the takeover. Towards the end of that particular year he had let it be known that he was very much in the hunt to buy back his former company from Coral.

People have said that Sir Fred was smiling, because of Coral's difficulties, but he maintained that he was genuinely concerned. He could see that the parent company could be in serious trouble in terms of cash flow and the adverse effect on their borrowing ratios if they lost their casino gaming licences.

He stressed that he wanted them to know that he was a very interested party. Unfortunately there were some very big guns on the battlefield. He had no real chance of matching the bid which eventually came from Bass. Grand Metropolitan had been on the scene a little earlier, the negotiations having been conducted by Maxwell Joseph and Michael Hoare at a figure of 106p for each Coral share.

There was, however, the problem of a reference to the Monopolies and Mergers Commission, which ruled that Grand Met would not be permitted to buy Centre Hotels, which were in Coral's ownership.

Grand Met subsequently withdrew and Bass came to the forefront, having already been engaged in negotiations with Trevor Hemmings, who was representing Coral. Bass's earlier offers had been rejected by the Coral board, but when they came back at the same level as Grand Met's figure in a more favourable market – and also added a dividend – the deal was done.

It will be appreciated that the management and staff of Pontin's had now entered yet another period of uncertainty, having been bought and sold twice in a comparatively short time scale.

Although the Pontinental business had continued under Coral's ownership, Peter Hopper resigned from the board of Coral Leisure in October 1978, according to Sir Fred, as a result of an ex-director of EMI Leisure and Mecca, Peter Delaney Smith, having been brought in over Peter's head as managing director of Pontinental in July 1978.

This, alongside other circumstances, had triggered Sir Fred's own premature departure from the Coral Group.

Sir Fred maintained that at that time he was very anxious to explore the possibility of renewing his association with his former business as a means of providing a stabilising factor. Derek Palmer of Bass did not respond favourably, however, to Sir Fred's approaches in this respect. Sir Fred had in mind the position of President of Pontin's, but there was no support for such an idea amongst the decision-takers at Bass.

By early 1980 he came to accept the fact that Pontin's could no longer be of any concern of his. He witnessed from afar the eventual sale of the Pontinental side of the business, with the exception of Pineta Beach, Sardinia. He concluded that Bass had no regard for the group as a holiday and leisure business, and took no real interest in what he had created in those post-war years.

To them it seemed to be just a "free house" with enormous sales. Sir Fred's view was that Bass never demonstrated to him any real understanding of the industry in general or Pontin's in particular.

In the Pontin's company there were changes in the location of office premises, involving a move within Bournemouth and then on to Banbury in Oxfordshire, which resulted in many staff leaving the company. There had also been a succession of Bass-appointed chairmen and directors. Mike Austin left the company in 1984, as did Graham Parr and one or two other leading executives who had been trained under Sir Fred's leadership and who he would have described as key players.

Graham Parr had a spell as operations director with Warner Holidays, part of Grand Metropolitan Group from 1983 to 1987. He was also influential in the development of Harry Ramsden's plc and became a non-executive director.

Mike Austin, who had a two year running consultancy with Bass, also kept in touch with what was going on through Trevor Hemmings, but the latter also decided to leave in June 1985. Sir Fred understands that at that time Trevor had talked about a possible buy-out with Peter Williams, the Chairman at Pontin's, who was also in charge of Crest Hotels, another part of the Bass group of leisure interests.

This never came to anything. According to Trevor Hemmings, such a sale would have resulted in the need for a Class 4 circular under the rules applicable to a public company, and disclosure of price and current profitability at Pontin's might well have caused questions from Bass shareholders.

Trevor Hemmings returned to some of his outside interests and became engaged in new enterprises, but he never allowed his fascination for Pontin's to fall by the wayside. He could see that it might well be only a question of time before he would have another opportunity to get back into the frame.

He also knew that Sir Fred was also prepared to respond to any call to get under starter's orders again. In 1986 Trevor paid his former Chairman the compliment of letting him know his intentions, so perhaps Sir Fred could, in his opinion, be forgiven for concluding that Trevor wanted the former guv'nor to be part of the deal. There was, alas, no clear-cut line of demarcation and according to Sir Fred his personal overtures to Bass were getting back to Trevor, who was really engaged upon doing his own thing.

Sir Fred had brought close colleague and "company doctor" Ronnie Aitken into the picture, and there were meetings with Trevor on the subject of funding a buy-out, but Trevor concluded the deal on his own and Sir Fred was not successful in negotiating any part of the transaction for his particular corner.

As Trevor once described the situation, his former Chairman had been placed in a "suspense account". In other words, some form of "reserve" or perhaps "contingency arrangement", which, in the event, was never required.

The sums involved were enormous. The final figure was some £57 million, excluding Pontinental because the offer fell short of what Bass was seeking. Swallowing all of his considerable pride, Sir Fred had to concede that Trevor Hemmings proved that he was fully capable of arranging the complicated structure which was required to finance the acquisition.

Virtually the entire amount was borrowed and supported by the personal assets of all concerned.

Trevor had identified the people who were to make up his managerial team. Graham Parr left Warner's and became Pontin's managing director. Mike Austin was appointed marketing director. The fact that these two key members of Trevor's buy out team had been trained by Sir Fred was really irrelevant – they could not be in both camps and Trevor had established that the banks were not looking upon Sir Fred's presence as an essential requirement for completing the transaction. This is a significant point and not one which Sir Fred would have appreciated if he had been made aware of the situation. Sir Fred's personal opinion of his importance to Pontin's was not shared by the people who mattered – the financiers. This attitude in the City would not have been unconnected with Sir Fred's age. By then he was approaching his 86th birthday but it had to be admitted he remained full of vigour.

Every dog has his day. Sir Fred appreciated that it was his age that was against him, and that the business had moved on in the seven years since he had left the fold. Sir Fred was well past an age when most people would have been more than content to take things easy.

However, until the end, Sir Fred had never felt able to see himself being placed in that particular category.

Trevor Hemmings had become enmeshed in the world of "mezzanine finance", "zero coupons", and "deep-discounted bonds" . . . a far cry from what Sir Fred had been used to. It was a bitter pill to swallow, but he did not permit this further disappointment to deter him from further forays in the business which had been his life for so many years.

Sir Fred maintained that, at the time, he was not aware of the true nature of the interest of Scottish & Newcastle Breweries in Trevor Hemmings' negotiations with Bass. He had since learned that Scottish & Newcastle were given what amounted to a "call option" on the shares in Pontin's. Sir Fred was under the impression that they were in the background on some form of financial basis connected with the commercial opportunity which would be afforded to them in terms of supplying the sites. However, they were, in effect, acting as an astute form of security back-up, providing comfort to the financial backers.

Given that Scottish & Newcastle did exercise their option in two equal stages, thus achieving one hundred per cent control of Pontin's in 1989, the confidence demonstrated by Trevor's bankers can be clearly understood. This deal undoubtedly put Scottish & Newcastle also beyond the reach of Elders at the time they were seeking to acquire control of the group by virtue of their hostile bid.

Profitability assumed far better proportions once Bass had relinquished the business. Scottish & Newcastle had providentially decided to accelerate the exercise of their options, because to have delayed for too long could have cost them an even higher price.

The division of Scottish and Newcastle which included Pontin's and Center Parcs could offer upwards of 17 million bed-nights per annum. Sir Fred saw no reason why he should not make the somewhat debatable point that this massive business had grown from the foundation stone of Leslie Dean's former wartime site at Brean Sands. This division accounted for a useful proportion of the aggregate profits of the group but investment returns from leisure in more recent years had been under significant pressure which have led to major changes in management philosophy at Pontin's.

The morning after the buy-out deal had been completed, and Pontin's was under his control, Trevor Hemmings called at Sir Fred's apartment in Whitehall Court and offered his former Chairman the position of Founder President of Pontin's, the company Fred Pontin had established in 1946.

He told Sir Fred that it was the unanimous decision of all concerned and it was intended as an acknowledgement of a lifetime's work.

Sir Fred was more than happy to accept, and, despite any misgivings which may been entertained by Trevor and his team, there was never been any question of Sir Fred interfering with the way they ran the business, which he was convinced had passed into very good hands.

Sir Fred was flattered that his portrait still hangs in one of the meeting rooms at Sagar House, the centralised office premises in Chorley, Lancashire, and he mused that perhaps, just perhaps, a glance from time to time at the expression on his face may well influence or even inspire the senior personnel in their deliberations.

"Now what would Sir Fred have done?" Was he being unduly egoistic? Probably. Yet that's what they would all expect from the guv'nor – and who was he to let them down?

Up until comparatively recently it was comforting for Sir Fred to know that Pontin's was controlled by people who were brought into the business by him. He felt that they had a lot of fun working together and he became gratified to learn that they had been applying the Pontin's business acumen and managerial expertise in reorganising a totally diverse business.

Langdale, the site which Sir Fred had introduced to Trevor Hemmings some years previously, is now a four-star luxury Time Share development in the Lake district. Formerly a caravan site, it remained part of the leisure division of the Scottish & Newcastle group until the mid-nineties. Pontin's were called in to sort out a few problems.

Mike Austin tells the story that the up-market owners suffered what amounted to a total culture shock when they heard that Pontin's were moving in, but they were soon forced to agree that after Pontin's had made some changes the site operated on a very efficient basis and Sir Fred would have certainly added "Well done the lads!"

However, the site did not fit into Scottish & Newcastle's strategic plans and it was probably with some all-round relief that Langdale was sold to the owners in 1995.

As a footnote to this section it should be recorded that in recent times quite a few of Sir Fred's managerial appointees in the employ of the Scottish & Newcastle group have left their positions although they are by no means inactive in the leisure industry.

Trevor Hemmings relinquished his position as chairman of Pontin's in the early months of 1996 to pursue the advancement of his powerful and expanding personal business empire which includes a quoted company and a majority interest in Blackpool Tower, following the acquisition of the bulk of the resorts division from Michael Grade's First Leisure in August 1998.

Trevor was never likely to rest on his laurels, being an acknowledged workaholic. He is now a leading player in the UK's leisure industry and all that he has achieved has been as a direct result of the already mentioned Ambrose Builders deal with Fred Pontin in 1977.

Graham Parr, another former Pontin's executive director who started his career with Pontin's as a Bluecoat was until recently chief executive of Arena Leisure plc, a company controlled by Trevor Hemmings and his family interests. Arena Leisure enjoys a full quotation on the London Stock Exchange and with Lingfield Park, Folkestone, Wolverhampton, Southwell and Royal Windsor race courses as major assets is poised to make significant progress in the United Kingdom's leisure industry.

An added feature as far as the company's future operational activity is concerned is the fact that the board of Arena Leisure is confident that it has identified a significant revenue generating opportunity in the business of on-line gaming. Arena Leisure have led the world in developing an internet site which provides broadcast pictures of live horse racing alongside on-line betting activities.This website named www.attheraces.co.uk went live in December 2001.

Arena Leisure's expanding portfolio of race courses, including the United Kingdom's only all-weather tracks, combined with the magic of the internet connection drove investor interest in the company to the point of a Summer 1999 rights issue price of 15p for its shares rising to 210p in February 2000 which capitalised the company well in excess of £500 million.

As a result Lady Pontin, the former Joyce Hey and widow of Sir Fred Pontin, as at the above date had a holding in Arena Leisure valued in the region of some £12 million.

Arena Leisure plc was formerly known as Alpine Soft Drinks. Sir Fred Pontin reversed his Farringford Hotel asset into the company in the early 1990s and Trevor Hemmings joined him as part of a necessary rescue operation a few years later when the market capitalisation was as low as around the £4 million mark. Alpine's soft drinks business was proving to be an unwelcome drain on the company's resources and the decision was taken to sell the business on grossly unfavourable terms to another public company. This left Alpine, which was subsequently renamed Farringford before becoming Arena Leisure, with onerous obligations under the terms of leases on redundant warehouse and manufacturing premises.

Eventually, these liabilities were eliminated after negotiations with respective landlords and following Trevor Hemmings' cash injection of £250,000 but it was to be a few years later before Trevor Hemmings made his move to take control by the injection of the Lingfield Park assets.

Following the acquisition of The Fisherman's Cot, Sir Fred was interested in making similar investments in the West Country. He purchased the Palomino Pony Inn in Honiton, followed in 1983 by the Berry Head Hotel in Brixham, which commanded superb views across Torbay.

It was like old times to be back in Brixham applying for a licence from the local magistrates. He had last seen them when he acquired the Dolphin and St Mary's Bay Holiday Villages and the Wall Park Holiday Centre for Pontin's way back in 1961.

Elsie was again involved with supervising these latest purchases, and Sir Fred set about the task of improving the facilities and services on the basis of his long-standing maxim of providing value for money. By the time he had completed his small group of hotels he had also added The Trout Inn, on the water side and just across the road from The Fisherman's Cot.

All this had to come to an end after a few years when Elsie reached her seventieth birthday and her husband Bob was seventy-three. They felt that they had earned retirement. Regular visits to all four sites was becoming too much of an effort for them.

Quite apart from supervision, they handled the book-keeping, purchasing and VAT returns and there were always some problems requiring attention, especially those relating to staff. It had to be faced, too, that the properties needed continual capital investment to keep them up to modern standards.

This was the overall deciding factor in the decision to effect the disposals. Sir Fred was a reluctant seller, but he realised that he could not expect the West Country branch of his family to carry on for ever. He sold all four units during 1986 and 1987 and reflected once again on what he considered to be his, now hotly disputed, ill-fortune in not having his long-sought-after family succession firmly in place.

On the subject of the Fisherman's Cot Peter Hopper states that by 1985 his son, Kevin had started a catering course at Thanet Polytechnic, which has a reputation of being the best catering school in the country. Kevin had done some work at the Fisherman's Cot and subsequently demonstrated some budding entrepreneurial spirit by writing to his grandfather asking if he would consider letting him work there and even offering to make an investment from his trust fund monies as a contribution to necessary repairs and renovations which he knew were under discussion. According to his father, Kevin never received a reply to this letter and this has served to add to the bitterness which is felt by the Hopper family towards their close and very successful relative.

Before these sales were effected, however, another public company proposition had attracted his interest. Ronnie Aitken, wearing his company doctor hat, had been drafted into a fast-failing "rag trade" company known as Kunick Holdings. He quickly recognised that he was dealing with a hopeless case, but saw the potential in treating the company as a "shell". It could be brought back to life if the necessary assets and entrepreneurial expertise were introduced, with the ultimate blessing of the Stock Exchange. Ronnie agreed a moratorium with creditors and set about a reconstruction of the company.

The newspapers decided that Sir Fred's activities were still of some interest to their readers, apparently because *of* rather than *despite* his advancing years. "Next on 76-year old Sir Fred's menu?" "Yet another come-back by Sir Fred Pontin." "Sir Fred, a real stayer." These were quotes from the national Press in May 1983 when the Kunick deal was announced.

Sir Fred had been brought in to Kunick with Don Robinson, whom he regarded as a charming and most successful businessman from Yorkshire, who also chaired Hull City football club. He had sold Scarborough Zoo to Trident Television in 1973, but had retained his interest in leisure by his ownership of Scarborough Opera House, a showboat pub and a half stake in two discos. He injected these assets into Kunick for £138,000 cash and six million new shares.

Sir Fred contributed the Farringford Hotel in exchange for £200,000 in cash, plus three million new 10p shares at par, which he subsequently placed with institutions at a 50% profit.

Kunick had now become a leisure company, but it was to be some years before a quotation on the Unlisted Securities Market, and ultimately a full listing, was to be achieved.

Other deals were to follow later that year. In August, Don Robinson arranged to buy back Scarborough Zoo and Marineland Amusement Park from Trident Television. He introduced these additional cash producing assets into the renamed Kunick Leisure in exchange for more new shares, which gave Trident a 21.5% stake in Kunick.

In the meantime Sir Fred was concentrating his efforts on persuading Annabel Geddes to part with her ghoulish exhibition of torture, disease and violent death known as the London Dungeon, which she had turned into one of London's top tourist attractions.

Located under railway arches near London Bridge, this business was producing annual profits of £200,000 on a turnover of only three times this figure. It was Sir Fred's view that the actual returns could be far higher, given improved controls and a more disciplined approach to book-keeping. He was soon to be proved correct.

The negotiations were quite protracted and accompanied by the consumption of considerable quantities of champagne, but they got there in the end. The purchase price was a mixture of cash and shares amounting to £1 million.

Sir Fred also did well out of this deal. He took three million of the Kunick shares which were allocated to Annabel by paying her the par value of 10p for each share in cash. In other words, he underwrote the issue to a certain extent, thus smoothing the way to a satisfactory completion.

He eventually disposed of these shares at a very useful profit . . . so the London Dungeon has never held any terrors as far as he was concerned!

The Dungeon deal also hit the national Press with headlines such as: "Pontin's buy is quite a scream" and "From holidays to horror". This publicity served to increase the takings at the turnstiles. As a result it was not long before this new investment made a significant contribution to Kunick's overall profit performance and the market price of the shares.

Sir Fred stayed with Kunick Leisure for four years and left on a perfectly amicable basis. It is said that he also made a hefty profit on the disposal of his shares.

Another useful spin-off for him at that time was that he "inherited" Leon Andrews from the management. He continued to be a close associate of Sir Fred for some time afterwards and Sir Fred came to value his friendship and loyal support. Leon was secretary and director of most of Sir Fred's private companies and it was comforting for him to know at that time that they were in such good administrative hands.

Chapter Fifteen

'NATIONAL ASSET'

Many reasons are given by people in various walks of life for wishing to see their biography being written and published or having their reminiscences recorded for posterity. Sir Fred did not pretend to have any particular or exclusive explanation as to why he should have welcomed this book which takes into account not only the history of his former business and his extraordinary life but also his successes, not only in commerce but also with people and charitable activities.

He had come to appreciate that an inevitable adjunct to such an exercise is a personal tendency to reflect upon the following . . . Why did it happen? How did it all come about? How did I play my role? What have I achieved?

Perhaps for the first time in his life he had been able to give some consideration as to how he had seen himself; also an opportunity to speculate upon how others may have passed judgment on him.

Sir Fred had always been aware that he was very fortunate to have been given an extraordinary supply of energy. This was a significant contributory factor in helping him fulfil his very early ambitions to make a lot of money.

In his words, he found there was no set path; no signposts to be followed and no sources of advice to be heeded above all others. He simply proceeded along his own route, took his chances, which were mainly based upon his own judgment, albeit having discussed matters with others and he had undoubtedly been the master of his own destiny.

When asked if he would have done certain things in another way he would reply that if he had he would have been a "different person" – so the question does not really arise.

Some of his closest friends have described his character as "enigmatic". Sir Fred had not been able to accept this description in the truest sense of the word. There were certainly times when his conduct may have been considered to be unpredictable, but he felt that most people had known where they stood with him. In the final outcome they would have been aware that he had usually tried to be fair in dealing with the multitude of situations confronting him over the years.

His staff and colleagues became accustomed to the sudden explosion of anger, the invective and the barely controlled irritation at what he invariably recognised as incompetence. Unless he was dealing with something totally unacceptable, his display of what many would have regarded as petulance – but which he considered to be an essential weapon of discipline – would sometimes, but not always, be followed by the velvet glove. Perhaps represented by a hand on the shoulder and a drink at the bar.

Anyone at the sharp end of this type of performance knew that, more often than not, it was an ephemeral feature of his conduct. He did not tend to harbour any long term grudges as far as his staff were concerned but the events surrounding the disposal of the Pontin's business in the late seventies and the management buy out, or perhaps buy in was a more accurate expression, some years later have undoubtedly left him feeling considerably aggrieved and, at times, betrayed. Time is said to heal but the wounds were deep and the healing process was, in the writers opinion, never fully completed.

On the basis that he treated his "not guilty" plea to the charge of being an enigma as sustained, perhaps it would be worthwhile to offer Sir Fred's own comments upon some of the evidence which had been provided in support of the allegations alongside perhaps some more objective views.

His public image was said to differ widely from how his close friends and associates had come to accept him. Sir Fred put this down to one particularly important factor. If his staff had regarded him as some form of autocrat, it is probably because they had been severely criticised by their Chairman and asked to do something which they may have regarded as unnecessary or irrelevant.

They would have experienced the sharp edge of his tongue – but then be faced with that pat on the shoulder. It may have been conduct of a rather ambiguous or even bewildering nature but as far as Fred Pontin was concerned it got results.

Sister Elsie had always said that his greatest strengths were a determination to succeed and an ability to get people to do exactly what he wanted. Staff came to recognise and appreciate if not readily accept this style of management. Not always, though, before they had found it necessary to pour out their hearts to whoever happened to be near at hand, usually someone like Ann Miller, who must have been responsible for suppressing many a letter of resignation in her day.

Whatever other people may have thought about this style of managerial control, it was important that *Sir Fred* was confident that it worked.

It has been said that these methods would sometimes lead to him getting the wrong answers to important questions. Answers which were given out of fear, rather than frankness and sincerity. This may well have been the case, but Fred Pontin maintained that he could usually tell the "yes men" from those who would stand their ground and argue their case. The survivors soon learned to do this and they were usually rewarded with promotion and increased responsibilities.

To continue with this theme, Ann Miller reflected that she had seen him "wipe the floor with a person", but "he or she would still come back for more". Perhaps it was because some of the staff never really knew how he was likely to respond to a given situation, and this generated some perverse form of loyalty. Born, perhaps, out of the challenge of survival.

In writing a comprehensive account of Fred Pontin's life and times it might be expected that an uninhibited description or even an analysis of his personal and private affairs should perhaps enter the debate. In these circumstances, there will be some disappointment because he was very much of the opinion that a line had to be drawn if one were to respect the privacy and intimate feelings of some of the people who had been close to him over the years.

Sir Fred's late wife Dorothy had been tolerant, understanding, loving and even forgiving in respect of his admitted tendency to philander over many years. They were married in 1929, and it must be said that these seven decades or so were not easy for her, especially in later years when she suffered so much from arthritis.

Dorothy had made it clear that she thought her husband was mad to get involved with holiday camps in the first place and she later admitted that she found the rapid rate of expansion totally incomprehensible. However, she came to realise that if confidence was required to succeed Fred would not be lacking in this department and from the early days she played her own, very personal part in the family business. Dorothy became known as "Dollie" Pontin and everyone has spoken well of her. Her contribution to the Little Canada camp on the Isle of Wight was quite significant. Dollie was partnered by her sister and aided from time to time by what have been described as a bunch on nondescript managers. She did, however, acknowledge efficiency when she saw it and always found time to make her feelings known to the people concerned. To be thanked and even congratulated by the boss's wife was looked upon as a valuable accolade and much appreciated by those concerned.

Dollie worked very hard, probably as her own form of antidote to her husband's constant travelling and socialising which served to preclude even the slimmest chances of establishing a normal family relationship. According to Dorothy, their daughter Pat was not even aware she had a father until she had grown up. Fred hoped and trusted that this was an exaggeration, but there must be some truth in it.

Although Fred and Dorothy lived independent lives during the week, Fred would make a point of travelling to see her virtually every weekend. There were quite a few family homes over the years but, well into her nineties, Lady Pontin ended her days in Cranbrook, Kent surrounded by lovely countryside in a wing of a house which belongs to Sir Fred's daughter and son-in-law. During the week in more recent years, Sir Fred could usually be found in his apartment in London, but he maintained his regular weekend visits to Dorothy up until the time she died.

Whatever interpretations may be advanced for the exact nature of his relationship with Dorothy, and given his overwhelming number of friends and acquaintances, as long as Dorothy was still alive Sir Fred had always described his marriage as the sheet anchor of his life. Those who know Sir Fred Pontin are aware that he had never lacked the company of an attractive woman when he needed an escort on the numerous social and other occasions. Dorothy always said that she never took to the sort of social life her husband was leading when his business was expanding. He worked very hard, but he also knew how to relax.

As is known in the case of Bill Clinton, power undoubtedly attracts and Fred Pontin was accustomed to exploiting his own brand of power. Over the years of his company's phenomenal success he had a long list of conquests and no doubt considered these notches on his belt as the guv'nor's perks. His philandering and womanising were legend at Pontin's and most people could only admire his energy. But he tended to keep these casual relationships entirely separate from his public engagements.

Fred Pontin could always be relied upon to exercise a supreme gift for compartmentalising his life. Somehow he arranged that none of his regular, as opposed to casual, women friends, not to mention his own wife, ever met face to face in his presence, even at the annual reunions at the Royal Albert Hall where they would certainly be in attendance.

He enjoyed the company of others, and this gregariousness extended to just about everything which Dorothy found unappealing. Her husband was to be found in boxing halls, expensive hotels, racecourses, football grounds, private clubs and smart restaurants. Fred Pontin thrived on all of it and he became a very popular host as well as a guest who always gave value by his presence.

Fred Pontin's charitable activities necessitated attendance at a myriad of functions, and, as far as his business was concerned, it was important to be in a position to entertain important people at very short notice.

It was during this period of what can only be described as maximum exposure as far as his powerful personality was concerned that certain of his senior staff noticed that the guv'nor's accent was becoming, shall we say a little more refined, not to say verging on "posh". He was, after all, moving in very fashionable circles and mixing with royalty as well as many of the leading show business, media and sporting personalities of the day.

Although never a great public speaker he never shunned his duties under this heading and perhaps this is when he decided that he wanted to sound the part. Some people have speculated on whether or not Fred Pontin had been taking elocution lessons but whatever was the case he certainly did not always maintain the typical articulation of a lad from London's East End.

During these times and as far as his business was concerned he was fortunate enough to have been surrounded by people whom he came to trust and whose opinions he undoubtedly respected. He also enjoyed the loyal support of a devoted family, who became closely identified with the success of Sir Fred's career in the holiday camp industry. They could never be described as "fellow travellers" who had benefited from nepotism, because they worked just as hard as he did. Nevertheless, he was undoubtedly a family dictator but as long as he was being successful he got away with it and he brought a fair degree of prosperity to all members of the family who worked in his business.

Leslie Dean, the original owner of Brean Sands and Osmington Bay, remained a director and shareholder for some years, but left after a disagreement on policy during the 1950s. However, Fred Pontin remained in fairly regular contact with members of the Dean family.

The Deans retained connections with the holiday camp business at Southdean, Middleton-on-Sea, near Bognor Regis on a site purchased from Mr & Mrs Shaw-Porter on the insistence of Leslie's daughter, Valerie. Valerie was keen to become involved in the industry, having previously worked for Fred Pontin at Brean Sands. Leslie died in 1970 and until the last year or so his widow, the late Audrey Dean, was still living at Middleton, as was "Auntie Vi", the widow of Arthur James, who was Fred Pontin's first manager at Brean Sands

Valerie Barnett (née Dean), who opened the front door of "Fairfield" to Fred Pontin back in 1946, is now living in active retirement near Chichester with her husband John. Until the early 1990s, together they owned and operated the very attractive and popular Mill Hotel at Kingham, Oxfordshire, where they built up a successful business with a fine reputation.

Leslie Dean was an enthusiastic cricketer, whose play was of county standard. He was so keen that he even arranged for Audrey to travel to London for the birth of their first child, just in case it was a boy and so that he could qualify to play for Surrey.

In the event they had their daughter Valerie, but brother Brian followed within a year or so, although his preference has been for tennis rather than his father's beloved game of cricket.

Looking back on his life, Sir Fred had come to appreciate the extent to which he has influenced the lives of others in what must now be seen as a remarkable manner. This rather belated realisation had a somewhat chastening effect upon him, but his success had also been theirs.

He was not conscious of too many regrets being harboured along the way, except perhaps some very personal misgivings concerning Ann Miller and his late wife, Dorothy.

Sir Fred admitted that he was by no means a religious man, but he was aware that it was St Paul who wrote, admittedly in another context, that: "I am what I am". The common use of this expression has assuredly served as a form of justification for the equivocal actions of many men in similar circumstances, but this is not a justifiable excuse by any means.

Reflecting on what he was responsible for creating Sir Fred felt, with some justification, that the entire concept of Pontin's could well outlast more contemporary holiday and leisure pursuits, particularly in view of the fact that despite competition from other sources the formula still has considerable appeal to, what has appeared to some cynics, a dwindling band of devotees. To the people who have been returning to Pontin's for their family holidays, year after year, he and his former empire could well be considered as having become part of British folklore, such has been the appeal of this type of all-inclusive family holiday. Just how the present owners of the Pontin's business together with the executive management have been tackling the challenges facing the industry in the dying days of the twentieth century are discussed elsewhere in this chapter.

But what of Sir Fred's close family? Peter Hopper married his daughter Patricia in 1958 and according to Sir Fred, his son-in-law never demonstrated any real enthusiasm at that particular time for the holiday camps in England and Wales, although both Peter and Pat did spend some weekends at the newly acquired Little Canada Holiday Village on the Isle of Wight where they did unpaid work in the kitchens.

Peter and Pat had met earlier when both were on the same course at the London Bakery School at Borough Polytechnic and before Peter joined his family's bread baking and retailing business in Kent. Both Peter and Pat attained degrees in bakery and flour confectionery, the former with distinction and Pat was awarded first class honours.

Sir Fred's interpretation of Peter Hopper's attitude to the camps in the UK is hotly disputed by his son-in-law who confirms that each member of the board of Pontin's took a special interest in a group of camps. His were at Bracklesham Bay, Broadreeds, Camber Sands and Plemont Bay, Jersey. Peter insists that he had a good working relationship with the general managers of these sites and resents his father-in-law's views on what had become a touchy subject in the Hopper household.

When Peter sought his future father in-law's permission to marry Pat in November 1956 Fred Pontin saw this as an opportunity to introduce the young man to the holiday camp business. Fred was, quite naturally, having thoughts about succession. He maintains that he even went as far as to make it a condition of his approval of the marriage, but that Peter soon sought a release from any such understanding so he could take up an offer from Hovis McDougall to manage a factory they had built following their acquisition of 50% of the Hopper family's baking business.

Once again, Peter Hopper takes issue with his late father-in-law's recollections on the above subject. Peter Hopper now regards the suggestion of such a condition of the marriage as preposterous and more akin to what might have happened in Imperial India or amongst royalty during the late Middle Ages in this country.

Within two years Hovis McDougalls had been taken over by Rank and Peter approached his father-in-law with a view to obtaining a position in Pontin's in 1964. According to Peter, this was the first time there had ever been any discussions on his joining Fred Pontin's rapidly expanding empire. The new recruit soon became very much involved with Pontinental. Peter had left the family business, not because of the takeover, but for reasons connected with his father's advancing years and the need for his parent to realise his investment in the bakery business in order to support himself in retirement. Peter had no faith in the long term future of the bakery business in general and had no ambitions to succeed his father.

Pat and Peter Hopper have been happily married for over forty years and have seven grandchildren. They are now very well established on their farm at Cranbrook. At one time they had a total of almost 180 acres of land and a flourishing farm shop, all bursting with economic activity. They were fattening chickens, pigs and bullocks as well as producing lambs.

They had thousands of fruit trees, as befits the Garden of England and Sir Fred knew full well that Pat had never been happier. She has always worked as hard as her father ever did and enjoys every minute of it. However, the scale of the Hopper activities has now changed but Sir Fred remained very proud of her achievements.

Peter and Pat Hopper have now reduced their farm to 70 acres, mostly grassland with some wooded copses. The grass is let out to a sheep farmer but they retain half a dozen cattle. They still keep busy and enjoy their beautiful surroundings.

The Hoppers' four children, all boys, were educated in the Canterbury area and have been well looked after by a trust Sir Fred created many years ago. He understood that the aggregate capital value exceeded £1.5 million. The word PINK was how he remembered their names: Paul, Ian, Neale and Kevin. Two of them were involved with the farm and the shop, one as catering manager and the other in all manner of enterprises.

When in his nineties, Sir Fred reflected on what a pity it was that they could not be persuaded to enter his business as, according to him, they received no encouragement from their parents, especially their father, who wouldn't even let them work at the holiday camps during their summer holidays. Their grandfather felt that by offering them such an opportunity they might conceivably savour the atmosphere of the sites, become interested in the business, and possibly choose a career with the company. However, he maintained that he was not successful with his little ploy.

The above was Sir Fred's personal recollection which is again hotly disputed by Peter Hopper who points out that when Pontin's was taken over by Coral in 1978 his four sons were aged between nine and seventeen. Paul, the eldest was just entering his second year in the sixth form at St Edmund's School, Canterbury and he eventually went on to university and obtained his degree. Ian was just about to sit his "O" levels and Neale and Kevin were aged only eleven and nine respectively. This was hardly a new generation of the Pontin family waiting in the wings!

The four Hopper sons knew the holiday clubs in Majorca very well as they spent some of their holidays there and on occasions joined their father when he was visiting other sites in his business capacity, as joint managing director of Pontinental with Fred Pontin. Ian Hopper actually worked at Cala Mesquida during the school holidays of 1977 and stayed on for a month after his mother and brothers returned home. Peter Hopper recalls that Domingo Ordinas, manager of Tropicana Holiday Club had agreed to find Ian a job during the summer of 1978 but by that time Sir Fred had disposed of Pontin's to Coral.

Peter Hopper, quite justifiably, questions how Sir Fred could possibly complain about the children not being encouraged to enter the Pontin's business by their parents, especially when they were not at an age when they were able to do so. Moreover, it has to be said that Sir Fred had lost control of Pontin's before they were even in a position to consider the question of such careers in the industry.

It now seems clear that Sir Fred's memory in his later years had been failing him on subjects which are deeply important to certain members of his family who have been quite distressed by what they feel have been gross distortions of the truth about their attitude to Sir Fred's business empire. The entire Hopper family have every reason to be proud of his achievements and have profited by his generosity but, quite understandably, wish to set the record straight from their own point of view regarding such delicate matters which affect them.

Sister Elsie and husband Bob enjoyed a well-earned retirement at their lovely home in Devon, until Elsie died in 1995. Brother Len and his wife Hilda are also retired and living nearby. They spend most of their time gardening and playing bowls, rather successfully in both activities.

Stan Butt, formerly the manager of a butcher's shop in Bristol, who once sold his employer's wares to the labour camp Fred Pontin ran at Bedminster, became a major supplier of meat and related products to all of Pontin's units in the West of England. He could be said to have enjoyed the material benefits derived from a large turnover.

Sir Fred was instrumental in encouraging Stan Butt in what must have been one of the earliest management buy-outs, when Stan was uncertain as to whether or not he should buy the business from its owner. The asking price was £15,000, but Fred Pontin recommended that he should bid £10,000, payable over a period of three years from profits. He also told Stan to inform his boss that if these terms were not agreed, Fred Pontin's business would be lost to the firm. Stan did the deal on this basis – and never looked back.

Many other people have benefited from Fred Pontin's business enterprises: lawyers, accountants, breweries, wine and spirit merchants and other suppliers, and, of course, H. M. Collector of Taxes.

Throughout his long life Sir Fred claimed to have represented himself as just an ordinary man who had never sought to lose the common touch. This had been despite a long standing exposure to a way of life which had brought him into contact with some of the leading figures in many strata of British society.

Thumbs Up! could well have been a title for this book which would perhaps have been particularly appropriate, bearing in mind the television advertisement which showed Fred Pontin doing just this when extolling the virtues of "booking early" for his holiday camps back in the 1970's.

He arrived at the studios in late afternoon, not long before the director intended calling a halt to the day's proceedings in which they were preparing the final version of Pontin's latest television campaign. Fred had a look at what had been produced and decided that his own presence in the short advertising clip would be a positive improvement. Leslie Crowther was at the studio, and, being a fellow Barker in the Variety Club, he readily responded to Fred's request that he should make some form of introduction to the larger-than-life proprietor's appearance in the advertisement.

Fred Pontin recalled that the director did not take too kindly to his spontaneous intervention. However, as Fred was the boss the director had little say in the matter. What had not been decided, however, was what Fred ought to be doing on film.

Mike Austin had a ready answer: "For heaven's sake, just look into the camera, smile and say 'Book Early'. What could be more simple?"

It would have been easy for a professional, but it took quite a few takes before everyone was satisfied. Sometimes Fred got the smile right, but had his thumb coming up too late. Other times there was a rapid thumb movement but only a sickly smile.

All was well in the end. Those few seconds on the Pontin's TV advertisement brought the company more publicity and attention – not to mention increased bookings – than anything else, which might have cost hundreds of thousands of pounds. Corny maybe – but it worked. "That's all that counts when it comes to marketing a good product!" triumphed Fred Pontin, showman to the masses.

Fred Pontin was a self-publicist through and through, long before the days of Richard Branson's personal efforts on behalf of the Virgin group of companies.

As far as promoting Pontin's was concerned Fred felt that he was more capable and successful at doing so than anyone else But, by doing so did he think he was addressing his existing clientele? Or was he intent upon attracting new customers? It is difficult to decide but he would have been more than a little apprehensive if it had ever been suggested to him that he should drum up more business by attempting to circumnavigate the globe in a hot air balloon.

However, his regular guests certainly identified with the larger-than-life type of character of Fred Pontin.

He was, after all, to be seen mixing with them on a regular basis. He tended to give the impression of treating everyone as a personal friend. This went down extremely well but were the TV advertisements successful in attracting new business? The answer must be yes because the Pontin's empire continued to grow throughout the period when TV advertising was a new medium for the marketing men.

There is no particular moral to Fred Pontin's life story, even though Lewis Carroll wrote in *Alice in Wonderland*: "Everything's got a moral if you can only find it". Sir Fred had long confessed to having no religious beliefs, so if there is any Guiding Light it can perhaps be attributed only to a sense of being aware of and, on occasions, caring for the feelings, sensibilities and unfortunate circumstances of others. Hence Sir Fred's strong inclination towards support for charitable causes.

Over the years he had established probably an over-exaggerated reputation for helping any member of his staff or any special friend if he considered his assistance would be necessary, if it was deserved and hopefully would be appreciated.

This point is made as many odd stories had somehow found their way back to him under this particular heading and he would have to be considered as some sort of saint for them all to have been true.

It is correct that he had always had what could be described as an obsessional hatred of illness in any form, and he felt that any generosity he may have shown was probably linked to a need to purge the obsession by trying to assist in removing its cause.

Fred Pontin remembered helping out Walter Rowley, for example, when Walter's first wife became seriously ill in Majorca. The local medical facilities seemed incapable of coping with what proved to be a haemorrhage of the brain so Fred flew out to arrange for her immediate repatriation to England for treatment at the London Hospital, where he had excellent connections.

She survived no less than three serious operations and lived for a further six years, which gave everyone a great deal of satisfaction. Walter died in 2001.

Walter's wife was a very special person to Fred Pontin, but there have been other instances when he had been happy to be of assistance, where it was thought necessary to short-circuit the National Health Service to set certain minds at rest.

A business can only be successful if the management and staff are not distracted by extraneous circumstances and illness of a loved one can certainly come under this heading.

Tim Moorcroft, a member of Pontin's managerial team, became ill with cancer at a crucial time in his career. Being a director on the main board it was entirely justified that he should receive the best possible attention, but Sir Fred liked to think that, given similar circumstances, other valued members of the staff would have received and were sometimes afforded the same consideration.

There was an occasion when Fred Pontin appreciated at first hand what care from others in moments of distress can mean. This was when he was involved in a serious motor car accident late at night in 1957.

The car he was driving was in collision with a trolley bus stanchion in Billet Road, Walthamstow. It happened to be Ann Miller's new car, a Ford Consul which Fred had picked up that particular day, his Bentley being in for a service.

It would appear that Fred had fallen asleep at the wheel of the vehicle and the crash caused him to lose consciousness. It was very fortunate that the sound of the impact attracted the attention of a young mother who was attending to the needs of her baby. She had the presence of mind to call an ambulance and other emergency services.

There were no compulsory seat belts in those days and Fred Pontin suffered fractures to his sternum and every rib in his body, in addition to a punctured lung, which caused internal bleeding. It took two hours to release him from the wrecked car and get him to the casualty unit at Whipp's Cross Hospital. He transferred to the London Hospital early on the following day.

Fred learned much later that the disturbed journey by ambulance, over so many uneven cobblestones to Whipp's Cross probably saved his life – he coughed up the blood, which was dispersed rather than being retained in such a vulnerable organ of his body.

Sir Fred recalled that he must have looked as if he was on his way out. When he arrived at the casualty department he was asked for details of his religion. As he had never had any religious belief he felt that he may well have replied "atheist", but, in recalling this incident he maintained that "There must have been some form of guardian angel watching over me, despite my refusal to acknowledge the existence of a Supreme Being"

That young mother who had demonstrated such commendable alertness, but whom Sir Fred could recall only as Mrs Smith, undoubtedly saved his life. It was with a great deal of pleasure that for many years after he was able to show his appreciation by arranging for her and her family to have their choice of regular annual holidays as well as many successive packed Christmas hampers.

An incident such as this demonstrates just how significant a part luck and good fortune had played in his life, so it is little wonder that he was affected by the misfortune of others.

Fred Pontin needed an extended period of convalescence after the accident, during which time Dickie Doyle took over as acting chairman.

In Fred's absence, one of Dickie's tasks was to present the annual report to shareholders. Fred Pontin had created a tradition that this was done on 24 October annually, being the anniversary of his birth in 1906 and in 1957 Dickie Doyle was able to confirm the company's continued expansion by announcing the acquisition of a freehold holiday camp at Pakefield, near Lowestoft in Suffolk. This camp had been previously owned by Leslie Dean and his partner George Harrison and became the tenth camp in the growing Pontin empire.

24 October 1957 was also a date which proved to be a watershed in the life of David Gwyn. He lived near Lowestoft and in the following Spring he responded to an advertisement in the local press. Pontin's required a camp secretary and David wrote what he considered to be one of the finest letters he had ever written in his formative years by way of a formal application for the job. To his ever-lasting consternation he never received a reply but he persisted in his quest to join Pontin's and in 1963, following a personal approach to Ed Miller, the manager at Pakefield and a former Butlin's employee, he was offered a position at Bracklesham Bay where considerable operational difficulties were being experienced. David admits that it was quite a baptism into the Pontin organisation but his experiences there stood him in good stead for what was to come in future years.

The rest of his career is now history; David not only became a very successful manager at Pakefield as well as at other centres but he also made a considerable reputation for himself in promoting Big Band events at Pakefield, details of which appear elsewhere in this story of Sir Fred Pontin and his holiday camps.

David recalls that he often recounted to Sir Fred, whom he invariably addresses as the guv'nor, that it took all of five years for Sir Fred to enjoy the luxury of David Gwyn working for him. Sir Fred's response has never been made clear but David's operational performance has always spoken for itself, and not only under Fred Pontin.

The future owners also had cause to recognise David Gwyn's successful record up to the time of his retirement in 1997.

Fred changed literally thousands of peoples lives in one way or another but many of his long serving managers will readily confirm how they caught the "Pontin disease" and devoted virtually the whole of their working lives in the service of the Pontin holiday camp business, both at home and abroad.

Sir Fred justified his attitude to religion, to a certain extent, in the knowledge that most wars are born out of the intolerance of other people's religious beliefs.

He recognised that much has been said and written about the existence of a Supreme Being. Cardinal Newman ventured the opinion that there were only two supreme and luminously self-evident beings: "Myself and my Creator". Fred Pontin would not have argued too much with that when the dominant influence in his life had been his own personality and to which should surely be added, hubris, his nemesis being the sale of the company to Coral. However, being without an acknowledged faith has been a source of distress to some of the people who have figured prominently in his life.

Sir Fred felt that despite the lack of success experienced in some of his later projects he had achieved just about everything he really wanted with the main business interest in his life. There have been disappointments from time to time but these have been almost exclusively associated with the deeds of others, especially where he felt that his personal trust had been betrayed.

No one can ever take away the fact that Sir Fred Pontin's family company started out from very modest beginnings but when the business changed hands for the very first time in 1978 the purchase price was some £57 million.

There have been many commercial achievements to emulate this success but given the post war years of hardship and rationing, followed by periods of considerable strain as far as the nation's finances were concerned one particular family business grew and grew.

Sir Fred Pontin created this rather special phenomenon and its continued existence for what will surely be well into the twenty-first century is a remarkable memorial now that his long life has come to an end.

Many people have set out in ways very similar to Fred Pontin's, but the order of life is such that not all can succeed. It is inevitable that failure should be experienced by some in order that success can be achieved by others. Sir Fred was a great believer in the fact that if doors open it is usually for a purpose. You can decide either to go through . . .

or you turn and walk away. He never hesitated in passing into whatever happened to lie within. He was seldom disappointed. If he was, another door usually appeared before too long and he soon learned that it did not pay to look back. That would be a negative reaction.

Sir Fred had always sought to benefit from a previous experience and then press on to the next opportunity. He strongly recommended this philosophy to anyone really prepared to grab what life has to offer.

Sir Fred had enjoyed good and robust health for most of his entire life, but he was certainly hit for six some years ago when he discovered that he had cancer. He thought he knew all about hospitals after his car accident, but this was a totally different experience. He could not be certain whether he would survive, and if he did, what would be the quality of the remainder of his life.

Cancer of the bowel was diagnosed after he had been experiencing severe abdominal pains. The operation involved the removal of large areas of the bowel and a colostomy, which was undertaken in a highly skilled manner.

He had always hated any thought of illness, whether in himself or in others. Sir Fred did not react in the most positive of manners when he was released from the London Clinic. Part of his convalescence was spent with Elsie and Bob at their home in Stoke Gabriel, where he was by no means an ideal patient, feeling very wretched and miserable at the thought of the indignity of it all.

Sir Fred's late sister did all she could to inspire him to look on the bright side. She reminded him that he could have been looking out at a brick wall in the back streets of London rather than at her very attractive millpond and wildlife.

Many people will be aware of what is involved as a result of a colostomy and Elsie helped Sir Fred to deal with his psychological hang-up. She encouraged him to accept the condition he was in. She further reminded her brother that other public figures had gone through the same operation, yet still carried on once the uncomfortable routine had been accepted. Elsie helped Sir Fred adapt to a more disciplined way of life and, providing he was careful about when and what he ate and drank, he was able to cope with the inevitable limitations in a tolerable manner.

Unfortunately, Sir Fred's condition had required further surgery but he was thankful that his medical consultants had responded in truly magnificent fashion to the extent that although his later years were not comfortable they had at least been there! It was George Burns who said on a TV chat show "I'm not only pleased to be here, I'm glad to be anywhere at my age!". How true.

On the above subject, this account of Sir Fred's life would not be complete without a few words about Joe Mountrose and his charming wife Catherine. Doctor Joseph Mountrose had been Fred Pontin's personal physician and valued friend for some thirty years, over the course of which they maintained contact on virtually a daily basis. Not always for reasons connected with his health either.

Since Sir Fred had the operation for cancer, Joe's extremely competent ministrations from his Harley Street premises, in hospitals, clinics and at home had been more valuable than Fred Pontin could ever express. He considered that he had been very fortunate to have him, not only as a loyal friend, but also as an eminent practitioner.

Until Sir Fred was in his late eighties they still enjoyed very regular meals together. Joe and Catherine were excellent company over the years and it gave Sir Fred much comfort and satisfaction to know that he had been in such good hands. Although there is a long history of longevity in Sir Fred's family, there comes a time when everyone's life must come to a close. Joe did, however, play a considerable part in ensuring that Sir Fred lived well into nineties and was still going strong until very near the end.

Joe Mountrose died in August 1997 but Sir Fred remained in regular contact with Catherine.

Sir Fred's duties as Founder President of Pontin's were not onerous by any means. The position had provided him with an excuse to visit his former sites, not just as a visitor for nostalgic reasons – though these did play a part – but also to let everyone know that he was still around and keen to take an interest in what is going on.

Who knows? perhaps the children really were interested in catching sight of the man who started it all. Until recent years, when Pontin's halted their generous support to the British Red Cross Society, Sir Fred made a point of attending various functions at the invitation of the board, such as the Red Cross holiday weeks, which events had always given him great satisfaction.

He liked to feel that his disappointments were then behind him. It was comforting to know that he could really enjoy such occasions without the need to count the light bulbs and complain about the size of the measures of whisky dispensed by the bar men – unless they were too small in his particular case!

During site visits, especially when Fred Pontin was really in top form, his attention to detail was said to be legendary, although there are some managers who doubted this, especially those who had worked previously for Billy Butlin.

Fred was determined that every member of the staff, from the manager downwards, was fully aware that a personal inspection by the Chairman and Managing Director could take place at any hour of the day or night. Managers have described these unannounced visits as energetic which can perhaps be taken as a euphemism for a tirade of criticism and personal abuse for what the guv'nor would describes as crass, bloody inefficiency or more colourful phraseology, depending upon the state of his disposition at the time. Whatever was felt by those concerned, whether staff or guests, his presence was undoubtedly commanding and vigorous and it would be some while before the camps returned to normality after he had left for the next centre.

One former employee who completed two tours of distinguished service for Pontin's described the Chairman as a bully driven by the power of achievement. His management style would not, in her view, be tolerated nowadays. There would be far too many industrial tribunals and too many lawyers to pay.

She recalls the entire catering staff being sacked on the spot when Fred Pontin decided that what he found on one of his visits was not to his liking. When something like this happened it was the local management who had to pick up the pieces and draft in replacement catering staff from other camps in order to keep the campers from starving.

Sacking was the ultimate sanction for Fred Pontin. He had power and he used it. On one occasion at a Pontin's centre he saw a shabbily dressed man hanging around in the vicinity of one of the rose beds. Half an hour later the Chairman saw the same man doing nothing but "poking around the plants" as Fred put it so elegantly when he challenged the person concerned.

"You are not paid to be doing nothing but looking at flowers. Either get yourself a spade and do some worthwhile digging or collect your cards" he shouted at the startled individual.

When the man just stood there, quite speechless, Fred's voice boomed loudly "Right, you're sacked. Get out of here now".

"But I'm a guest" protested the terrified fellow. "All I am trying to do is to learn about species of roses so that I can put up a good show in the gardening quiz this afternoon."

Fred Pontin made up for it later by buying the guest and his family a drink. He laughed it off and as far as he was concerned he was just adding to his reputation for being a bit of a character. He felt that his guests expected him to act as the successful and unconventional showman with a warm and engaging personality. He did not let them down and they loved it.

These stories are by no means apocryphal and it is difficult to understand just how many of Fred Pontin's long suffering staff not only remained loyal but actually idolised him. They still talk about him today in glowing terms even though they had felt the rough side of his tongue on many occasions, whether justified or not.

Fred Pontin became known for his notebook which he kept in an inside pocket of his jacket. He could often be seen reaching for this book and appearing to scribble furiously after first looking over his shoulder and observing what might be going on in another part of any room he happened to be in the time.

Members of the management and staff never knew if it was their name and alleged misdeed which was being entered. Fred Pontin certainly gave no indication at the time so after he had left they were left waiting for what could well be a written rocket in the form of a memorandum from Head Office.

If nothing arrived they probably thought that they had got away with it, whatever it might have been. If anything arrived, at least they had a degree of warning.

However, the ones who had got wise to the guv'nor's little trick came to ignore the procedure. It was accepted that it was just Fred's way of keeping people up to scratch.

Sir Fred was almost consumed by the need for cost saving and some of his memoranda on the subject have survived today. Indeed, one or two general managers have filed them away for posterity, perhaps just waiting for someone to write a book about their legendary guv'nor.

Bearing in mind that Fred Pontin was running a public company, with the shares quoted on the London Stock Exchange from the time he first opened for business at Brean Sands in 1946 the communications received by the camp managers on a regular basis would be, to say the least, unlikely to have left the desk of one of today's captains of industry.

A selection of memoranda which deal with the guv'nor's hands-on style of management and a rather unique attention to detail now follow:

From: Sir Fred Pontin
To: All camp managers
Date: 26 October 1977
Subject: Christmas staff

You will shortly be recruiting staff for employment during the Christmas period. I am aware that already a number of past employees want to return for this period.

However, I realise it will be necessary to recruit additional staff. In this respect I insist that before engagement is made that references must be taken up and they must be satisfactory. In my opinion every crook in the country will be looking for such a good holiday job with plenty of opportunity for pilfering etc.

Please confirm to me that my instructions are understood.

Not only was Sir Fred's opinion of the potential calibre of his temporary staff somewhat jaundiced but he was also keen to make his camp managers aware that he expected them to make every effort to cut costs and that he would not tolerate slackness.

From: Sir Fred Pontin
To: All camp managers
Date: 17 June 1976

I recently paid several visits to the camps and I am dismayed in many instances of the lack of management, namely managers, assistant managers, catering and entertainment managers etc.

I wish the following duties to be undertaken by yourself and your various assistants:

You or your assistants should be in the kitchen each and every meal to see the standard and quality of food being served and presented, also the cleanliness and tidiness of waiters and waitresses. The hot plate covers should be switched on when needed and this should be supervised. Supervision shall be given to the staff room, dining room and at all meals.

The Staff menu that has been sent to you by Mrs Brown should be served and served without exception. Ensure that the best meal for the staff is served in the evening. It is necessary for the live-in staff to have a substantial meal to carry them through to the next morning. The mid-day meal should be a light meal as this will keep the cost down as this meal is taken by numerous part-time and live-out staff.

On analysing the wages which you know by law have been substantially increased I find these in many cases are very excessive.

I wish the kitchen in future to operate on a one shift only over a period of six days with no overtime. I wish to know the names and duties of every one of your staff in the kitchens, and also their days off.

I wish to know also the hours that they have to work in order that myself, other directors or crime prevention officers can ensure they are working the correct hours. They are to be on duty for the number of hours they are getting paid for and there must be enough work for such kitchen staff on duty to carry out.

In one instance at 9.30 a.m. in the morning I saw the evening's pudding being prepared – sponge cakes being taken out of wrappers,
placed on a tray and some hot custard being poured on. At
the same time the bacon was being trayed for the following
morning's shift. There were at least a dozen so-called chefs doing
this. How bloody stupid can we be? I wish you also to control your
food costs.

In one instance I found that the staff were permitted to help themselves to as much bacon and braised steaks as they wanted – three
portions were seen being taken. There was no supervision and
they were allowed to help themselves. This must not happen.
Supervision must be present for all staff meals, as I have said
either by yourself or one of your assistants.

I also want you to concentrate on petrol, fuel and transport costs.
These have risen substantially and the greatest economy must be
practised.

Lastly, no overtime, other than essential overtime for maintenance work, i.e. on the sixth or seventh day as arranged.

Please confirm to me that everything is understood as I intend that
the management of my establishments conform to my wishes.

These memoranda have been reproduced, word for word and in the
form in which they were first issued from the office of Sir Fred Pontin
who controlled over twenty holiday camps (note his use of the word
"camps" well into the late seventies) in the United Kingdom and
many abroad through Pontinental. You may wish to contrast this
level of detailed supervision with what might be expected from
modern day managing directors who are more accustomed to poring
over computer printouts of monthly management figures with
perhaps no real understanding of what is happening in the front line.

At the time these missives were dispatched Sir Fred's shareholders
were enjoying the fact that the company in which they had invested
was earning pre-tax profits of some £6,600,000 on an annual turnover of £39,000,000. The present owners of Pontin's would certainly
welcome such magnificent returns on the increasingly large amounts
of capital that have been employed in the business.

The 1970s shareholders would not be too interested in how Sir
Fred achieved such high profitability as long as they were receiving
their dividends but if they had been privy to the contents of such
memoranda from the managing director's office they could well
have been impressed by just how effective good, old-fashioned
management could be, particularly as the mid-seventies were far
from trouble-free in terms of industrial relations.

Sir Fred also kept an eye on any initiatives from his managerial team and the following memorandum, written to his brother Len Pontin, again demonstrates his passion for cost-effectiveness with at least two children's items being described as "nothing cheaper".

From: Sir Fred Pontin
To: Len Pontin
Date: 9 November 1976
Subject: Trampolines

Recently I sent you a photocopy of a memo from Vic Davis to Miss Miller regarding trampolines. We must give consideration to these recommendations and I think that we should have new wire 6' high fences erected at all sites that require them. The wire should be barbed wire, extending outwards, in order to prevent any drunken hooligans causing wilful damage to the trampoline beds. I think you should get a price from our suppliers giving them a sketch of the areas that require such treatment.
Certain camps require additional trampolines. I suggest the large camps, Camber, Southport, Prestatyn, Tower Beach, Blackpool and Brean Sands. In my opinion there is nothing cheaper than trampolines for entertaining children. It tires them out and sends them to bed early. Incidentally in future children's play areas are to be open from 9.30 in the morning until 9.30 at night, with a lunch break of 12.00–1.00. There must always be a Bluecoat or part-time pensioner in attendance throughout this 12 hour session.
Further, a lot of our Noddy trains are on their last legs and either require a new engine or repainting. In fact I know that at Tower Beach we advertised Noddy trains but did not have any, this causing a lot of aggravation and reference to the Trades Descriptions Act.
These trains must operate between 9.30 a.m. and 6.30 p.m., with a lunch break of 12.00–1.00. Nothing is cheaper than Noddy trains. I would like all camp managers to inform you if they require any attention to their Noddy trains.
Please keep me advised on progress.

It will be seen from the above that Sir Fred's guests were not always happy families enjoying a non-violent summer break. Hooliganism was a problem but Sir Fred, being the businessman he was, appreciated that a large proportion of Pontin's profits was represented by receipts from the bars. The staff became experienced at dealing with trouble as and when it arose but it will be seen that the Chairman was also intent upon damage limitation even if barbed wire could have been thought to be more reminiscent of prison camps than holiday camps.

Laundry bills at Pontin's camps would have been running at a considerable level if all camps used outside contractors. It appears that there was an internal laundry service but this was not without its problems. Reading the following memoranda it is not difficult to picture the chalet girls in *Hi-De-Hi* and what action Joe Maplin might have taken in similar circumstances. Joe Maplin never made an appearance in this popular TV show but his presence was always felt in one form or another.

One wonders why the writers of *Hi-De-Hi* decided on this approach to the fictional owner of Maplin's. It must have been tempting to create a character based upon either Billy Butlin or Fred Pontin (please take note of the last two letters of all three of these names which give some clue as to the writers' source of inspiration) but perhaps it was felt that these two larger than life pillars of the holiday camp industry were too well known; too much loved as well as respected by their loyal campers. In such circumstances any attempt at caricature would have been found wanting and even perhaps less believable than the real thing.

From:	Mrs E. M. Brown
To:	G. Parr, Brean Sands
Date:	11 January 1977
Copy:	Sir Fred Pontin

I must bring to your attention the diabolical state of the outside sheets of your bundles, when they arrived at the laundry this week. How we are ever going to get them clean, I do not know. This would answer the reason we have found so many of your sheets falling into holes, when obviously the laundry in the past have had to use bleach to get out the staines (sic).

We must get the sack system into operation before the forth-coming season. If you have on your staff a machinist, please contact Dave Wardell direct for some sacking, so that she may get on making them immediately. I am enclosing a sample pack.

May I also mention at this time the number of small tears that are in your sheets. This is obviously from the springs on your beds which need immediate attention. Would you please make sure that one of your maintenance staff make a complete overhaul, before the commencement of the season.

From: Sir Fred Pontin
To: Mr G. Parr
Date: 18 January 1977
Subject: Laundry – Brean Sands

I refer to my sister's memo dated 11 January 1977. I would say
that I do not blame you entirely for the criticism of your laundry.
This obviously must have been going on for quite some time in
spite of repeated warnings that dirty linen was not to be thrown
down outside the chalets to get wet and muddy.
Next season there will be numbered bags available and in no way
will I allow sheets to arrive at the laundry in such a state as
described by Mrs Brown. I know that you have considerable
duties to carry out and this is undoubtedly an important one. I
would add for some degree of comfort that Brean Sands is not
the only culprit as far as muddy and torn sheets are concerned. I
hope to effect a remedy for the 1977 season.

Here was Sir Fred Pontin trying to soften the blow following the
admonition inflicted by his sister who was, after all, a director of
the company. She had sent a copy of her memorandum to her
brother, no doubt expecting total support, but this episode is indic-
ative of how the company was run on family lines. She got her
support but the Chairman and Managing Director felt the need to
reassure Graham Parr that he was not being unduly singled out
for criticism.
    Graham progressed well in Pontin's and was general manager
at some of the group's largest and most profitable camps. He
subsequently became part of Trevor Hemmings's management
buy out team and made a considerable fortune on his shares
when Scottish and Newcastle Breweries bought Pontin's in the
1980s.
    In May 1997 Graham was appointed Chief Executive of Arena
Leisure Plc, a company controlled by Trevor Hemmings and
whose shares are quoted on the London Stock Exchange and
as mentioned elsewhere in this book, with a capitilisation in
February 2000 well in excess of £500 million. Not bad for someone who had problems with his dirty linen when he was a much
younger man.
    It will be seen from the next selection from company communi-
cations that surplus and unsaleable stock could be a problem but it
will be noted that Sir Fred had no time for euphemisms.

From: Sir Fred Pontin
To: All camp managers
Date: 25 July 1977
Subject: Gift Shop Stock

I understand that Vincent has sent you recently some unsaleable rubbish for your gift shops. It has been suggested that these should be made up into a pack similar to that produced in the past by Donkey Roberts and sold at a knock-down price. Please give me your views on this.

I must emphasise that all this type of rubbish and unsaleable stock must be included in your raffles, giving if necessary 20 different items for prizes which makes the raffle more interesting and gets rid of the stock at cost price.

From: H. F. Dowell Area Supervisor
To: Sir Fred Pontin
Date: 28 July 1977
Subject: Gift Shop Stock

I would suggest that if the bags of sweets given out free to children each Friday (on Catering Camps) were withdrawn, then we could give out in their place packs of "Books of Knowledge" (one of the lines that all sites have heavy stocks of). This could be done when present stocks of bags of sweets are exhausted, and any outstanding orders from Nestles could be cancelled.

On Self-Catering Camps, if the 25p vouchers given out for various competitions were withdrawn then the Books of Knowledge packs could be substituted for the vouchers, this will help to clear our stocks.

I think that we could get complaints if we included in the raffle the "rubbish stock" you mention, but after the usual raffle prizes have been given, an announcement could be made stating something like "Hold on to your raffle tickets as we are now having a quickie raffle". We could then raffle about 20 of the stock you mentioned i.e. scent, Shari gift sets, hand cream etc. The money for these would of course be deducted from the main raffle to cover the cost of these prizes.

In an effort to clear stocks I held a "Mini Market" at Pakefield last Friday. There are several local markets in this area, therefore why not one on the Camp?

From 2.00 p.m. until 4.00 p.m. we took £157.00. Apart from the goods we are selling at cost any other "slow selling" items could be included at a reduced price, a record of these reduced goods to be kept so that shop could be credited with any reductions in retail price.

I am enclosing photographs of the Mini Market held here last Friday. I shall be doing another one this week, also one at Hemsby and Seacroft. If any other sites adopt this method of selling I would suggest they do not advertise it until lunch time of the day of the market. Otherwise, if customers know of this beforehand they may keep out of the shop until market day hoping for a bargain and our normal shop sales could suffer.

From:	Sir Fred Pontin
To:	Mr H. F. Dowell, Pakefield
Date:	21 August 1977
Subject:	Gift Shop Stock

Thank you for your memorandum dated 28 July 1977.

I was delighted to read its contents and I do congratulate you on your initiative. Naturally I approve that you continue these mini-markets in your area. I am hoping that this idea of mini-markets would be feasible in other camps and would help to get rid of surplus stock, especially the rubbish.

I am sending a copy of your memo to all my managers in order that they may be able to follow your example.

After Coral acquired Pontin's in early 1978 Sir Fred remained managing director and his somewhat individual brand of management appeared to continue unabated. In this final example of a memorandum from the guv'nor he demonstrates his solicitude for the welfare and comfort of his campers.

From:	Sir Fred Pontin
To:	All self-catering camp managers
Date:	10 May 1978
Subject:	Single persons

As some of our early and late bookings in self-catering camps are very poor I now give you permission to book three single persons maximum in a chalet for four or five persons occupancy in order that we may improve our bookings.

Try as far as possible to maintain equal numbers of men and women in order that they both give each other satisfaction during their holidays.

In the boom years Fred Pontin drove thousands of miles each month in order to keep in touch with what was happening in his empire. He was always instantly recognisable and the campers invariably greeted him with cheers and applause. They looked upon him as a man larger-than-life. In his own way he was and he enjoyed every minute of the adulation.

It's just as well that the contents of the above memoranda were not leaked to the unsuspecting guests; otherwise perhaps Fred Pontin's reception at the various camps might have been just a little less rapturous

A former managing director of Pontin's was Stephen Haupt and although the chances were he was not seen and instantly recognised by the vast majority of the Pontin's guests "on patrol" or in the bar after a day's activities it is reassuring to know that he spent a good deal of his time at the various sites. He recognised that this was by far the best way of keeping in touch with not only his loyal staff but also his guests. It will be seen elsewhere in this chapter that this is how he was able to bring about a major transition in the Pontin's business and thus secure its prosperous entry into the twenty-first century.

Regardless of who runs the business nowadays Fred Pontin is still a household name and until he died he remained an easily recognisable personality. His former guests still talk of him in a touchingly fond and thoroughly approving manner whenever his name is mentioned.

People could identify with Fred Pontin and it is highly significant that the Pontin name survives, although the former owners have certainly toyed with the idea of creating a brand new image and consequently introducing a new name to the business.

When Stephen Haupt was persuaded to leave his job as operations director of Chef and Brewer, another part of the Scottish & Newcastle Breweries group and become managing director of Pontin's he was mindful of becoming associated with a brand name which could well have passed its sell-by date. He had experienced a similar situation when dealing with comparable problems at Berni Inns. He felt at the time that his previously successful career could be on the line at Pontin's. There had been years of neglect and he was aware of the low morale at all levels of the business. However, he overcame his misgivings after being finally persuaded by Trevor Hemmings and other members of the Scottish & Newcastle board.

He spent over five years in the top job at Pontin's when he became fully aware of the true worth of the brand name which was looked upon as being irreplaceable as long as the guests were enjoying what the company was giving them. Stephen Haupt's view was that a brand name which had endured over five decades could not be easily cast aside and at the start of the new millennium rather than showing any sings of diminution the brand name of Pontin's seems to be going from strength to strength.

Pontin's as a business is undoubtedly as unique today as it was in 1970, when Southport, one of the new generation of holiday camps, was constructed and introduced to the market. Subsequent owners have brought this site, and most of the others, up to date and have steered the fortunes of the company through the changing economic conditions, including periods of recession since the late seventies when Fred Pontin completed his fateful deal with Coral.

In the industry people were talking about the way earlier successive owners had neglected the Pontin's business and had not recognised the need to back a famous brand name with hard cash. The feeling amongst the staff was that too much cash had been taken out. This had never been the case in Fred Pontin's day. He had a programme of constant reinvestment and his personal decision to forego the full extent of his remuneration package added weight to his policy of ploughing back the profits whilst retaining the support of his shareholders.

1996 was Pontin's Golden Anniversary and also the year of their founder's ninetieth birthday; a unique combination which deserved a greater level of celebration than it received.

The Pontin name has been retained for the simple reason that it still sells, although perhaps not so well as in Sir Fred's day. It seems clear that the current management team has inherited Sir Fred's feeling for a business where, on the company's own admission, its essential product hadn't changed much over the years. Pontin's success had been due mainly to the unique holiday atmosphere which is created by staff and guests alike. The loyalty factor remained because the camps were still camps, although chalets are now termed as apartments. But even fervent supporters of Pontin's are not immune from the ageing process. What of the new generations?

It had at last been recognised that there was a need to take into account the changing needs of the guests and in 1999 Pontin's completed what was said to be a three year £55 million investment programme in the shape of new and refurbished buildings and facilities which were, in turn, linked to a new and improved style of operation. The fact that the original programme was for four years, the speeding up of the operation was seen as how successful the results had been which was in turn a reflection of the increased expectations of Pontin's guests at the start of the twenty-first century.

This money had been invested in each of the eight family holiday centres and was seen by the staff and guests alike as long overdue. Pontin's is an enormous business and it would not be totally uncharitable to reach the conclusion that if the investment had not been made the company may well have tottered on the brink of a solid fall-off in its loyal support.

Pontin's guests, and I was told that there were well over 700,000 annually in 1998, consumed three million eggs, 34 tons of bacon, some 68 miles of sausages, 600 tons of fish and chips and 15,000 gallons of fruit juice.

These statistics serve to illustrate the sheer size of the problem which confronted Stephen Haupt when he was appointed managing director of the company. Would the people who consume such a vast volume of food and drink wish to continue to spend their family holidays at Pontin's if something wasn't done about what the company calls "the estate"?

In the jargon of modern managers Stephen talked of 'hardware and software'. What he really meant was premises, facilities and accommodation on the one hand and the Pontin's product and staff services on the other.

He reasoned that expensive improvements in the hardware would be totally wasted if the guests were not provided with facilities and services in a manner which met the needs of a clientele which reflected changes in life styles.

On arrival at Pontin's Stephen Haupt's first impression had been one of horror. He had been warned about the serious of lack of investment through the chain of successive ownerships of the company; Coral, Bass, the management buy out and then Scottish & Newcastle. This deprivation of cash had caused the deterioration in standards of accommodation and facilities which in turn led to a high level of complaints from the guests.

He was also shocked to discover that the management culture was almost feudal, no doubt a throw-back to Sir Fred Pontin's family regime although he was also impressed by the fact that the company had so many long serving and loyal employees who had a long tradition of huge personal commitment to the company. A boost in their morale would not come amiss but Stephen recognised that this could not be achieved overnight.

He had much work to do and lost no time in getting started.

During 1995 Stephen Haupt and his Pontin's team spent a great deal of time, money and energy in identifying their target market. Children were put at the top of the list on the basis that if the children were happy the parents would also be happy.

Stephen Haupt toured various holiday resorts in the United States of America such as Disneyland in California and DisneyWorld in Florida. He studied the management techniques employed at Ritz Carlton and was very impressed.

The results of his travels made an enormous contribution when deciding upon the strategy and Stephen was encouraged by the fact that it was soon to be seen that the staff at Pontin's had drawn inspiration from the new methods then in daily use within their company. He succeeded in getting them involved and they responded magnificently.

After all, as far as they were concerned it was Stephen Haupt who had first led the way by demonstrating that he was also prepared to listen to what they and the Pontin's guests had to say regarding what was needed in the late 1990s. Products and services had to be brought in line with modern demands.

It was pleasing to hear that particular managing director of Pontin's expressing the view that their clientele '... deserved something better. They work hard and want to be looked after and entertained on their holiday with the children'.

Accommodation is always an important factor and it was decided that this needed to be comfortable, but not essentially luxurious. From this the company developed their three standards of accommodation; Club, Classic and Popular, of which the mid-range Classic is in the most demand.

But the top priority was deemed to be entertainment and within that brief the children's needs were considered to be paramount. The management at Pontin's were then maintaining that they had achieved the status of the United Kingdom's leading authority on children's holidays and they insisted that they never got complaints from the children.

"Value for money", Sir Fred Pontin's often repeated slogan was not forgotten by the research consultants and once the strategy had been agreed Stephen Haupt secured the Scottish & Newcastle group's financial support for his proposed investment programme.

As far as the parent company was concerned Stephen Haupt was the man chosen to revitalise Pontin's and it was essential that it was seen by the staff of Pontin's that he was given strong support.

Pontin's was very important to the group in terms of retail sales of alcoholic drinks but there was also a desperate need on the part of Scottish & Newcastle to be seen to be doing all it could to restore the company's profitability to acceptable levels if their errant subsidiary was to continue to be an important part of the group's leisure division.

Improvements were made not only to the guests' accommodation but also in terms of new and refurbished restaurants, ballrooms and nightclubs. Each family centre at Pontin's now boasts a "Queen Vic" themed pub as part of that particular improvement programme.

As the century drew to a close Pontin's guests could choose what they wanted from a selection of sites which had been carefully and expertly programmed to meet their particular needs.

Under Stephen Haupt the families had a choice from eight centres, described on a cover of a promotional brochure with words such as "awesome", "cool", "brilliant" and "wow". Yes, it was the children who were being targeted and six costume characters such as Captain Croc, MegaMix Mick, Florence the Ostrich, Zena the Zebra, Chuckles the Monkey and Safari Sam figured prominently in the inside pages.

The children were offered Actionpack for the 8–11 year olds and MegaMix for the 12–15 year olds. There was supervised abseiling, snorkelling, zip wires and off centre mountain biking for the adventurous; there were computer rooms for surfing the Internet, opportunities for quad biking, stunt kite flying and much more to excite even the most timorous of children who can be difficult to entertain.

Publicising these activities with modern marketing techniques was a far cry from Fred Pontin's much more modest leaflets of the early years when the emphasis was on packing them in and organising just about everything, for parents and children alike.

Although under Stephen Haupt's regime the children were receiving what must be considered as unprecedented priority entertaining the parents was by no means overlooked but fully organised events for the adults as in former days were virtually non-existent. There are no more knobbly knee contests, no more beauty queens and "glamorous grans" competitions. These activities no longer form part of the Bluecoats' repertoire although talent contests remain very popular.

Adults were left to choose for themselves what to do as all the necessary and popular facilities were readily available. The Queen Vic pubs have been mentioned and there were also bingo games, lunchtime and evening cabarets, Bluecoat spectaculars and the incredibly popular Karaoke. Some centres were making use of a significant proportion of their annual entertainments budget to book show business stars of the calibre of Freddie Starr or Rolf Harris to entertain their guests during a normal holiday week at the height of the summer months.

Pontin's were insisting that it was for the parents to decide what they wanted to do on their holidays and there was no longer any of what Sir Fred always described as 'alleged' compulsion to participate in group or individual activities. What the company was doing was to ensure that non-stop entertainment was readily available on an all-inclusive tariff, just like in Sir Fred's days.

However, in the late 1990's it was the new Pontin's product that was perceived as the major attraction and the promotional literature provided both regular and would-be guests with a dazzling array of mouth-watering and colourful information in abundance. Pontin's was printing and circulating no less than one and a half million brochures each year but the company had also sharpened up its selling techniques.

Pontin's then made a point of concentrating an increasing proportion of its marketing energies on hosting "educationals" for agents in order to have the "New Pontin's" (shades of Tony Blair's "New Labour") message broadcast in the High Streets. Journalists from the national and regional newspapers were encouraged to take their families and sample what the new Pontin's had to offer.

The resultant articles and features were not always flattering in connection with the overall ambience as far as adults were concerned but the children's activities were voted top every time. It is clear that the children really took to the magical atmosphere created by the six costume characters which figured so prominently in the Pontin's publicity material.

Instead of the run-of-the-mill fancy dress competitions of the past the children were then encouraged to dress up and take part in the Grand Parade around the centre with their favourite characters in the style of Disneyland which culminated in a spectacular event in the ballroom where the new style fancy dress competition for the children took place.

However, about ten per cent of the Pontin's sales turnover was then derived from what is termed as the "empty nester" market which is said to comprise parents whose children have left home. Four locations at Barton Hall, Devon, Riviera, Dorset, Sand Bay, Somerset and South Downs, Sussex were dedicated to catering specifically for adults.

Modern day attractions for the older generation included themed and special interest breaks which varied from jazz music entertainment, Christmas Crackers which were staged before the actual festive season approached, murder mystery weekends, bridge and bowling and there was not a child in sight.

This was highly organised targeting and provided a total contrast to what Sir Fred had in mind when he opened his first ever holiday camp at Brean Sands in 1946 when only the summer months were paramount as far as making money was concerned. There was no careful study of demographic profiles in those days and market segments was not a term in everyday usage. Fred Pontin was providing budget holidays for war-weary families and their popularity was the foundation of a thriving business which has, however, found it necessary to change with the times.

In the final months of the twentieth century Pontin's was perceived as a service oriented company which "invests in people" and had chosen its specific market sectors. There was total focus on the market and their chosen segments and a declared aim to provide quality which the management firmly believed could lead only to what they were seeking to achieve; high levels of sales and profitability.

However, any optimism created by the above remarks was tempered by a financial journalist's comment that "Pontin's is gradually being whittled down". This was written in *The Times* of Tuesday 2 December 1997 and followed the publication of the parent company's profits for the first half year which disclosed an overall increase of 15% following the acquisition of Courage which resulted in the chief executive of Scottish & Newcastle reporting that the brewing division's beer performance "is out of sight".

It should perhaps be explained that in dealing with audited profit performance as far as Pontin's was concerned it was much more revealing to review the interim figures as the Scottish & Newcastle annual reporting date is usually at the end of May or the beginning of April. Although Pontin's centres operate virtually on an all-the-year-round basis it is the summer months which produce the highest level of sales. On this basis the interim results for the period ending at the end of October in each year give a far better impression of how the Pontin's business is performing.

This point is best illustrated by revealing that the full year's operational results for the Pontin's business as reported in Scottish & Newcastle's annual report for 1998 (actual year end 3 May 1998) was a loss of £1.5 million following a four per cent decline in the volume of trading as compared with the 1997 full trading year.

The group's interim results were for the six months to the end of October 1997, a period in which even the group's Center Parcs business joined Pontin's in turning in a disappointing performance, due mainly to the strength of the pound and a consequential fall off in demand from Continental Europe.

Scottish & Newcastle were well aware of the worth of top brands as far as its beer products and pub outlets were concerned and had backed them heavily with cash. But Pontin's was surely a brand name which deserved the accolade of continued investment in order to offer their traditional customers the increase in standards which the business so clearly needed.

Although an investment programme of a minimum of £55 million, depending on the source of information, in respect of the period 1995–1998 did seem to be an appropriate and timely response to falling profits at Pontin's it is tempting to suggest that their senior management could perhaps have taken an even broader cue on how the industry was moving in other sectors when they were seen to be taking a look at the superb level of accommodation and facilities being offered by one their smaller but long serving competitors, Potter's at their award winning unit near Great Yarmouth.

"The Resort", as Potter's have named their much improved site is now a very popular venue for members of a particular generation who have come to expect higher standards and do not shrink from paying the premium over the Pontin's tariff which accompanies such a generous level of investment from the operator.

Potter's have shown great faith in what Brian Potter describes as their re-invented product as a result of their own market research initiatives and demographic profile studies. They have taken the necessary risk when employing their capital resources and it is to be hoped that they will continue to reap the benefit as it takes people of the calibre of the Potters' family, who have the longest history in the industry, stretching back to the 1920's, to set standards for a business which would otherwise be showing all too evident signs of decline.

It is also interesting to note that Bridie Reid, who spent many years recruiting "class acts" for Pontin's and now works as a full time entertainment consultant in partnership with Don Jones, has supplied Potter's with cabaret acts for their magnificent "Atlas" theatre building. But whatever the act the person who really organises the guests' enjoyment at Potter's is the entertainments manager, Mark Brewer, who was formerly a Pontin's Bluecoat. He certainly knows what the customers at Potter's enjoy and heads up a team of resident talent, over twenty strong, which is said to be the largest team amongst the smaller independent centres.

But Pontin's, having inspected various products offered by the opposition throughout the United Kingdom, were then taking the view that Potter's catered for a niche market which would not be appropriate for their size of business which was still attracting over 700,000 guests each year. This had the appearance of a wise decision as the Potter's product would be unlikely to attract young families and the owners have made no discernible attempt to do so.

Potter's still think in the old-fashioned term of bed nights of which they offer over 160,000 each year. With a 90% occupancy rate during 1998, since said to be more than upheld, all has been achieved without national advertising. It is not difficult to understand how the Potter's performance is the envy of all within the industry.

Contrast this undoubted success with Pontin's lower profit returns as already reported and it will be seen that sheer size is not necessarily profitable.

When issuing their interim report for the six months trading period to 1 November 1998 the Pontin's business did not rate a mention in the Scottish & Newcastle group's statement to shareholders under the names of Sir Alistair Grant, chairman and Brian Stewart, chief executive. Perhaps they were hoping to give some reassuring news in their next annual report.

Overall, the group's results for the first half of the 1998/99 financial year showed a 4.5% decline in first half pre-tax profits to £251.3 million, blamed on the poor summer weather and the uncertain economic climate combining to restrain consumer spending.

Scottish & Newcastle Breweries' chief executive, Brian Stewart was quoted in *The Times* as saying that the group was seeing returns of 17% on investment but he could not have been referring to Pontin's under this heading when he responded to a question by hinting that a sale of the Pontin's business was 'a possibility'.

'Oh no! Not again!' was undoubtedly the cry from the Pontin's staff and there would have been much sympathy for such a reaction following perhaps what could be thought of as a somewhat ill-considered remark coming so soon after what was said to be expenditure of £55 million on the Pontin's estate and trumpeted by the Pontin's management in a press release date-lined 19 October 1998. A 17% return on this figure would need to see Pontin's full year profits running at something like the £10 million level. Taking inflation into account even this level of profits would not compare favourably with what Sir Fred was achieving in the time leading up to the deal with Coral.

When Pontin's was put up for sale by the disgruntled parent company which had lost patience with a troublesome and unprofitable subsidiary it was not difficult to speculate that Trevor Hemmings would be willing to consider reacquiring the business in order to exploit the improved Pontin's estate and enhanced product. Trevor had and still has a very sure touch in the leisure industry and his enormous wealth and powerful asset position placed him firmly at the forefront of would-be "Pontineers" for the twenty first century.

This subsequently proved to be accurate forecasting in that Trevor Hemmings' leisure interests subsequently acquired one hundred per cent control of the Pontin's business undertaking and his team took over management on 15 September 2000. Yet another new approach to the task of making Pontin's provide an attractive return on capital employed was soon to be undertaken. Just how Colin Homer, Trevor Hemming's choice of managing director, has been addressing this crucial issue will be described later.

But getting back to the Stephen Haupt era what was the competition doing now that Pontin's had been seen to reinvent themselves?

Butlin's was still attracting the national headlines as a result of Rank, the parent company, being without a group chief executive at the end of 1998 following Andrew Teare's resignation and the investing institutions declaring their worries about the company's overall direction and poor trading results. With a £140 million "make over" refurbishment of accommodation and facilities at their "theme park" type centres and their redcoats being clad in trendy uniforms, created by celebrity designer Jeff Banks, Butlin's appeared to be seeking to recapture the family market as part of their image overhaul.

An article in the *Sunday Times* at the beginning of 1999 described Butlin's latest venture into American comic-book characters as a "last throw of the dice to woo back families that have been displaced in recent years by drunken stag parties". This is probably an exaggeration of the true facts but the introduction of Spiderman, the X-Men, Casper the friendly ghost and the popular British puppet, Otis the Aardvark appeared to be an expensive effort by way of retaliating against the success of characters which are exclusive to Pontin's such as Captain Croc, MegaMix Mick and Actionpack Jack.

Butlin's were no doubt paying expensive licence fees for staging shows by these established characters in what are described as "skyline pavilions" at three of their centres following an investment of £23 million.

There was even talk of the traditional redcoats being displaced by "reds" in the form of 200 young actors who would perform in musical shows. It is perhaps tempting to suggest that this transformation came about as a result of Butlin's managing director, Tony Marshall spending the August bank holiday weekend in 1998 in the role of a redcoat at Butlin's Somerwest centre at Minehead, a camp which can accommodate 8,000 guests serviced by 1,300 employees, far larger than the biggest Pontin's centre.

Tony Marshall's undercover activity was for one of BBC 2's "Back to the Floor" series of TV programmes entitled "Seeing Red" which certainly proved to be the case as far as he was concerned when he discovered the many deficiencies in the Butlin's operation at Minehead, said to be their most profitable site.

He declared that he was making use of his temporary role as a redcoat in order to find out what the public really wanted from Butlin's in the late 1990s as his mission was 'to create a paradise for the family'. The commentary in this certainly unflattering TV programme introduced Marshall as a man 'brought in to save a legend'.

Stephen Haupt took longer than a bank holiday weekend over the same exercise and the public will have judged the results of their respective investigations for themselves. However, in October 1999 Mike Smith, Rank's chief executive made his own decision. Tony Marshall lost his job and his replacement as managing director of Butlin's was George Rushton, head of Rank's Oasis brand, the group's answer to Scottish & Newcastle's Center Parcs.

In the meantime Warners, also under Rank ownership and one of Pontin's main competitors and coincidentally previously headed by George Rushton, had also identified what they perceived as their own target market and were concentrating their efforts accordingly.

Warner's no longer take children at their centres and cater for adults only. They have been buying listed buildings and converting them into hotel accommodation with added bedrooms in the grounds and constructing and installing good quality leisure facilities to consolidate their new image. A good example of this new breed of holiday centre is the site of the manor house at Cricket St Thomas, Somerset which came to international prominence by being the location for shooting BBC TV's award winning series 'To the Manor Born'.

Warners' holiday camps, not being suitable for the company's new profile, were being sold thus heralding the end of yet another era in the holiday industry. Gone are the days when Fred Pontin, Billy Butlin and Harry Warner dominated the family holiday camp market.

When discussing the activities of the likes of Potter's and Warner's who were once considered to be close competitors the Pontin's view at that time was that there was a question mark over the long term continuity of the adult market as opposed to the family and children's markets and that they had made the right choice when considering where to direct their future promotional activity. This was largely Stephen Haupt's policy and it will be seen that this strategy was not to figure too long when Trevor Hemmings took over Pontin's in September 2000.

Later trading results at Pontin's, although falling short of targets as a result of a downturn in UK economic activity and a poor summer in 1998, were, however, up on a year-by-year basis and this must surely have provided significant encouragement to Stephen Haupt and a management team which appeared to have been given renewed inspiration by his leadership.

In the meantime, Rank had found a new chief executive in the form of Mike Smith from Ladbroke but in February 1999 with the company's shares standing at less than half of the value they reached in 1996 it seemed clear that the future ownership of the group could lead only to further speculative comment after a report that a consortium of private equity investors was formulating a bid at some £3 billion. How this was to affect the future of Butlin's was anyone's guess at that time but after massive investment by both Pontin's and Butlin's the era of the holiday camp had by no means come to an end, regardless of the actions of the high-rolling investors in the City of London, where Sir Fred Pontin first made his mark in the business world, if only as a lowly clerk. But talk of 'people knocking on the door' and 'circling sharks' from Rank's former acting chief executive and company chairman did nothing to silence the speculation regarding the group's future and consequently the future of a leading holiday camp operator in the time leading up to the start of the twenty first century.

The sequel to all the speculation was the sale of Butlin's, Warner's and Haven Holidays to the Bourne Leisure Group and Butlin's now operate from only three centres; Minehead, Bognor Regis and Skegness. The times have certainly been changing but Mike Smith's decision to sell these leisure interests found favour in the City if only because of the significant reduction in group borrowings.

To return to the story of one of the dedicated entrepreneurs of holiday camps, Sir Fred must surely have wondered what to make of all this. He would certainly have been encouraged by the recent improvements in his former business as he for one had never lost confidence in the "value for money" concept but he would not have been impressed by such poor profit figures which compared very badly with what he achieved when at the helm.

Sir Fred once saw it written that "A Pontin's holiday has become part of the British way of life". He would have felt that a way of life should not be subjected to constant threats regarding its survival. Until Trevor Hemmings had reappeared on the scene there had been four owners of Pontin's since 1978 and a reasonable period of stability would unquestionably have been welcomed following the period of transition under the innovative but by no means overwhelmingly successful stewardship of Stephen Haupt.

The above quotation dates back to 1961, just fifteen years after a war which cost a great number of lives and during which the British people made many sacrifices. Sir Fred always felt that the holiday camp industry had made an important contribution to national recovery and he was proud to have played his part in the process.

Sir Fred also had the quotation in mind in the Spring of 1991 when he was told by Prime Minister, John Major that he had been a 'National Asset'. There is no doubt that he had succeeded in leaving his mark on the United Kingdom during a half-century of the family holiday industry.

The founder of the business may no longer have been a shareholder in Pontin's, but his heart was still very much with the entire operation which still carries the family name and shows no sign whatever of being consigned to oblivion; just as the Butlin's name lives on under the new ownership.

Hopefully, Pontin's will continue to provide what their loyal, if decreasing number of customers, bearing in mind the reduced number of centres currently being operated, have come to appreciate over the years – value for money. Time can never stand still, but Sir Fred very much hoped and trusted that the unique atmosphere which is Pontin's, especially with their new products or offerings as they are now described, will continue for many seasons to come.

However, the signs in later years and the well publicised quotes from top management at Scottish & Newcastle Breweries towards the end of their ownership could perhaps have been described as more than ominous. Talk of "whittling down" the sites and perhaps even putting the entire business up for sale did not fill even the most enthusiastic supporter of Pontin's with confidence. Scottish & Newcastle was soon to preside over the sale of Sand Bay, Weston-Super-Mare, Seacroft and Elsie Pontin's beloved Barton Hall. I heard the current managing director, Colin Homer murmur 'I wish we had them now'.

Stephen Haupt certainly had his doubts about accepting his appointment as managing director but he was a sound and convincing advocate of a prosperous future for Pontin's. Although he admitted that sites had been sold he maintained that these disposals were based on sound commercial principles and were in no way connected with asset realisation leading to a break-up of the business. I suppose that had to say something for his loyalty to his employers.

In discussing these matters, however, Stephen Haupt made a valid point. Both Sir Fred Pontin and Trevor Hemmings (with his Scottish & Newcastle Group responsibilities in mind) had been what he termed as "property-minded, not product-minded" whereas his view was that a modern manager must concentrate on ensuring that real estate, whatever its desirability in terms of its location and environment must provide levels of profitability commensurate with its capital value. Otherwise, the company's cash flow would suffer and investment even more difficult to obtain let alone justify.

In Sir Fred's day and even after the management buy out led by Trevor Hemmings in the mid-1980s there was no targeting within Pontin's and no focus. Both bosses had been trying to provide through the entire spectrum and in Stephen Haupt's words, Pontin's was 'neither one thing nor the other'.

Sites had certainly been disposed of as Pontin's felt that some areas were over-bedded but they took care not to sell properties to an organisation which would compete with their other local centres. Middleton Tower was a good example of this policy and Seacroft at Hemsby in Norfolk left the group because investment at a level to bring it up to the standards of other sites offering the up to date Pontin's product was simply not viable.

Stephen confirmed that the proceeds from sales had been reinvested in other parts of the Pontin's estate and had not been lost in the general pot of group funds. On the contrary, the vast majority of the finance for the multi-million pound investment programme emanated from the coffers of the Scottish & Newcastle parent which was also faced with the task of finding the investment needed to upgrade the Centre Parcs sites in continental Europe. Centre Parcs continue to report lower profits but not on the scale of downturn experienced by Pontin's and it must be admitted that these two leisure subsidiaries of the brewing giant did not share quite the same problems.

So, what of the morale at Pontin's after they had experienced two full seasons of the new image and product? The good news was that most seemed very happy with what had been done and the company's former entertainments manager, after years of being ashamed of a deteriorating level of service and facilities was then immensely proud of what had been delivered by the latest management regime.

Under Stephen Haupt's leadership Sir Fred's hastily recruited troubleshooting teams had become history. Pontin's was far more proactive and the customer services teams worked on the basis of doing everything they could to ensure that things did not go wrong. If, however, the teams did come across a genuine complaint or grievance certain members of the staff were given the necessary power to settle on the spot by cash compensation to a predetermined maximum figure. The fact that this unprecedented remedy, as far as Pontin's was concerned anyway, was rarely if ever applied stood testimony to the sea change in the company's management philosophy brought about by Stephen Haupt.

However, the managing director was still not entirely satisfied. 'We are getting there' he mused 'but the transition has taken time'. He was relaxed, even quite bullish and he was generous in praising his team. However, it was he that led the way, generated the teamwork and restored morale. But time does not stand still and today's Pontin's, under Trevor Hemming's ownership is changing course again. More will be written about this later; after I have dealt with some other features from the ongoing Pontin' story. The king may be dead but his former realm is still very much alive.

The process for recruiting the Pontin's Bluecoats was vastly improved in the late 1990s in that that a separate organisation within the group known as Super Choice, and now renamed 3D, had taken over responsibility for children's highly organised and supervised activities and sports events, leaving the Bluecoats free to concentrate on pure entertainment for the guests and the much sought after Equity card can be earned as a result of a full season of employment at Pontin's. This is subject to the Bluecoats concerned demonstrating by the quality and popularity of their performances that they have earned such a badge of recognition for their talents.

Pontin's are accustomed to having as many as 1500 applicants for the Bluecoat positions each year but only 120 make the grade and are offered employment with the company.

Bluecoat shows at Pontin's have now become much more professional and a competitive element between nominated shows at the various centres has served to raise standards even higher. The Bluecoat teams compete for a much coveted silver cup and there are also attractive bonuses to be earned for the winners.

Pontin's now offer a minimum of two Bluecoat shows each week with some centres staging at least four evening entertainment spectaculars with at least two performances at lunch time during the week. Guests love to see the Bluecoat personnel on stage and performing in a professional manner after mixing with them during the course of other activities throughout the day.

The company's efforts to achieve an even greater reputation for family entertainment included the employment of a professional choreographer and director for the 1999 season. He attended rehearsals at the various centres and provided expert advice to all concerned. The Bluecoats write and produce their own shows but this extra dimension will be much appreciated by people who see their role as a Bluecoat as a necessary rung on the ladder to stardom.

Jim Kennedy, the former entertainments manager at Pontin's, stated that after thirty years service with the company, during the course of which he had cause to admit that the holiday camp business must be in his blood, that he had never been more excited about what they were then offering the guests who he confirmed were returning in increasing numbers.

He confirmed that 'having lost it' in terms of offering their guests what they really wanted the company had changed direction and that it was a new era for Pontin's. Although Sir Fred's creation of a family company earned years of devoted service from his employees who appreciated and even revered such an atmosphere it was admitted that the changes had to come.

Jim Kennedy felt that the company had previously lost sight of its market and although Pontin's called their sites "family centres" there was no vision and consequently no investment. It was then that Stephen Haupt appeared on the scene and after a period of detailed assessment of the company's as well as the market's needs and convincing the parent company of the urgency to back his ideas and recommendations changes were put in hand.

It was then recognised that Pontin's was being run on straight business lines by professional management and that this was absolutely necessary for the company's long term survival. Jim Kennedy acknowledged that although the old days were wonderful in that everyone felt part of the family, with Sir Fred the father figure, his reign had become history and it was the future that was so important.

Jim conceded that his new managing director, Stephen Haupt, was never considered as a father figure but he was certainly looked upon as not only very approachable but "one of the boys" who placed staff relations well up in his list of priorities. Stephen sent out birthday cards to his staff, could talk about football, enjoyed a friendly drink but above all he had demonstrated by his actions that he listened and listened attentively to what staff and guests had been telling him about the state of the business he had inherited.

The result was an amazing transition in the Pontin's enterprise which the staff could not possibly have envisaged through the late eighties and early nineties when morale descended to catastrophically low levels of despair.

There was then a general feeling that Pontin's had got it right again and it was up to the marketing people to bring back the crowds.

However, looking back to the old days, Jim Kennedy recalled what he described as the special aura which surrounded Fred Pontin. 'He was a star who had tremendous presence' he reminisced. But Jim could recollect the frustrating times when the guv'nor would tear up the contracts for the entertainers into little pieces, just as he had done for Bridie Reid, and dispose of them like confetti. At the same time the Chairman took great joy in pronouncing the artistes concerned "talentless and useless" and not worth anything like the money he was being asked to pay.

These artistes were not lost to Pontin's as Jim Kennedy tended to revamp the contracts and present them for signature at the next signing session, hopefully when Sir Fred was alone. As most of these entertainers went on to become big stars and are still in show business Jim Kennedy should perhaps be congratulated on saving their careers.

Jim also remembered that when his employer was not playing to the gallery he could be a wonderfully warm person who made his staff feel very special. Many was the time on a Friday evening, after signing the contracts, Sir Fred would reach for a bottle of his favourite wine and two glasses. It was on these occasions that Sir Fred would reminisce about the old days, just after the war, and Jim Kennedy would leave to catch the train home with the feeling that he had just left the considerable presence of a great man.

However, not all of the senior staff at Pontin's experienced Sir Fred in this mood and still refer to their employer's unfortunate and quite deplorable habit of seeking to humiliate and demean them when the guv'nor had other people with him. It was not only Jim Kennedy who recalled that when visiting head office hearts would sink if they could hear the sound of voices in Sir Fred's office. This was a sure indication that they were in for a bad time.

The boss of Pontin's in those days seemed unable to resist the temptation to find fault with anything put before him and his conduct has left marks even to this day.

It was a regular routine for management and staff to suffer quite badly as a result of Sir Fred's bullying demeanour which can perhaps be explained as some form of need or compulsion to demonstrate to his visitors that he was the boss and would not tolerate inefficiency. It appears that if he was in female company his behaviour could be extravagantly macho. One is tempted to speculate on whether or not these ladies were really impressed by these frequent demonstrations of power management which would not likely to be tolerated nowadays.

On the other hand, would Sir Fred have behaved like this if it had not suited him to do so? It does appear to offer evidence of a Jekyll and Hyde type of character as far as his employees were concerned but such conduct must surely have brought the desired reward.

Otherwise there seems to be little point in this type of behaviour unless some form of machiavellian conduct was in play.

All of these stories, being told several decades after the events, seem to have a common thread. Whatever had been done beforehand to avoid incurring the wrath of the Chairman and Managing Director was rendered futile if he was in the company of people he wished to impress and, as a result, the guv'nor was determined to find fault, however trivial the alleged shortcoming.

Jim Kennedy once went to extraordinary lengths to pave the way for an enjoyable evening for Sir Fred and his party of six to watch a cabaret performance which, on that particular occasion, was represented by a skilful display from a group of Ukrainian Cossack dancers.

Careful preparations had been made so that the orchestra's break did not coincide with the Chairman's arrival. All members were told to wear their best black evening suits and the conductor wore a white tuxedo in honour of the occasion.

Sir Fred almost invariably made a point of giving a short speech if the cabaret had been well received by the Pontin's guests. His theme tended to be 'What a marvellous show. That's the calibre of entertainment you can expect from Pontin's. Don't forget to book early for next year'.

Once the Cossacks had left the stage, on Jim Kennedy's signal the orchestra struck up with "For he's a jolly good fellow" and on to the stage swaggered Sir Fred Pontin.

He made his usual speech and Jim Kennedy breathed a sigh of relief. 'Everything went well' he thought to himself. 'The guv'nor's pleased his guests and he'll be happy'.

Jim looked across to Sir Fred's table. The Chairman was crooking his finger at his entertainments manager. Jim felt that he was about to be praised for a great evening's entertainment. He should have known better.

'Absolute rubbish' remonstrated Sir Fred Pontin, not too loud for the vast majority of the Pontin customers to hear but distinct enough for his guests to get their hosts' message.

'What was wrong?' asked an astonished Jim Kennedy.

'The band was a shambles; they weren't even wearing the same clothes'. Jim could hardly believe his ears. Sir Fred was acting true to form but all he could find wrong on this occasion was the difference between what the conductor was wearing and how the members of the orchestra were dressed. It really was too much and Jim must have revealed his feelings by his body language as Sir Fred went out of his way to apologise for his rather outlandish conduct the next time they met.

By all accounts Sir Fred was well aware of this notoriety and seemed to savour any consequence on the grounds that his employees needed to be reminded that it was his business and he was the boss who made all the decisions.

It will have been seen that Fred Pontin could never be accused of not knowing what was going on in his organisation and one can only wonder at what was his astonishing capacity for stamina and passion in just about everything he did.

He was known for consuming vast amounts of alcohol, staying up until dawn after a long night of carousing and womanizing in a foreign resort and still be back in his London office at the start of normal business hours on the same day wondering why on earth his companions over the course of the previous night's jollities were still in bed back in Majorca, Ibiza or perhaps Torremolinos.

Even in his early nineties and over fifty years after he started his holiday camp business the guv'nor continued to anticipate that doors of opportunity would continue to open and prevent him from giving any thought to retirement. He used to say that if such an idea should ever occur he was pledged to stretch out on a couch in a darkened room until such time as the desire left him ... placing his faith in the quotation from Milton's *Paradise Lost*: 'And short retirement urges sweet return'.

However Sir Fred had also been heard to confess that 'I've accepted retirement. I feel that I have earned it'. Who could possibly have quarrelled with that having regard to the fact that it was being said over 50 years after he started at Brean Sands in 1946, well into the maestro's ninetieth year.

In October 1996 Mike Austin organised a 90th birthday party for Sir Fred Pontin. This took place at Wick Ferry, one of Pontin's earlier camps and now owned by Trevor Hemmings.

George Webb, one of the invited guests, recalls 'Anybody who was anybody in Pontin's was there'.

There were no organised speeches but several people did get up to say a few words on what was, after all, a momentous occasion. 1996 was not only the year of Sir Fred Pontin's 90th birthday, it was also the 50th anniversary of founding of the Pontin's business.

Sir Fred responded to various tributes by recalling in general terms what he felt that he had achieved during the course of his long career. It was perhaps fitting that on this special occasion he had entered the dining room, after everyone had been seated, arm-in-arm with Ann Miller, the person who had been so close to him during those successful years from 1946 to the late 1970s and, of course, during the war on the Orkney Islands.

George Webb, who will be mentioned a little later, felt that this grand entrance recalled the days when Fred Pontin was accustomed to descending the stairs at the Royal Albert Hall whilst hosting the company's annual reunion.

In 1997 and after his wife's death, Sir Fred set up home in Blackpool, almost literally within a stone's throw of one of his most successful holiday centres. He was then able to live quite openly with Joyce Hey, a lady who subsequently became Sir Fred's wife and whom he described to me as being "quite wonderful". He added on that particular occasion 'I am a very lucky man to have such a wonderful partner at my time of life'. Sir Fred and Joyce's relationship commenced in 1962 and had been one of the mainstays of a remarkable career and its aftermath, particularly in the later years when his state of health had been far from tolerable.

I was a witness on many occasions when Sir Fred would be in some difficulty with his movements and general comfort and Joyce was always readily at hand to make him more comfortable and attend to his immediate needs. Without such loving care and support he would have found it impossible to undertake both social and business commitments towards the end of his long life. I am pleased to record these facts as they will not be generally known. Joyce was never seen to behave in other than in a caring and loving manner in the company of Sir Fred during the last decade of his life when he became increasingly infirm and there was never a complaint or any sign of irritation. It was pleasing to be witness to such devoted and tender conduct.

Until Sir Fred's death he retained his apartment in central London and although his memberships of Variety Club, Saints and Sinners and the Water Rats continued until the end his occasional attendance was confined to luncheon events in later years, evenings then being a little too burdensome for a man who celebrated his 93rd birthday in 1999. Indeed, he very nearly reached the 94th anniversary of his date of birth.

He outlived all of his contemporaries in the holiday camp business who helped him create the mass British holiday market after the war. He could look back upon an eventful life which had brought him an abundance of extraordinary and wonderful experiences. Inevitably, these were rewarding as well as disappointing but it can be said with every justification that he had made his own luck, both good and bad. Although he had regrets these can be seen to be far outnumbered by the happy memories of his achievements in a competitive world which takes very few prisoners.

A regular visitor to Sir Fred's home in Blackpool was George Webb, formerly Bronislav Baczkowski, who is still living in retirement in nearby St Anne's. His wife, Elsie died in 1994 but he keeps active and plays golf regularly on a nearby course.

George parted company with Pontin's in 1968 after a three bouts of serious illness. Fred Pontin did not take too kindly to the resignation and offered George an extended period of recuperation. It was quite unusual, not to say unheard-of, for a successful executive to leave Pontin's but George was not financially dependent on the company and he had been disappointed not to be appointed to the main board a little earlier in his career.

At one time George was a local director at Pontinental's Sardinia site, being also an Italian speaker, and he had always understood that a full board appointment was a definite prospect, especially after a successful spell as Pontin's regional controller for the north of England where he was responsible for "putting the Pontin's stamp" on the new acquisitions. This elevation to full director status was, however, not to come about and one is left wondering if perhaps Fred Pontin had sometimes been a little careless in dropping hints of promotion which never came to subsequent fruition.

George Webb is a proud man who achieved much by his own efforts after leaving Pontin's. His presence would have been sorely missed after his resignation. Ann Miller had made a point of keeping in touch with George up until she died only quite recently but until much later years, indeed on his return to reside in Blackpool, Sir Fred Pontin never did. This seems typical of his attitude to people who had, in his view, crossed him or let him down.

However, after the extended period of estrangement it was pleasing to learn that George Webb and his former employer were able to meet on a regular basis and reminisce over times past, any differences then forgotten. Sir Fred had many acquaintances but very few close, personal friends, having outlived most of them.

The British Travel Industry honoured Sir Fred at a dinner at the Savoy Hotel in May 1998 when his excellence and outstanding achievement were recognised by affording him membership of the industry's Hall of Fame. Other members, similarly honoured, include Lord Forte of Ripley, Sir Billy Butlin, Christel DeHaan, founder of the Saga group and the Rt. Hon. Lord King, formerly chairman of British Airways.

It's not everyone who would be able to reflect on the fact that their very name has become a household word, instantly recognisable by millions of people of all ages. Indeed, it has even been said that just like Hoover or Biro, he became the product himself. Sir Fred was doing his own advertising and promotion, long before the likes of Richard Branson appeared on the scene.

Brand names are established nowadays by expending millions of pounds in promotion. Sir Fred created his own brand name by sheer personal magnetism and gladly, there is still no sign that Pontin's are intent upon changing to something more trendy. Their customers would be unlikely to countenance such heresy.

Perhaps young John Sharples summed it all up when he cried 'Come on Mum, let's get out there'. Sir Fred knew very well, along with his shareholders, that there would be every chance that the loyal guests will still be "getting out there" well into what he would describe as the next millennium as there could be no substitute for the Pontin's formula, still based upon value of money, fun-filled family holidays, first created by a man who always knew what his guests wanted and provided it with abundance.

Up until the time of Sir Fred's death it might have been appropriate to have left the last word to Sean Woodgate, who was in charge at Brean Sands in 1998 and then one of the latest breed of general managers at "New" Pontin's, specially selected to deliver the much sought after return to the high levels of profitability which were the norm when Fred Pontin's stewardship of the company was in full train.

When I left Sean after a conducted tour of his bailiwick in late December 1998 he surveyed the milling throngs of guests getting in the mood for the New Year celebrations and boasted 'We're fully booked for the millennium'. I found myself speculating that his then managing director, Stephen Haupt, would have responded by musing 'If only Sean, if only ...'

In the event, Stephen Haupt left Pontin's in September 1999, only a short time before Scottish & Newcastle Breweries announced the sale of the group's leisure interests. He is now with Regent Inns and he was succeeded as managing director of Pontin's by David Grace who acted as "night watchman" for Sir Fred's former business until such time as a buyer was found. During this period it was just a question of a ticking over operation and it must have caused considerable anxiety amongst the Pontin's staff. It was to be nearly a full year before the new owner emerged although there had been much speculation in the press as to his identity.

Although the new millennium is very much in its infancy, Colin Homer, Trevor Hemmings' choice as as the first managing director under his new ownership, is under no illusions. He is charged with producing an acceptably high level of return on the capital employed in the Pontin's business and he must achieve this goal by trading profitably for at least 35 weeks during each calendar year, a far cry from Fred Pontin's early days. He talks of "shoulder periods", away from the traditional school holidays when Pontin's cater for people, probably aged over 55, who wish to enjoy themselves without being accompanied by children as well as parents with youngsters under school age. Pontin's meet this challenge by operating two catering and six self-catering sites and by organising special events.

Colin is fully aware of what is expected of him. He has known Trevor Hemmings since 1969 when Trevor's construction company was rebuilding the accommodation at the Prestatyn Sands site for Fred Pontin. However, Colin did not become a Pontin's employee until 1975 and it was in 1982 that he received his first appointment as a general manager at Morecambe. Since then he has been employed in a number of responsible executive positions, both for Pontin's following the management buy out by Trevor in 1987 and for the Trevor Hemmings group of companies whose leisure interests extend from public houses to Blackpool Tower and a number of UK racecourses.

Taking over responsibility for Pontin's following a period of time when Scottish & Newcastle were reporting the business as a problematic part of the groups' leisure division on a regular basis would be a daunting task for anyone but Colin has risen to the challenge. He talked of the £80 million investment yielding negligible returns for the brewery group but at least he has the comfort of knowing that Trevor Hemmings secured control of Pontin's for a sum rumoured to be around half of this figure. So, in that respect alone, he can perhaps be said to have a somewhat easier task than was faced by Stephen Haupt who recommended the huge investment to his parent company in the mid-1990s.

Colin makes the point that the company's loyal customers do not take too kindly to major changes in the product as they want to be able to recognise what they have always remembered about Pontin's. So, although he is taking a different route from that initiated by Stephen Haupt this is being done with care and attention to detail. He was proud to show me the monthly returns for the 2002 season for one particular centre which were well up on the previous year's figures. He added that this was a general trend which indicated to me in the finest possible manner that they were on the right track.

Pontin's has now been trading for over 50 years and still going strong. Colin Homer feels that this is a strong publicity slogan and it is being used in current press releases. This must be music to the ears of staff and customers alike and when Colin added that 'There will still be a Pontin's offering for a good while yet' it would be nice to know that Sir Fred was aware that his former business was in a safe pair of hands. But this is not to say that the new management is not aware of the need to concentrate on keeping up with changing markets. Colin makes the point that people who have given up travelling long distances for their holidays look for a more comfortable style of holiday, closer to home. Pontin's will address this market and still provide value for money which remains a watchword, just as it did in Sir Fred's day.

Notwithstanding the expenditure of £60 million on the sites which remain in Pontin's ownership following the disposal programme instituted by Scottish & Newcastle in the later years leading up to their sale of the business Pontin's continue to invest in their centres. Improvements took place at Brean Sands, Camber Sands, Southport and Wall Park in the winter of 2001-2002. Brean and Camber were the first two centres to undergo refurbishment and enhancement in 1994-95 and were due to have renewed attention. Colin Homer made the point that refurbishments have a limited shelf life and Pontin's intend to keep on top of this vital aspect of managing the estate.

The Blackpool centre, lacking a suitable room for social activities such as ballroom dancing for the senior adult market, had this deficiency remedied in 2001–2002. Colin was keen to make the point that 'Pontin's continue to listen to their guests' when confirming that they have also provided a resident band for live music in order to meet popular demand. I like to think that Sir Fred would have liked that.

Meanwhile, back at Brean Sands, Sir Fred Pontin's first and quite possibly his most nostalgic, if not his favourite site, the new general manager Jane Loveys, who has graduated from being a Pontin;s trainee, is keeping up the old traditions whilst managing and operating the centre on very professional lines. Her predecessor, Sean Woodgate, has returned to Ireland to manage Trabolgan which is no longer within the Pontin's empire. Let us hope his millennium expectations will be off to a good start. He will have learned a lot with Pontin's and he will probably be aware of the part Trabolgan played in the Pontin's story, not to mention Sir Fred's notable horse racing successes.

I revisited the Brean Sands site on a fine day in March 2002 and found 1,200 adults guests enjoying a weekend on the Somerset coast with a planned evening's entertainment of rock music. On this particular occasion there was not a Bluecoat in sight as an outside organisation had hired the centre for this special weekend. The Pontin's role was to supply the accommodation, food and booze which is a service they provide on a very efficient basis.

This was not an isolated event because such activities take place throughout the UK but it is a clear indication that Pontin's sites, in addition to playing host for a variety of holiday activities, also fulfil a popular social function. There is a genuine demand for people sharing similar interests getting together under one roof and enjoying themselves. If Pontin's did not exist it is difficult to know how this need could be met and at such relatively low cost to the participants. Long may it continue and once again it is certain that Sir Fred would have been pleased to see just how popular these events have become.

I am wondering if those 1,200 guests at Brean Sands, like me, also enjoyed the spectacular sunset over the Bristol Channel. Even if they didn't it is gratifying to be able to report that there is no sign of the sun setting on Sir Fred Pontin's business empire. As long as families similar to the Sharples continue to enjoy setting off for action-packed, fun-filled activities at Pontin's centres, even if it is only at a moment's notice, there will be traditional Pontin's hospitality waiting for them even if the guv'nor is no longer around to keep a wary eye on things. As long as it's Pontin's he has no need to do so. The tradition lives on and there is a lot to be said for a safe pair of hands.

SOURCE MATERIAL

The British Barker – The Official Journal of the Variety Club of
Great Britain
The Millionaire Mentality – by Michael Pearson, Secker & Warburg
The Pound in Your Pocket – by Peter Wilsher, Cassell & Company
Limited
Good night Campers – The History of the British Holiday Camp – by
Colin Ward and Dennis Hardy. Mansell
Holiday Camps Directory and Magazine – 1948 and 1949 editions
Holiday Time at Butlin's – 1951 edition
Daily Telegraph Library – newspaper cuttings
New Encyclopaedia Britannica, Volume 5, Micropaedia – ready
reference edition
Dictionary of National Biography – Oxford University Press
Dance News and *Recall* – publications for ballroom dancers
David Gwyn's personal archive
Offer Document – Recommended Offer by Charterhouse Japhet
Limited on behalf of Coral Leisure Group Limited for the whole
of the share capital, issued and to be issued of Pontin's Limited
Records at the National Horse racing Museum, 99 High Street,
Newmarket by kind permission of the Curator
Who's Who 1990
Extel Statistical Services Limited – Stock Exchange News Cards
BBC Television Light Entertainment Publicity – viewing figures
Pontin Family Tree – Mr L. Pontin
Annual and Interim reports Arena Leisure plc
Website – Scottish & Newcastle Breweries

INDEX